Two Millennia
of Memorable
Christian
Women
Showing Strength without Power

Stanley M. Burgess and Ruth Vassar Burgess

WESTBOW
PRESS®
A DIVISION OF THOMAS NELSON
& ZONDERVAN

WestBow Press books may be ordered through booksellers or by contacting:

WestBow Press
A Division of Thomas Nelson & Zondervan
1663 Liberty Drive
Bloomington, IN 47403
www.westbowpress.com
1 (866) 928-1240

Picture on front cover is Pandita Ramabai, whose bio appears on pg 165-7.

Scripture taken from the King James Version of the Bible.

ISBN: 978-1-9736-9782-4 (sc)
ISBN: 978-1-9736-9783-1 (hc)
ISBN: 978-1-9736-9781-7 (e)

Library of Congress Control Number: 2020913467

Print information available on the last page.

WestBow Press rev. date: 08/17/2020

Contents

Dedication ix

Preface xi

Editors and Contributors.. xiii

Introduction: Ancient Christianity...................................... 1

Mary, Mother of Jesus of Nazareth 7

Mary Magdalene.. 10

Junia/Junias: Ancient Female Apostle? 12

Mary, Mother of John Mark.. 14

Priscilla 16

Lydia of Thyatira: a First Century Business Woman........... 18

Thecla 20

Philip's Daughters: Early Prophetesses................................ 22

Irina of Macedonia: Martyr: 1st – 2nd century..................... 24

Early Montanist Women: Maximilla and Prisca................... 28

Blandina of Lyon: The Martyrdom of a Slave Girl.............. 31

The Martyrdom of Perpetua and Felicitas........................... 33

Zoe of Rome 36

Helena: Mother of Constantine... 38

Elizabeth the Wonderworker... 40

Nino of Iberia 42

Marcella of Rome.. 44

Macrina the Younger... 46

Egeria Pioneer Pilgrim.. 48

Introduction: Medieval Christianity....................................51

Scholastica 57

Mary of Egypt... 59
Brigid of Kidare, Ireland 61
Clotilda of France 63
Theodelinda 65
Leoba 67
Irene of Athens Byzantine Empress 69
Dhuoda.. 71
Princess Olga of Kiev (c.890-969) 74
Saint Petka-Paraskeva 10th-11thcenturies 81
Clare of Assisi.. 86
Margaret of Scotland.. 88
Hildegard of Bingen Universal Genius 90
Esclarmonde of Foix... 93
Gertrude of Helfta 95
Elizabeth of Hungary... 97
Brigitta of Sweden 99
Julian of Norwich 101
Catherine of Siena 103
Margery Kempe, 1373-1438.. 105
Joan of Arc 109

Introduction: Reformation Era and Early Modern Era......................113
Teresa of Avila... 117
Katherine Von Bora... 119
Idelette Calvin...121
Anna Reinhart Zwingli 123
Katharina Zell.. 125
Pocahontas Rebecca Rolfe 127
Susanna Annesley Wesley... 129
Ann Lee 131
Soeur (Sister) Françoise and Seour Marie: Jansenist Girls 133

Introduction: Nineteenth Century 137
Bernadette Soubirous of Lourdes..141
Florence Nightingale 143
Phoebe Palmer 145

Fanny Crosby..147
Catherine Mumford Booth 149
Harriet Ross Tubman..152
Elizabeth Cady Stanton..155
Amy Beatrice Carmichael...157

Introduction: Twentieth Century 159
Elena Guerra 163
Pandita Ramabai Mary Sarasvati.......................................165
Dr. Lilian B. Yeomans... 168
Lizzie Robinson: Founder of the Church of God in Christ
    Women's Departmeni 176
Dr. Ida Sophia Scudder 181
Alice Reynolds "Mother" Flower 183
Lillian Hunt Trasher 189
Anna Eleanor Roosevelt 191
Marie Burgess Brown 194
Mahalia Jackson...197
Mother Teresa: 'Saint' of the Gutters.................................199
Lenora Isabel Scott Vassar 204
Aimee Kennedy Semple Mcpherson 207
Margaret Gaines 212
Corrie Ten Boom...218
Kathrn Johanna Kuhlman 220
Billie Clare Davis 225
Betty Peterson 227
Elisabeth Caspari and Marie Montessori 231
Mary Ann Louise Hoover 233
Soong Mel-Ling Madame Chiang Kai-Shek 236
Jashil Choi 238
Maya Angelou 242
Helen Adams Keller 245
Coretta Scott King...247

Glossary 251

Dedication

This tome is dedicated to the great Christian women of the past, whether remembered or not, who had the courage and foresight to bring a more just and lasting recognition that we are all made in the image and likeness of God. It is with positive anticipation that we believe our five children and ten grandchildren will continue the positive movement we see in recent history to remember and to celebrate women of noble character.

Preface

For over 2,000 years, Christian women have struggled with inequities between the genders. This certainly is true in matters religious. Christian women have shown ethical, moral, and spiritual strength, while being deprived of leadership or power positions, reserved for their male counterparts. This tome celebrates a wide variety of such female heroines, drawn from early Christian, Roman Catholic, Orthodox, Protestant, Pentecostal and Charismatic groups, as well as a sprinkling of "heretical" individuals. These women often have become saints, martyrs, visionaries and spiritual voices-models to all generations.

At the same time, it must be remembered that many of them also carried and gave birth to children, raised them, and fulfilled the other functions required of them in their social contexts. This work is intentionally trans-spatial, trans-temporal, and trans-cultural. Of course, it is necessarily only representative of the women throughout Christian history, and certainly not fully comprehensive or exhaustive. We are aware that millions of outstanding Christian women have lived and died without leaving permanent records, and thus have been lost to our memories.

Inevitably, most readers will ask why certain women have not been included. Others will ask why less-than-perfect individuals have been chosen. Clearly, selective judgment has been exercised in determining those selected for inclusion. Above all else, our selections are truly memorable, as much for their struggles as for their achievements. As such they are significant figures to emulate, both now and in generations to come.

We now begin a process which will take us from times of origin, to persecution, to seclusion, to intolerance, and finally, to significance and influence. It is the ongoing heritage story of Christian women at their best, worthy of remembrance and of emulation.

Editors and Contributors

Burgess, Stanley Milton. Co-Editor and contributor. Ph.D, University of Missouri-Columbia. Professor Emeritus, Missouri State University, Springfield, MO.

Burgess, Ruth Vassar. Co-Editor and contributor. Ph.D., University of Missouri-Columbia. Professor Emeritus, Missouri State University Springfield MO

CONTRIBUTORS

Artman, Amy. Ph.D., University of Chicago. Instructor, Missouri State University, Springfield, MO.

Berg, Robert. Ph.D., Drew University. Professor, Evangel University, Springfield, MO.

Friesen, LaDonna M.A. Missouri State University, Springfield, MO. Assistant Professor of English, Evangel University, Springfield, MO.

Hristova, Rumyana. Ph.D., Nottingham Trent University, Nottingham, UK. MS, library Science, University of Illinois. Catalog/Outreach Librarian, Evangel University, Springfield, MO.

Johnson, Todd M. Ph.D., William Carey International University. Co-Director, Center for the Study of Global Christianity at Gordan-Conwell Theological Seminary, S. Hamilton, MA.

Ma, Julie, Ph.D. Fuller Theological Seminary. Associate Professor, Oral Roberts University, Tulsa, OK.

Newberg, Eric. Ph.D., Regent University. Professor, Oral Roberts University, Tulsa, OK.

Olena, Lois E. D. Min. Assemblies of God Theological Seminary. Free-lance writer and editor.

Peterson, Eric K. B.S. Augustana College, BBA, University of Illinois-Urbana-Champaign. President of Peterson Wealth Advisors, Springfield, MO.

Ringer, David. D. Min., Assemblies of God Theological Seminary, Evangel University, Springfield, MO. Professor Emeritus, College of the Ozarks.

Rodgers, Darren. J.D., University of North Dakota School of Law. Director, Flower Pentecostal Heritage Center, Springfield, MO.

Rodgers, Desiree. Ph.D. Cand., MDiv., Assemblies of God Theological Seminary. Adjunct Professor, Evangel University, Springfield, MO.

Satyavrata, Ivan. D.Phil. Oxford Centre for Missions Studies, Oxford, UK. Associate Professor of Intercultural Studies, Evangel University, Springfield, MO. Pastor of Buntain Memorial Church, Kolkata (Calcutta), India.

Satyavrata, Sheila. M.S. Biology, Bangalore University, Bangalore, India. Co-pastor, Buntain Memorial Church, Kolkata, India. Social worker in prevention, rescue, and restoration of victims of sex trafficking.

Zurlo, Gina A. Ph.D., Boston University. Co-Director, Center for the Study of Global Christianity at Gordan-Conwell Theological Seminary, S. Hamilton, MA.

Introduction

Ancient Christianity

T o fully understand the place of memorable Christian women during the past two millennia, we must first put their stories into context. We begin at the beginning, with the women who were part of the earliest Christianity, who knew Jesus of Nazareth and were involved with him in founding the religion which has grown to be the largest in the history of the world.

Our study cannot be meaningful unless we recognize the extent of patriarchy before and during this period of Christian origins. Men ruled in government, in local society, in their tribes, in their families, and in religion. This was a time of patriarchal monopoly. Women, of course, were essential in maintaining this monopoly. They had to continue the human race. As with Eve in the Garden, they provided companionship to men, to raise and to nurture the next generation. They were expected to be faithful to the lot that they inherited at birth.

Even Jewish women suffered from this Patriarchal press. While they learned from their holy book that their Almighty God had created them in HIS image and likeness (Genesis 1:26-27), they were reminded that they were responsible for leading man astray (Genesis 2-3). Necessary, but flawed and weak-certainly too weak to lead, too weak to teach (outside their natural environment, their home), too unsteady and too temperamental, too.... Their true place had been determined by their birth, by their gender.

Of course, it was always possible for women to be consoled with the non-Jewish elements that surrounded them. Were there not goddesses, as well as gods? Were there not women of beauty, such as Helen of Troy, over whom men shed their blood for seemingly endless decades? But there seemed to be no bridge between the immortals and struggling mortality, especially the women.

The Roman Empire dominated the era of early Christianity. The empire—the size of which had never before been experienced-during the time of Jesus, was dominant. But once again, patriarchy on every level seemed to characterize the landscape. Women knew their roles and their destinies, and their men seemed content to remind them how to avoid stepping out of line.

Then came Jesus of Nazareth, the greatest iconoclast human history has ever witnessed. If God had birthed humanity in His image and likeness, Jesus rebirthed humanity, male and female, in His likeness. He recognized women as leaders, as well as productive followers. He walked and communicated with those he chose, both men and women. He taught them together on the hills of Galilee and from boats on the waters. They anointed his head with perfumed oils. They financed his ministry and accompanied him on his journeys. They were his friends and, it seems, his almost constant companions.

Women, not his male followers (with the exception of John), were with him as he hung on the cross and died. They were the first to witness his resurrection. One of them, Mary Magdalene, because his first apostle to the male disciples. They met with him in a woman's home (Mary, mother of John Mark). They were with him as he proclaimed the good news of the Resurrection in the same home. They were with the other disciples on the Day of Pentecost, in the home of the same Mary. They experienced the same transformation as did the men in that Pentecost moment, when the Church was born.

Even the newly created apostle, Paul, in his Galatians epistle, proclaimed that we are neither Jew or Greek, neither slave or free, *neither male or female,* but we are one in Christ Jesus (Galatians 3:28).

In Paul's letter to the Romans (16:7) he sends greetings to Adronicus and his wife, Junia, "who are of note among the apostles." Clearly, this was a reference to another early woman apostle. But we have archeological evidence that the female "Julia" was changed to the male "Julias" on one statuary. Yet another attempt to tamper with the Biblical evidence to serve the patriarchal purposes.

Of course, we must recognize that this same Paul would seemingly shift his message in his Ephesian epistle, where he instructs wives to be subject to their husbands (5:22ff) and in First Timothy 2:11-12 where he insists that women be silent in the churches and not to lord it over their men.

In those early years of the Church, the Ascension commands of the angelic messengers that all Christians (regardless of class, race or gender) should go into all the world to preach the gospel to all people dominated the thinking of Christians, whether male or female. But before long there was another concern that surfaced, namely that of keeping the new faith pure and without heresy.

It must be recognized that Christianity was varied from the beginning. Having been founded on the Day of Pentecost with a multi-varied collection of Jews present from all parts of the world, the Church soon expanded to Gentle populations, beginning with the group present at Cornelius' house (Acts 10} in Caesarea Maritima (by the sea). As a result, the followers of Jesus travelled the world over to spread his good news.

We live in an age of increased research, and with that have come discoveries of additional materials that were not considered fit for inclusion in Holy Scriptures, writings of the losing sides in the struggle against diversity by the conformists on the winning side. Gnostics, Donatists, Montanists, and numerous other groups had challenged the Catholic/ Orthodox world. In our world of curious scholars, it has become common to discover long-hidden scrolls from the distant past, scrolls from the losing sides in many doctrinal power struggles occurring in the early Church.

It is most interesting to note that numerous recently discovered scrolls directly address our question of the place taken by women in the first and second centuries. When we read scrolls devoted to Mary Magdalene, for instance, attention will be paid to Gnostic source materials, where new information is given.

At the end of the first century CE, Gnosticism was challenging Catholic/Orthodox Christianity in numbers. There seems to have been uncertainty as to which side would win out. As such, it seems quite reasonable that the side which eventually lost this power struggle-the

Gnostics would attempt to save their tablets by burying them in the deserts of Egypt (now called the Nag Hamadi Codices).

Through the entire history of the early Christians, to the time of Constantine the Great in the early fourth century, believers have been under persecution. Finally, a place for women to lead! In the pages which follow, we will be tracing the lives of women who gave their lives in service to Christ. From Blandina of Lyons to Perpetua and Felicitas to Zoe of Rome in the late third century, Christian women stood out for their compassion and their bravery during their death passions.

There is clear evidence that there were female prophetesses in both first, second, and third centuries. Philip's four daughters are certainly examples, as the famed historian, Eusebius, provides evidence. Then we have even more evidence that the Montanists (early Pentecostals) were led by the male, Montanus, and two prophetesses, Maximilia and Prisca (or Priscilla). Later, Tertullian, after being converted to Montanism, reports that an early third century Montanist woman was silent during the services, but afterwards declared her prophecies to the male leadership. It is fair to argue that prophecy, not tongues, has been the most dominant feature of Pentecostalism in the Church throughout two millenia. In these enthusiastic movements, women have often led, and certainly outnumbered the men in their congregations.

On rare occasions, women have risen to positions of influence, if not of power, to affect the history of Christianity. Chief among these in the ancient Church was Helena, mother of Emperor Constantinople. Through her influence and a variety of fortunate circumstances, Constantine converted to Christianity and issued a decree, the "Edict of Milan" which proclaimed that Christians were to be treated more humanely. Before long, Christianity was declared the official religion of the Roman Empire.

But that Empire was beginning to decline. By 476 CE Rome fell to invading Germanic tribes. Despite this imperial collapse, the Church continued to advance. During the fourth and fifth centuries, several of the greatest ancient Christian leaders emerged, including Augustine, the three Cappadocian Fathers (Basil, Gregory of Nyssa, and Gregory of Naziansas) and at the transition to the sixth century, Benedict of Nursia. Lost in the story are leading women, such as Mary of Egypt, Macrina the Younger (sister of Basil and Gregory of Nyssa) and Scholastica (sister to Benedict), who lived the ascetic ideal which bought a higher level of Christian character to the late Empire.

BIBLIOGRAPHY

Aune, D. E. *Prophecy in Ancient Christianity and the Ancient Mediterranean World*. Grand Rapids, Ml: Eerdmans, 1983.

Burgess, Stanley M. *The Spirit and the Church: Antiquity*. Peabody, MA: Hendrickson, 1984.

Clark, Elizabeth and Herbert Richardson, eds. *Women and Religions: A Feminist Sourcebook of Christian Thought*. New York: Harper & Rowe, 1977.

Cruse, C. F., trans. *Eusebius of Caesarea: Ecclesiastical History*. Peabody, MA: Hendrickson Publishers, 1998.

Ehrmann, Bart D. *Lost Christianities: the battle for Scripture and the faiths we never knew*. New York: Oxford University Press, 2003.

Frend, W. H. C. *Martyrdom and Persecution in the Early Church*. Garden City: Doubleday, 1964.

Hultgren, Arland J. and Steven A. Haggmark, eds. *The Earliest Christian Heretics: Readings from their Opponents*. Minneapolis, MN: Augsburg Fortress, 1996.

Oden, Amy, ed. *In Her Words: Women's Writings in the History of Christian Thought*. Nashville: Abingdon, 1994.

Pagels, Elaine. *The Gnostic Gospels*. New York: Random House, 1979.

Torjiesen, Karen Jo. *When Women Were Priests: Women's Leadership in the Early Church & the Scandal of their Subordination in the Rise of Christianity*. New York: Harper Collins, 2003.

Stanley M. Burgess

Mary, Mother of Jesus of Nazareth

M ary or Miryam (named after the sister of Moses) was the mother of Jesus Christ. According to tradition, her parents were Joachim and Anne. She lived in Nazareth, a village of about 1,600 people, in the northern region of Galilee in ancient Israel. She was betrothed and later married to Joseph of the House of David. According to Matthew (1:18-20) and Luke (1:35} she conceived Jesus miraculously without Joseph's involvement. She gave birth to a son named Jesus or Joshua (Matt 1-2, Luke 2:1-21), who is revered as the savior of humankind by virtually all Christians.

According to Matthew's gospel (1:18-25), Joseph intended to divorce Mary when he learned of her pregnancy and having not known her, until an angel informed him in a dream to be unafraid and take her as his wife, because her unborn child is "from the Holy Spirit." This leads to the teaching about the "Immaculate Conception", which actually refers to grandmother Anne and the miraculous birth of Mary, thus born without sin.

Meanwhile, Luke (2:1) tells us that a decree was issued by the Emperor Augustus, requiring Joseph and Mary to proceed to Bethlehem for an enrollment. There they found no place for them in the inn, thus leading to the birth occurring in a stable, with an animal manger as a crib. The actual dating of the first Christmas is uncertain, but clearly before 4 BC, when King Herod died. Scholars still debate the precise time, and we still have a variance of celebrations for Christmas-December 25th for most Roman Catholics, Protestants and Greek Orthodox; January 7th for other Orthodox (accounted for by difference in Julian and Gregorian calendars).

In the northern hemisphere, we currently place the first Christmas during the night, because angels are said to have appeared to the shepherds at night rather than daytime. However, having personally experienced Christmas in Bethlehem (1985-6), we discovered that it was far too cold "for shepherds to watch over their flocks by night"!

We know of King Herod's killing of the infants and of another dream experienced by Joseph leading him to take Mary and baby Jesus to Egypt (Matt 2:13-23). After Herod's death, yet another dream prompted the holy family back to Nazareth in the Galilee, where Jesus lived until the beginning of his public ministry at about the age of thirty. Meanwhile, we do have the incident of Jesus being brought to the temple when he was but twelve, confounding the sages there, while his mother and Joseph travelled a day back to Nazareth, only to discover that he was not with them (Luke 2:41-52).

Although she is not named in two scenes in the Gospel of John, Mary appears as Jesus's mother. First, she is with Jesus at the wedding at Cana (John 2:1-11), where she tells the servants to "do as he would have you to do," resulting in his first recorded miracle of turning water into wine. The second occasion is at Jesus' crucifixion, where Jesus on the cross looks at his disciple John and insists that his mother, Mary, is now John's charge (John 19:25-27).

In Mark's gospel (6:3) Jesus is identified as a carpenter, the son of Mary, with brothers James, Joses, Judas, and Simon, together with unnamed sisters.

Without question, Mary of Nazareth remains the most famous and the greatest woman is the two millenia of Christian history. At the Council of Ephesus (431) she was venerated as *Theotokos* (Mother of God), and as Queen of Heaven and Earth (first c. 1485 in an oil painting, later with explanation and justification by Pope Pius XII <1939-1958> in his *Munificentissimus Deus* 1950. In the same apostolic constitution Pius XII declared that Mary was assumed both body and soul into heaven). Orthodox Christians have a feast celebrating the Dormition (death, resurrection, and ascension into heaven). Protestants are divided on these issues, although most honor her above other saints as mother of Jesus the Christ.

BIBLIOGRAPHY

Cronin, Vincent. *Mary Portrayed*. London: Longman and Todd, 1968.

Pelikan, Jaroslav. *Mary Through the Centuries: Her Place in the History of Culture*. New Edition. New Haven, CT: Yale University Press, 1998.

Stanley M. Burgess

Mary Magdalene

Mary Magdalene was a native of Magdala, a village on the western side of the sea of Galilee in ancient Israel. She is identified in Luke 7:37-50 as the one out of whom Jesus cast seven demons. Her grateful response was to minister to Jesus as he traveled and preached, making provision for him out of her resources (Luke 8:2-3), indicating that she was relatively wealthy.

In all four canonical Gospels, she is present at the crucifixion of Jesus, and in Matthew, Mark, and Luke, she was present at his burial. All four gospels identify her as first witness to Jesus' resurrection, whether coming alone or in a larger group of women. We read that Jesus spoke to her at that time, giving her instructions to tell his other disciples that he had risen from the dead. For these reasons, she has been identified in many Christian traditions as the "Apostle to the apostles" (Apostolorum apostola).

Mary has been mentioned in the subsequent Gnostic writings: *The Dialogue of the Savior* (138-11- 13;140.17-19; 142.11-13), the *Pistis Sophia* (26.17-20; 218.10-219.2) the *Gospel of Thomas* (114), the *Gospel of Philip,* and the *Gospel of Mary* (18.14-15). These texts portray Mary as Jesus' closest disciple and the only person who truly understood his teachings. However, they do not necessarily agree on details. For example, the *Gospel of Thomas* offers that Jesus offered to turn women into men, so that they might be a living spirit like his male apostles. In contrast, the *Gospel of Mary* suggests that women are on the same plain as their male counterparts, and so do not need to be changed.

In 591 AD (or CE, common era) Mary's reputation took a sudden turn when Pope Gregory I ("Gregory the Great") declared in a homily (#33) that Mary Magdalene was the same person as the anonymous sinner with the perfume in Luke's gospel, and the same as Mary of Bethany, sister of

Martha and Lazarus. Thereafter, the Roman church connected her with the act of penance, and it was common to place her in Southern Gaul during her last years of life, while others suggested that he joined John in Ephesus and was buried there. The reformers of the sixteenth century were not united in their treatment of Mary Magdalene.

In 1969 the identification of Mary Magdalene with Mary of Bethany and the "sinful woman" was removed from official Catholic calendars by Pope Paul VI. On July 22, 2016, at the request of Pope Francis, a new decree was issued, in which her memorial was declared a feast (annually on July 22).

One further note: Dan Brown's bestselling mystery thriller novel, *The Da Vinci Code* popularized a number of erroneous ideas about Mary Magdalene. These fictions included the suggestion that she was Jesus' wife, that she was pregnant at the crucifixion and that she gave birth to Jesus' child ("Juda"), founding a bloodline which survives to this day. There is no historical evidence for any of these claims, although the Gnostic *Gospel of Philip* (Antonov, 55 on p. 33) alludes to Jesus kissing Mary Magdalene often on her face and loving her more than his other students.

BIBLIOGRAPHY

Antonov, Vladimir, ed. *The Gospel of Philip*. Pdf e-books, 2008.

Ehrmann, Bart D. *Peter, Paul, and Mary Magdalene: The Followers of Jesus in History and Legend*. New York: Oxford University Press, 2008.

Grant, Robert. *Gnosticism: A Sourcebook of Heretical Writings from the Early Christian Period*. New York: Harper and Rowe, 1963.

Pagels, Elaine. *The Gnostic Gospels*. New York: Random House, 1979.

Thompson, Mary R. *Mary of Magdala, Apostle and Leader*. New York: Paulist Press, 1995.

Stanley M. Burgess

Junia/Junias:
Ancient Female Apostle?

A t the end of his letter to the Romans (16:7) Paul sends greetings to Andronicus and his wife, Junia, "my relatives, who have been in prison with me, **who are of note among the apostles,** who also were in Christ before I was." A literal reading of this passage suggests, if the female name "Junia" is accepted, that she would be the only female apostle mentioned in the New Testament.

Evidently Junia had been a leader in the early Christian Church even before Saul the Jewish persecutor was converted and became Paul, a prime leader of the Jesus movement. Notwithstanding, no further mention is made of her in the New Testament. It is known that Junia and her husband travelled throughout the Roman Empire, as missionaries preaching the gospel. Church fathers, Origen of Alexandria (185-254) Jerome (347-420) and John Chrysostom (347-407) recognized Junia as a female apostle. Chrysostom argued that she must have been a person of great wisdom in order to be considered among the apostles. Even the twelfth century theologian, Abelard (1079-1142) agreed in his support of Junia's apostolate.

But in the thirteenth century, a change occurred with Archbishop Giles of Bourges (1247-1316) who referred to the "honorable men" Andronicus and Junias. Giles was a contemporary of the misogynist Pope Boniface VIII (1235-1303) who wanted all nuns safely locked away in their convents. Only Gertrude the Great (1256-1302), a German Benedictine nun, correctly translated Romans 16:7 naming Junia an apostle.

In the sixteenth century the great Renaissance scholar and humanist Desiderius Erasmus (1466-1536) and the famed Bible-translator William

Tyndale (1494-1536) both translated the original Greek (because it was available for the first time in centuries) and recovered Junia's name (Muir, 1-6; Torjiesen 33).

Two names, but with great significance. Currently, many translations (including the KJV) opt for the female translation, although the R.S.V. and others persist with using Junias. Why does it matter? Clearly, the inconsistency between versions reflects editorial views on the acceptable roles of women in the Christian Church.

BIBLIOGRAPHY

Muir, Elizabeth Gillan. *A Woman's History of the Christian Church: Two Thousand Years of Female Leadership.* Toronto: University of Toronto Press, 2019.

Pederson, Rena. *The Lost Apostle: Searching for the Truth About Junia.* San Francisco: Jessey Bass, 2006.

Torjiesen, Karen Jo. *When Women were Priests: Women's Leadership in the Early Church and the Scandal of their Subordination in the Rise of Christianity.* San Francisco: HarperSanFrancisco, 1991.

Stanley M. Burgess

Mary, Mother of John Mark

Among the numerous Marys mentioned in the New Testament, Mary, the mother of John Mark who wrote the second gospel, is spoken of but once (Acts 12:1-19). Notwithstanding, we can assume that she was the aunt or sister of Barnabas, the one-time companion of Paul (Col. 4:10). Such a relationship accounts for Barnabas' choice of Mark as his companion, a selection over which Paul and Barnabas parted.

Mary's large house is also a major part of her legacy. According to tradition, it was the site for the Last Supper and shortly thereafter, the place where post-resurrected Jesus appeared to his disciples. It also is the location where the Holy Spirit descended on the Day of Pentecost. Then it was the house that Peter came after his release from prison, only to be met by the uncertain damsel, Rhoda. All of these events speak to the generosity of Mary in providing the first house church for the followers of Jesus. Today this site can be visited in Jerusalem. It is called the "Cenacle" or "Upper Room".

We now have evidence that Mark travelled to many cities in his missionary journeys (including Libya and Egypt), eventually locating in Alexandria in 41 or 43 AD. He is credited by a credible ancient historian, Eusebius of Caesarea, in founding the Coptic Church in Egypt at that time *(Ecclesiastical History* 2:16). Mark was martyred in Alexandria in 68 AD, when pagans of Serapis, an Egyptian god, tied him to a horse's tail and dragged him through the streets of that city for two days, until he was torn to pieces.

Mary, mother of John Mark, can certainly be claimed as one of the mothers of the early Church. This because of her hospitality, her encouragement of the apostles, her presence in the "Upper Room" and her association with John Mark, who is very much responsible for the origins of North African Christianity. As Thomas Oden has pointed out (*The African Memory*, p. 107), Independent Pentecostal Christianity is in the twenty-first century the fastest growing form of worship in Africa. Demographers have discovered that Africa now leads the world as the continent with the greatest number of Pentecostals and Charismatics (Johnson and Zurlo, 2019). It is fascinating to note that Mary and John Mark, together with the apostles Peter and Paul, sparked the beginnings of that early movement.

BIBLIOGRAPHY

Cruse, C. F., trans. *Eusebius' Ecclesiastical History.* Peabody, MA: Hendrickson Publishers, 1998.

Johnson, Todd M. and Gina A. Zurlo, ed. *World Christian Database.* Leiden/Boston: Brill, July 2019.

Oden, Thomas C. *Early Libyan Christianity: Uncovering a North African Tradition.* Downer's Grove, IL: 2011.

_____. *The African Memory of Mark: Reassessing Early Church Tradition.* Downer's Grove, IL: 2011.

Stanley M. Burgess

Priscilla

The story of Priscilla is one of missionary activity in the first century Christian church. She was a Jewess, married to Aquila, who lived in Rome until the couple was expelled from the city by the Roman Emperor Claudius in 49 BC. The ancient Roman historian, Suetonius, reports that there was an expulsion of Jews by the Emperor who reacted to the turmoil caused by their teaching about Jesus in Jewish circles (Suetonius, *Claudius* 25 in *Lives of the* Caesars, pp. 184, 203; the same passage states that the turmoil was caused by the instigation of Chrestus <or Jesus Christ>; Acts 18:1-2).

The couple ended up in Corinth. Perhaps because they also were tentmakers and certainly because they were Christians, Paul lived with Priscilla and Aquila for approximately eighteen months. Then they started accompanying Paul when he proceeded to Syria, stopping first at Ephesus in the western part of Asia, now Turkey.

In I Corinthians 16:19, Paul passes on the greetings of Priscilla and Aquila to their friends in Corinth, suggesting that the couple was in his company when he founded the church there. While in Corinth, we know that Priscilla was the teacher of Apollos, who had learned of the teachings of John the Baptist, but needed the full story of Jesus Christ (Acts 18:26, 1Corinthians 3:4-9). The three missionaries then traveled to Ephesus, staying for over two years there (I Corinthians 16) before heading to Rome (Romans 16) after Claudius died in 54 AD and the expulsion of the Jews from Rome was lifted.

Christianity did not come to Rome originally with Paul's arrival. It seems to have come as early as when pilgrims from Rome at Pentecost in Jerusalem carried the message back to the Eternal City. Some scholars speculate that Priscilla might have been present for Pentecost in the Upper

Room. According to tradition, after returning to Rome, both Priscilla and Aquila were martyred there.

Priscilla certainly was an important minister to the Gentiles. Hers is a significant chapter in the history of early Christian missions. In addition, because she was referred to before Aquila in the writings of both Luke and Paul, at a time of rigid patriarchal tradition, she is a most memorable woman in Christian history. It is speculated that she authored the book of Hebrews because of her high scholarship and teaching ability. She needs to be celebrated for her contributions.

BIBLIOGRAPHY

Edwards, Catherine. *Lives of the Caesars.* Oxford: Oxford World's Classics, 2000.

Witherington, Ben Ill. "Priscilla-An Extraordinary Early Christian Life,'" *Biblical Archeology Review* 45 no. 6, November/December 2019.

_____. *Women in the Earliest Churches.* London: Cambridge University Press 1990.

Stanley M. Burgess

Lydia of Thyatira: a First Century Business Woman

ydia (Acts 16:14-15, 40) a businesswoman in Philippi dealing in expensive purple cloth, became the first of Paul's converts in Europe. She was originally from Thyatira, where the muricid mollusk flourished, the source of the dye for the cloth she produced. We know that she worshipped God in the Jewish tradition until she met Paul and his companions. It was in the Greek region of Philippi that she heard Paul preach. She and her entire household were converted to Christianity, and baptized by Paul. Lydia persuaded Paul, Silas, and Timothy to stay in her spacious home together with her household for a period of time.

It appears that Lydia was a noble woman, likely a widow, who demonstrated Christian hospitality. Certainly, her home also was an early house church, because of its size and her persistence in providing for the missionary group. This act of hospitality, certainly on the list of the highest Christian virtues, resulted in the Church at Philippi, one of the strongest and healthiest that Paul founded.

Paul was most appreciative of this congregation, which sent him assistance when he was in prison later in his ministry. This we learn from the letter of appreciation he sent to them, now known as "Philippians" (4:15-23).

This is also an example of a first century converted Jewess, who, obviously without restraint by a male partner, was able to accomplish much for her God and the Church.

The latest scholarship about Paul and Lydia at Philippi is Asen Chilingirov's new book, still only in Bulgarian. I am grateful to Rumyana Hristova for her assistance with this material.

BIBLIOGRAPHY

Ascough, Richard S. *Lydia: Paul's Cosmopolitan Hostess.* Collegeville, MN: The Liturgical Press, 2009.

Chiilingirov, Asen. *Apostle Paul, Philippies or Philippopolis.* Sofia: Bulga Media, 2019.

Cumming, John. *Butler's Lives of the Saints.* Collegeville, MN: The Liturgical press, 1998.

Muir, Elizabeth Gillan. *A Woman's History of the Christian Church: Two Thousand Years of Female Leadership.* University of Toronto Press, 2019.

Stanley M. Burgess

Thecla

Thecla was a contemporary of Paul the Apostle, born ca. 30 AD in Iconium in Asia Minor (Turkey today) to a wealthy family. She was expected to marry, and marry well. Her mother had already picked out the young man, who had an excellent position and could offer Thecla a secure and stable place in society, with children to carry on the family name.

But her mother's dream did not materialize. The apostle Paul, who had been in Antioch, traveled to Iconium, lodging at a place near Thecla's home. There she heard his "Discourse on Virginity", came to espouse his teachings and became estranged to both her fiance, Thamyris, and her mother. Thamyris was furious and demanded that Paul be imprisoned. Because the fiance was so prominent, Paul was arrested and imprisoned. Late at night Thecia secretly went to the prison, bribed the guards, and stayed to hear Paul's teaching. Her family turned her and Paul over to the authorities. Paul was driven from the city and Thecla was sentenced to death.

Thecla was miraculously saved from burning at the stake by the onset of a storm. She found her way to Antioch where she was reunited with Paul and helped him preach. But there again a nobleman named Alexander desired Thecla and attempted to rape her. When she hurt his pride by refusing his advances, he denounced her to the authorities who sentenced her to die in the arena. Again, she was spared when the wild animals refused to harm her. Even an attempt to drown her failed, and the Antiochians let her go free.

Thecla rejoined Paul in Myra, travelling with him and preaching to women, encouraging them to live a life of chastity. In one tradition, she then lived in a cave in Seleucia Cilicia for 72 years. However, it is more likely that she passed the rest of her life in Maaloula, a village in Syria. She became famous for her healing ministry, but remained persecuted until her death late in the first century (although she is said to have reached the age of ninety in the *Acts of Paul and Thecla).*

Much of our knowledge of Thecla comes from the *Acts of Paul and Thecla,* a late second century text. Several men came to oppose these writings, most notably Tertullian, well known for his rejection of women in ministry. Notwithstanding, Thecla became a patron saint of virgins in the early church, and an antecedent of the monastic movement.

BIBLIOGRAPHY

Ehrman, Bart D. *Lost Christianities: The Battles for Scripture and the Faiths We Never Knew.* Oxford: Oxford University Press, 2005.
Oden, Amy, editor. *In Her Words: Women's Writings in the History of Christian Thought.* Nashville, TN: Abingdon Press, 1994.

Stanley M. Burgess

Philip's Daughters:
Early Prophetesses

A mong the oft forgotten individuals alluded to in Luke's Acts of the Apostles are the four daughters of Philip the Evangelist, living with their father at Caesarea Judea. The four were known for being "prophetesses". While today the term tends to mean a foretelling of the future, in the first century church it had a broader meaning: to teach and to proclaim difficult but necessary truths to the people.

Luke (Acts 21:8-9) relates that, around 58 AD he and Paul were travelling through Palestine when they came to Caesarea by the Sea. They located in the house of Philip the Evangelist, one of the seven, where they stayed for a period of time. There they encountered Philip's four unmarried and virgin daughters who had the gift of prophecy.

Perhaps most interesting is that the passage does not give the names of the four prophetesses. Fortunately, other ancient non-Biblical sources provide this information. Our ancient sources include the very early church historian, Papias (70-163 CE) and the eminent Eusebius of Caesarea (of the third and fourth centuries). This presents the problem that these sources are not consistent. Most modern scholars have concluded that the four were Hermione, Eukhidia, Irias, and Chariline.

We know the most about Hermione, who studied the philosophy of medicine while living with her father in Caesarea. It is likely that her interest in medicine reflected her father's concern for those who suffered illnesses among Christians there. Shortly after Luke and Paul's visit, Philip's family and others were driven out of Caesarea by anti-Christian forces. They settled in Hierapolis, an inland city in what is now central

Turkey, known for its healing mineral waters. Hermione may have stayed for a time there, or as the tradition suggests, proceeded on to Ephesus to see the apostle John. Although she arrived in Ephesus after John had already passed away, she stayed on in that city with the strong Christian community there. She apparently founded a medical clinic there, devoted to the treatment of the poor and homeless. The clinical services were offered without cost.

Eukhidia also came to Ephesus, although she apparently fell ill while serving her clients there, and may have returned to Hierapolis, to be with her father and other sisters there. The four daughters of Philip were but the first of a long line of prophetesses, including the two prominent female leaders of the New Prophecy (Montanism), Prisca and Maximilia.

BIBLIOGRAPHY

Bass, Debra Moody. *The Female Prophets of the Bible: Who Were They and What Did They Have To Say.* Bloomington, IN: WestBow Press, 2018.
Bruce, F. F. *The Acts of the Apostles.* Grand Rapids, Ml: Eerdmans, 1951.

Stanley M. Burgess

Irina of Macedonia:
Martyr: 1st - 2nd century

Saint Irina (feast day 5 May) lived most probably in the second half of the first century. She was the first woman recognized by the Church as a "great martyr" of the Christian faith. Her hagiography does not tell us much about her life, but it does inform us what God did through St. Irina. In general, the hagiographic literature does not belong to the "historical genres;" rather, it belongs to the theological moralizing (didactic) and ethical literature.

St. Irina (birth name Penelope) was the daughter of Licinius, the pagan ruler of Mygdonia, a region in Macedonia, and was known for her exceptional beauty. She was educated by her mentor Apelian, who was a secret Christian. He was the one who also instilled in Penelope Christian virtues and values. According to the legend, the young girl was warned of her future conversion by three birds who flew into her room one by one and each left something for her: a dove left an oil branch, an eagle - a wreath of different flowers, a raven - a small snake. Her teacher Apelian foretold that the Lord would crown her with a wreath of glory in His Kingdom and that she would suffer persecutions because of Christ, who wants to betroth her to Himself. Soon after that event Penelope was baptized by the Apostle Timothy, a disciple of the Holy Apostle Paul, who gave her a new name – Irina (derived from Ancient Greek: Εἰρήνη, "peace," "prosperity"). Then Irina openly confessed herself a Christian. Her infuriated father ordered her to be thrown under the hooves of wild horses. However, instead of harming his daughter, they trampled Licinius. Through the prayer of St. Irina he was resurrected and became Christian together with all his nobles and about 3000 people who witnessed that miracle.

During her stay in Mygdonia, St. Irina tirelessly preached the name of Christ and performed many miracles. Not only did she heal the sick, cleanse lepers, and chase away demons, but she also resurrected a dead young man. After Mygdonia, St. Irina continued to preach the Christian faith among the inhabitants of Macedonia and Thrace in the cities of Kallipol, Constantine, Messemvria. She suffered inhumane tortures by the rulers of all these cities for refusing to bow to pagan idols, but Irina's torment was accompanied by miraculous signs that attracted thousands to the Christian faith. Even some of her tormentors accepted Christ and were baptized. In total, more than 10,000 pagans were converted by St. Irina.

When the Lord indicated to Irina the day of her death, she retired to a mountain cave near the city of Ephesus, whose entrance, at her request, was blocked with stones. On the fourth day, her friends returned to the cave and, opening it, did not find the body of St. Irina in it. Everyone understood that she was taken by the Lord to Heaven.

The fundamental principles of the Lord's Kingdom, which Christ taught through parables, such as love, peace, wisdom, light, resurrection are complex and multilayered. This is why these concepts were simplified so that they could be understood by the ordinary people. One of the steps in this direction was to personify these ideas borrowing the method from the classical antiquity. In Christian context, however, this was done not through allegorical characters, but by embodying the ideas in the lives and images of the saints. In this manner we can see how the idea of the Kingdom's peace - "Peace I leave with you, my peace I give unto you: not as the world giveth, give I unto you. Let not your heart be troubled, neither let it be afraid" (John 14:27) - was merged with the image of St. Irina. Thus, there is little doubt that the development of the legend of the great martyr Irina was aimed at replacing the cult of Eirene, the ancient Greek goddess, a personification of peace. The latter was very popular in the Late Antiquity and the image of the goddess was probably what the Romans associated with when St. Irina's name was mentioned. The spread of the cult of the great Christian martyr was reinforced by the gradual imposition of her iconigraphy over the pagan personification of

Eirene. In the Byzantine art St. Irina was depicted with a cross in her hand, in a richly decorated royal robe, and with a crown, sometimes even with gold ornaments and precious stones. The image of the Saint is found on icons in monasteries and churches in Sinai, Cappadocia, Georgia, Byzantium, Kosovo; in miniatures of Greek manuscripts, in miniatures created in Kievan Rus', where Irina was one of the most revered saints, as well as on frescos in Balkan churches and monasteries (e.g., in Veliko Tarnovo and Gracanitsa). In Constantinople the cult of St. Irina was part of the Empire's propaganda supporting the sanctity of the New Rome and New Jerusalem as the Byzantine capital was called after the middle of the fourth century. Furthermore, the name "Irina" became very popular in the Eastern Orthodox world. For example, this was the name given to Byzantine princesses who married foreign rulers, as well as to foreign princesses who were married to Byzantine emperors. Thus, it can be seen how the concept of the divine peace was partially profaned, while successfully utilized in the ideological work whose goal was to renew the old pagan Rome and to convert it into the New Christian Rome.

BIBLIOGRAPHY

Vachkova, Veselina, and Mariyana Shabarkova-Petrova. *Misteriyata na Balgarskite Stenopisi: Sveshtenata Istoriya i Istoriyata* [*The Mystery of the Bulgarian Murals: the Sacred History and History*]. Sofia: Inle, 2015, pp.46-50.

Saenkova, E. M. "Irina." *Pravoslavnaya Entsiklopediya* [*The Orthodox Encyclopedia*], 15 May 2012, http://www.pravenc.ru/text/673929.html. Accessed 28 May 2020.

"Svetaya Velikomuchenitsa Irina Makedoskaya" ["Holy Great Martyr Irina of Macedonia"]. *Ruskaya Pravoslavnaya Tserkov* [*The Russian Orthodox Church*], 2005-2020, http://www.patriarchia.ru/db/text/911894.html. Accessed 28 May 2020.

Rostovsky, Dimitri. "Stradanie Svyatoi Velikomuchenitsiy Iriny" ["The Suffering of the Holy Great Martyr Irina"]. *Zhitiya Svyatyh po Izlozheniyu Sv. Dimitriya Rostovskogo* [*The Lives of the Saints According to St. Dimitry of Rostov*], Wikisource Library, 16 May 2019, https://ru.wikisource.org/wiki/. Accessed 28 May 2020.

Rumyana Histova

Early Montanist Women: Maximilla and Prisca

The Montanists (second to eighth centuries) were founded about CE 153 by Montanus, a former priest of Cybele, who had converted to Christianity and began to prophesy in his new context. His prophecies attracted much attention partly because he is said to have lost control of himself, falling into a state of frenzy and ecstasy. He is reported to have raved, babbled., and uttered strange things (certain modern scholars have identified this as glossolalia, although we have no proof). We do know that he prophesied in a manner contrary to established custom.

Of greatest significance to our study, Montanus was joined by two women, Maximilia and Prisca, or Priscilla, who left their husbands with Montanus' approval, and claimed to have the same prophetic gifts their founder enjoyed. All three of these early Montanist leaders believed that their prophecies would be God's final word to humans. Montanus identified a new holy place Pepuza in Phrygia (west central Asia Minor, Turkey today)-where Christ would return, and there he gathered his followers to await that event. In the process of writing his prophecies, both Old and New Testament were superseded. However, in the period of persecution that followed, his new tome was lost.

The initial three "New Prophets" claimed to be embodiments of the Holy Spirit or the Paraclete mentioned by Jesus in John 14:16 (Jesus speaking, "And I will pray the Father, and he shall give you another Comforter, that he may abide with you forever" KJV). The authority of the mainstream Catholic church for imparting grace was rejected, having been replaced by the authority of the New Prophets and their more demanding discipline and intolerant exclusiveness. The new Montanist lifestyle required additional fasting and rejection of second marriages, with the promotion of other forms of self-denial and preparation for martyrdom.

It seems that Montanist women continued to exercise a prophetic gift after the death of these three, for Tertullian, himself a convert to Montanism, tells of an early third-century woman who became ecstatic during services, but did not deliver her prophetic message until the congregation departed. It is interesting to note that late in Tertullian's life (he died c. 225) he left the Montanist movement, choosing an even more severe lifestyle (the Tertullianists). Donald Gee has argued that Tertullian was the first great teacher of doctrinal orthodoxy who dared to suggest that the church is not a mere conclave of bishops, but the manifestation of the Holy Spirit (quoting *De pudicitia* <On modesty> 21:17).

In the late second century, a bishop of Rome (either Eleutherius or Victor) was inclined to approve the new prophecies, according to Tertullian, but was dissuaded by Praxeas. Despite continued attempts, the mainstream Church was impotent to wipe out the new prophecy until it was itself legitimatized by the state.

From the beginning of the fourth century, however, the Montanists suffered acute persecution by the orthodox faithful, until at last in the sixth century under Justinian they barricaded themselves in the churches (including one in which the original three Montanists had been buried), and burned them down. A few Montanists remained throughout the empire for the next two centuries.

While Montanus' testament has been lost, a number of sayings of the early Montanists have survived in the writings of Tertullian, Epiphanius, and Eusebius of Caesarea. Here is a sampling of the sayings of Maximilla and Prisca:

Prisca: "A holy minister must understand how to minister holiness. For if the heart gives purification, says she, they will also see visions, and if they lower their faces, then they will perceive saving voices, as clear as they are obscure." (Tertullian, *De Exhort, Cast.* 10.5)

Prisca: "In the form of a woman, says she, arrayed in shining garments, came Christ to me and set wisdom upon me and revealed to me that his place (Pepuza) is holy and that Jerusalem will come down hither from heaven." (Epiphanius, *Haer.* 49.1.2-3)

Maximilla: "The Lord has sent me as adherent, preacher, and interpreter of this affliction (burden) and this covenant and this promise; he has compelled me, willingly and unwillingly, to learn the knowledge of God." (Epiphanius, *Haer.* 48.13.1)

(The Spirit says through Maximilia:). "I am chased like a wolf from the <flock> of sheep. I am not a wolf; I am word and spirit and power." Eusebius, *Eccles. History* 5.16.17).

BIBLIOGRAPHY

Burgess, Stanley M., ed. *Christian Peoples of the Spirit: A Documentary History or Pentecostal Spirituality from the Early Church to the Present.* New York and London: New York University Press, 2011.

Christie-Murray, David. *A History of Heresy.* Oxford: Oxford University Press, 1990.

Heine, Ronald E. *The Montanist Oracles and Tertimonia.* Macon, GA: Mercer University Press, 1989.

Trevett, Christine. *Montanist: Gender, Authority and the New Prophecy.* Cambridge, England: Cambridge University Press, 1996.

Stanley M. Burgess

Blandina of Lyon:
The Martyrdom of a Slave Girl

Blandina of Lyon, Gaul (France) was martyred in her home city in CE 177 during the reign of Emperor Marcus Aurelius. She was but fifteen years of age, a slave, and known to the local population to be a devout Christian. The great Christian historian, Eusebius of Caesarea, devotes extensive time and space to the lives and deaths of a band of martyrs *(Ecclesiastical History,* 5:1-2}.

While the imperial legate was away from Lyon, the chiliarch, a military commander, and the duumvir, a civil magistrate, threw a number of Christians into prison. All had confessed their faith in Christ. When the legate returned, the imprisoned believers were brought to trial. Among these was the young slave girl, Blandina. Her companion victims feared that her physical frailty would result in her giving in under torture. Although her torturers attempted a wide variety of horrible and painful indignities on her, she simply insisted that she was a Christian and that she and her companions had done no wrong.

The Emperor ruled that if the prisoners denied their Christian faith, they were to be released. Those who held to their faith, and were Roman citizens, were to be beheaded. Those who were Roman citizens were to be tortured. Blandina was then bound to a stake and wild beasts were set on her. We are told that the animals would not touch her. Then she was led into the arena to see the sufferings of her companions. Finally, when all of them had been killed, Blandina was scourged, placed on a red-hot grate, enclosed in a net, and thrown before a wild steer who tossed her into the air with his horns. When all else had failed, she was killed with a dagger.

The slave girl now became a hero in the Church. She has been venerated in the Roman Catholic Church, Eastern Orthodox, Eastern and Western Rites, Eastern Catholic Churches, and the Anglican Communion. St. Blandina is celebrated on June 2, her annual feast day.

BIBLIOGRAPHY

Cruse, C. F., trans. *Eusebius of Caesarea: Ecclesiastical History.* Peabody, MA: Hendrickson Publishers, 1998.

Goodine, Elizabeth. *Standing at Lyon: An Examination of the Martyrdom of Blandino of Lyon.* Piscataway, NJ: Gorgias Press, 2014.

Eusebius of Caesarea. *Ecclesiastical History.* C. F. Cruse, trans. Peabody, MA: Hendrickson, 2006.

Stanley M. Burgess

The Martyrdom of
Perpetua and Felicitas

On March 7, 202, during the reign of Septimius Severus, five Christians gave their lives for their Christian faith in the arena at Carthage. Among these were Vivia Perpetua, a twenty-two-year old matron, noble born and well educated, and her handmaiden Felicitas. Their final hours are reported in *The Passion of the Holy Martyrs Perpetua and Felicitas,* written by an unidentifed apologist (perhaps their countryman Tertullian of Carthage}, who has unmistakable Montanist or New Prophecy leanings. The same Tertullian five years before had penned the famous phrase: "The oftener we are mown down by you, the more in number we grow. The blood of the martyrs is the seed of the Church" (*Apology 50,* ANF 3:55).

It is likely that Christianity had arrived in North Africa at the time of the persecution by Nero, when both Peter and Paul had been martyred. At first there seems to have been little formal opposition to the preaching about the Christian God and Jesus Christ. However, as members of the urban elite began to abandon their native gods, the Roman gods, and emperor worship, the Christian faith became increasingly dangerous. In 180 AD seven men and five women were beheaded at Carthage. In 202 AD the Roman Emperor Septimius Severus (emperor from 193-211), who had been born in North Africa, issued an edict that prohibited any further conversions to Christianity. He wanted no disruption of the peace of Carthage, for the port was a key to Roman prosperity. In addition, there were minor insurrections on the borders of North Africa, for which the emperor blamed Christians. The Montanists were the likely offenders since they were politically and militarily anti-Roman. At this point, they do not seem to have yet become anti-Roman, although they refused to worship the emperor or engage in military service,

In North Africa, the proconsul Scapula applied the decree with great cruelty to women and men alike. Women as well as men, children as well as the aged, were part of the early church of the martyrs. If they died, their religion could not help them. Then, if the tortures and deaths were disgusting enough to onlookers, they might be dissuaded from joining the cult of Christians. Finally, the crowd would relearn who held ultimate power in Carthage.

Three authors combined to write *The Passion of the Holy Martyrs Perpetua and Felicitas,* and this is evidenced by the use of three different Latin styles. The opening section deals with an understanding that as life extends, so do the criteria for sainthood, although holiness always is the overarching key. In the second portion, Perpetua writes her own diary, describing actual events, feelings, and prophetic visions. She will not receive the clemency that was sometimes shown to pregnant women or mothers of infants (and we know that she was carrying an unborn child}. She also alludes to the "second baptism" or "baptism in blood" as her promise that she would be received into Christ's heavenly kingdom as soon as she died.

The third section tells the story of the enraged cow who attacks both Perpetua and Felicitas, and includes a revelation that in the final moments of the execution, the young gladiator hits the wrong part of her throat, thus prolonging both her pain and time of death. Perpetua actually guides the executioner's hand during his second attempt. We read that throughout her passion, she experiences an ecstasy in the Holy Spirit, and seems not at first to have known that she is mortally wounded.

The document concludes with a lofty utterance of the writer's confidence that the Divine Spirit remains at work in the Church providing strength and other spiritual virtues to believers who are summoned to martyrdom.

BIBLIOGRAPHY

Ehrman, Bart D. "The Martyrdom of Perpetua and Felicitas." In *After the New Testament: A Reader in Early Christianity,* 42-50. New York and Oxford: Oxford University Press, 1999.

Salisbury, J. E. *Perpetua's Passion: The Death and Memory of a Young Roman Woman.* New York: Routledge, 1997.

Stanley M. Burgess

Zoe of Rome

Zoe of Rome was a noblewoman, married to Nicostratus, a high Roman court official. Her husband was the jailer of Sebastian, who was to be martyred with her ca. 286 AD. What little we know of her comes from the story of Sebastian. He was imprisoned with others who were awaiting execution because of their faith in Jesus Christ.

For six years Zoe had been unable to speak, communicating only with gestures. According to medical specialists, Zoe had probably suffered either from a disabling stroke or from a severe emotional incident. Sebastian in prison learned of Zoe's desire to become a Christian, called for her and made the sign of the cross over her. She immediately regained her speech, proceeding to glorify Jesus. Her jailer husband and she asked to be baptized. Sebastian told Nicostratus to serve Christ rather than the evil emperor Diocletian. He also asked the jailer to assemble his prisoners so that those who wished to be baptized could be. Sebastian then told the priest Polycarp to prepare them, forbidding the baptismal candidates to eat until that evening when 64 new Christians were baptized.

Diocletian learned of this Christian group, and chose to arrest Zoe first, while she was at the tomb of the Apostle Peter. Then Sebastian was taken, placed on trial, and found guilty. He was tied to a tree, then shot with numerous arrows, and when he did not die, was beaten to death.

At her trial, Zoe bravely confessed her faith in Christ. She died, hung by her hair over the foul smoke of a huge dung fire. Her dead body was then flung into the Tiber river. She is considered a saint in the Roman Catholic and Eastern Orthodox Churches. She is celebrated on July 5 by Roman Catholics and on December 18 by Eastern Orthodox.

BIBLIOGRAPHY

Acta 5. Sebastiani Martyris, in J. P. Migne, *Patrologiae Cursus Completus Accurante* (Paris 1845), XVII, 1021ff.

Hofer, J. and K. Rahner, eds. *Lexikon fur Theologie und Kirche.* Second edition, 1957-67. IX: cols 957ff. (Bibliography in English)

Stanley M. Burgess

Helena: Mother of Constantine

Helena (ca. 246/248-ca. 330), was the wife (or concubine) of the Roman Emperor Constantius Chlorus (250-306), and the mother of Emperor Constantine the Great. She is credited after her death with having discovered the fragments of the "True Cross" and the tomb in which Jesus was buried near Golgotha.

According to Ambrose of Milan in the late fourth century *(De obitu Theodosii* 42), she was born a commoner, later to be a "stable-maid" in the Greek city of Drepanum in Bithynia (Asia Minor). It is unknown when she married Constantius, nor is the precise relationship beween the two. Some suggest that she actually married him, others that they had a common-law marriage, recognized in fact but not in law.

Helena gave birth to the future emperor Constantine I on 27 February probably in 272. In order to obtain a marriage compatible with his rising status, Constantius divorced Helena before 289, when he married Theodora. Helena and her son were moved to the court of Diocletian at Nicomedia, where Constantine grew to be a member of the inner circle. Helena never remarried and remained in relative obscurity until 306 when Constantine was proclaimed Augustus of the Roman Empire by Constantius' troops after the latter had died. According to Eusebius, she did not convert to Christianity until after her son became emperor.

She received the title of "Augusta lmperatrix" in 325, enabling her to use the imperial treasury in her quest to locate the relics of the Christian tradition (Eusebius, *Vita Constantini* 3:42-47). Helena was now nearly eighty years of age, heading off to the east and to Jerusalem (327-8).

She ordered the 200-year-old Temple of Venus built during the reign of Hadrian be torn down. It was here that the tomb of Jesus and the relics of three crosses were found. Helena demanded proof of the "true cross", and proceeded to bring a dying woman from Jerusalem to touch the three crosses. Tradition has it that the ill woman was not changed until she touched the third cross, which Helena then declared to be the Savior's cross.

On this site, Constantine ordered the building of the Church of the Holy Sepulchre. Historians Sozomen and Theodoret reveal that Helena also found the nails of the crucifixion. To aid her son, she placed one on Constantine's helmet, and another in the bridle of his horse. She also visited Bethlehem, where she ordered the Church of the Nativity to be built. Helena died around 330, with her son, Constantine, at her side.

The Feast of St. Constantine and Helena, celebrated on May 21 in Bulgaria, combines pagan and Christian customs. On the one hand, on this day people honor the memory of the two saints, go to church, where they donate their icons with gifts, pray for health and good harvest. On the other hand, it is the feast of "nestinari"-people dancing barefoot on glowing embers, a ritual still preserved in some parts of the Strandzha mountain, but almost only as an attraction. Legend tells of a man named Constantine who went barefoot into the fire to protect God. Then God chose him as his helper. Constantine's task was to send to the embers anyone who had committed any sin to be purified.

BIBLIOGRAPHY

Drijvers, Jan Willem. *Helena Augusta: The Mother of Constantine the Great and her Finding of the True Cross.* Leiden and New York: Brill, 1992.

Histova, Rumyana. Personal archives, 2020.

Odahl, Charles Matson. *Constantine and the Christian Empire.* New York: Routledge, 2004.

Stanley M. Burgess and Rumyana Histova

Elizabeth the Wonderworker

E lizabeth Thaumaturgus ("wonderworker") was born to aging parents, Euphemia and Eunomianos, in the mid-fifth century AD. Her family owned an estate in Thrace and was known for their hospitality to the poor, giving liberally to those in need. Elizabeth was learned in scriptures, and was highly educated because of her parents' investment in her training.

Her parents died early in her life, with her mother dead when she was twelve, and her father when she was fifteen. Although she was left with considerable wealth, Elizabeth decided to give all to the poor, to set her slaves free, and to join her aunt's monastic community on "Little Hill" in Constantinople. George, famed for allegedly killing the dragon, was their patron saint. As time passed and Elizabeth's reputation for healing the sick grew, she also came to be known as the "dragon slayer". She also became famous for her many fasts and for going without shoes, which was quite unique for her social class. When her aunt died, Elizabeth became abbess.

Elizabeth soon became known for prophetic and healing ministries. She was especially effective in prayer for blind women, for those with bleeding disorders, and for driving out demons. She wore a coarse hair shirt all year round. For many years, she ate only grass and vegetables, rejecting all bread, wine, and oil.

She made a final visit to her family and to pray at holy sites. Now well advanced in years, she became aware of her impending death through a dream. After returning to her monastic community, Elizabeth died of an intense fever on the 24th of April (year unknown), and was buried in the Cathedral of St. George.

BIBLIOGRAPHY

Schussler Fiorenza. Elizabeth. *In Memory of Her: A Feminist Theological Reconstruction of Christian origins.* New York: Crossroad, 1993.

Swan, Laura. *The Forgotten Desert Mothers: Sayings, lives, and stories of Early Christian Women.* New York, Mahwah, NJ: Paulist Press, 2001.

Stanley M. Burgess

Nino of Iberia

Nino was born to a Greek-speaking Roman family from Kolastra, Cappadocia, although an alternate version of her story claim that she was from Rome, Jerusalem or Gaul. The Orthodox story is that she was the only child of a famous family, related to St. George on her father's side and to the Patriarch of Jerusalem, Houbnal I, on her mother's. She was raised by a nun from Bethlehem, and went to Rome with the help of her uncle, when she decided to preach the Christian gospel In Iberia, bordering the Persian Empire and Armenia on the south and the Black Sea on the East. According to an early legend, she was commissioned by the Virgin Mary to enter Iberia, the supposed resting place of Christ's tunic.

She entered Armenia with 34 other virgins, and with the exception of her, all were slaughtered (beheaded) by the pagan King Tiridates Ill However, shortly after reaching Iberia, Nino was summoned by Queen Nana, who was suffering from a severe illness. Through her prayers, Nino brought healing to Nana, who officially was converted to Christianity, along with her attendants. King Miriam of Iberia was well aware of his wife's conversion, but resisted Christianity until he, while on a hunting trip, suddenly lost his eyesight. In anguish, Miriam prayed to Christ Jesus, asking for deliverance. He was instantly healed, and immediately became a Christian. In 326 King Miriam made Christianity the state religion of his kingdom, Iberia thereby becoming the second Christian state after Armenia. He commissioned the building of the first Christian church in Iberia, and sent an ambassador to Emperor Constantine I to have a bishop and priests sent to Iberia.

Nino withdrew from the Mtskheta into the surrounding mountains, where she died c. 332. She is venerated in the Eastern Orthodox Church, the Oriental Orthodox Church, the Roman Catholic Church, and Eastern Catholic Churches. Her feast is on January 14th.

BIBLIOGRAPHY

Dowling, Theodore E. *Sketches of Georgian Church History*. Boston, MA: Adamant Media, 2006. Wardrop, Margery. *The Life of Saint Nemo*. Piscataway, NJ: Gorgias Press, 2006.

Stanley M. Burgess

Marcella of Rome

Marcella (325-410) was born to a noble family in Rome, with a large Aventine Hill palace. This place became a center of Christian activity, including serving as an academy for the study of Sacred Scripture and a school of prayer. As a young girl Marcella heard Saint Athanasius speak of the Desert Fathers. This grew in her spirituality to the point that she eventually became an ascetic. Marcella married but was widowed after only seven months. Thereafter, she chose to devote her life to prayer, charity, and mortification of the flesh.

Her large home soon attracted Saint Paula and other Roman ladies, eager for the pursuit of holiness. Marcella frequently visited the shrines of the Roman martyrs. She distributed her considerable wealth to the poor. When the Goths invaded Rome in 410, she was brutalized by their leader, Alaric, who assumed that she was still wealthy, and tortured her in order to uncover the location of "the hidden wealth", which no longer existed. As a result of the scourging, she died shortly afterwards.

Saint Jerome corresponded with her, and he called her "the glory of the ladies of Rome." Most of what we know about Marcella comes from the letter of Jerome, especially letter 127 to Principia. It was written on the occasion of Marcella's death, paying tribute to her life and consoling her beloved student. He remembers that she was constantly questioning him about the Scriptures, and other issues. Never doing so for the sake of argument, she grew when he grew, the two relating to each other as scholars and believers. He indicated that when he travelled to Jerusalem from Rome, he felt secure leaving Marcella in charge of the Christian community in Rome. In the many scholarly arguments that ensued in the period, Marcella tended to support Jerome against Origen.

Marcella is best remembered as the founder of the first religious community for women in the Western church. She should also be noted for her cognitive strategies and her constant questioning. One is left with the uncertainty of whether these strengths were generated from the Christian or the Jewish communities in Rome. Or was she stimulated cognitively by Jerome? She is venerated by the Roman Catholic Church, the Eastern Orthodox Church, and the Western Orthodox Church. Her feast is on January 31.

BIBLIOGRAPHY

Butler, Alban. *Butler's Lives of the Saints.* 12 vols. Edited by David Hugh Farmer and Paul Burns. Tunbridge Wells, UK: Liturgical Press, 1995-2000.

Wright, F. A., trans. *Jerome: Selected Letters.* Cambridge, Mass: Harvard University Press, 1933, 1999.

Stanley M. Burgess

Macrina the Younger

Macrina the Younger was born c. 330 AD in Caesarea, Cappadocia, Asia Minor (Turkey today). Her parents were Basil the Elder and Emmelia, and her grandmother was Saint Macrina the Elder. She had nine siblings, including two of the three Cappadocian Fathers, Saint Basil the Great and Saint Gregory of Nyssa. Macrina's father arranged for her to be married, but her fiance passed away before the wedding. After having been betrothed to her fiance, Macrina did not believe it appropriate to marry another man. She saw Christ as her eternal bridegroom, and, as a result, devoted herself to her religion, becoming a nun.

Her strict adherence to an ascetic ideal had a profound influence on her brothers and her mother. In response to her sanctity, her brother Gregory of Nyssa wrote a work entitled *Life of Macrina*. She lived a chaste and humble life, devoting her life to prayer and the education of her younger brother, Peter. Apparently, she consciously rejected all Classical education, choosing instead to devoted study of Scripture and other sacred writings.

Meanwhile, her brother Basil was elected bishop of the great church of Caesarea at Mazaca (now Kayseri in Turkey). A man of great intellect and strong academic preparation, he became famous for his writings, including his writing on the Holy Spirit. He also known for the Basilian Rule, which remains standard for Eastern ascetics even until today. Basil died in 379 AD.

Gregory of Nyssa determined to visit his sister, Macrina, to comfort her for the loss of her brother, Basil. He was shocked by the realization that she was also on her death bed. Notwithstanding her physical condition, she engaged in a spiritual dialogue with him, which he thereafter recorded. Macrina also passed away in 379 AD. She is venerated as a saint by Eastern

Orthodox Christians, as well as Oriental Orthodoxy, the Roman Catholic Church, the Anglican Communion and Lutheranism.

BIBLIOGRAPHY

Dury, John L. "Gregory of Nyssa's Dialogue with Macrina: The Compatibility of Resurrection of the Body and the Immortality of the Soul." *Theology Today 621:* no.2 (2005): 210-222. P.G. XLVI, 12 sq.

Gregory of Nyssa, *Life of Macrina,* in Elizabeth Alvilda Petroff, ed., *Medieval Women's Visionary Literature.* New York and Oxford: Oxford University Press, 1986.

Wilson-Kastner, Patricia. "Macrina, Virgin and Teacher," in *Andrews University Seminary Studies,* 17:1 (Spring 1979), pp. 105-18.

Stanley M. Burgess

Egeria
Pioneer Pilgrim

Egeria (also known as Etheria or Aetheria) was a Western European pilgrim, probably from the western coast of Spain or France (she refers to her home as "Ocean"). In the late fourth century AD she travelled for three years to the Holy Land. While others may have preceded her in such a pilgrimage, she is the first to have recorded her travels, in a long letter now known of as **Itinerarium Egeriae,** probably written to the nuns of her community. The historical details she includes place the trip in the early 380s, during the reign of Emperor Theodosius.

The two surviving parts of Egeria's book begin as she approached Mount Sinai and end in Constantinople, and in the second portion with descriptions of the services in Jerusalem. She appears to have enjoyed mountain climbing, having scaled Mt. Sinai, as well as Mt. Nebo. In addition, she travelled to Haran and other Old Testament sites, as well as the Sea of Galilee and other places where Jesus performed miracles. On her way back to Europe she stopped at Hagia Thekla, the shrine of Saint Thecla's near Seleucia Isauriae (now Silifke, Turkey}, a place especially venerated by women. After returning to Constantinople, she writes of her plans to visit sites in Ephesus, including those related to St. John's life and ministry. Because this section does not appear in materials discovered to date, we have no proof that this side trip ever occurred.

The second portion of her itinerary report deals with liturgical services and church observances in Jerusalem. This information is most valuable in understanding the development of liturgical practices in the fourth century, including Lent, Palm or Passion Sunday, and Pentecost, at a time when the implementation of liturgical seasons was reaching universal practice. It is noteworthy that this is before the acceptance of a celebration of a December 25 celebration of the nativity of Jesus.

The only surviving copy of Egeria's book is a manuscript included in the *Codex Aretinus* copied in the eleventh century. After many centuries, it was translated into Russian in 1889, and into English in 1891.

BIBLIOGRAPHY

Oden, Amy, ed. "Egeria, Pilgrimage," *In Her Words: Women's Writings in the History of Christian Thought.* Nashville, TN: Abingdon Press, 1994.

Wilson-Kastner, Patricia., et. al. eds. *A Lost Tradition. Women Writers of the Early Church.* Lanham, Mass: University Press of America, 1981.

Stanley M. Burgess

Introduction
Medieval Christianity

I t is virtually impossible to find a consensus on an exact dating of the so-called "Middle Ages." The present practice is to "round off" the beginning and ending dates to encompass the millennium from CE 500 to 1500. Historians of Rome argue the question of when Rome "fell." Some would suggest CE 410, when Alaric, the Vandal king sacked the city. Others, including the venerable Edward Wakefield Gibbon, chose CE 476 when the Ostrogoths overthrew the last Roman-born Emperor of Rome, Romulus Augustus. But even this answer is confusing. The Roman Senate continued to operate during the Ostrogothic period. Another problem with this date is that the capital of the Western Empire had moved from Rome to Ravenna. Then of course the Eastern Empire already existed, soon to be known as Byzantium. The Eastern Emperors claimed to be rulers of the entire Roman Empire, East and West. The ancient world certainly ends before the rise in the sixth century CE of Islam. Much of this confusion results from an absence of adequate evidence, including the issue of hagiography (uncritical treatment of stories of saints and miracles)—a problem that plagues historians in their attempts to understand the entire Medieval period.

The same problem exists in our effort to define the "end of the Middle Ages." Church historians often claim CE 1517, when Martin Luther nailed (or mailed!} his 95 Theses to the Church door at Wittenberg. But the Reformation Era actually had its start some decades before, as Italian and northern Europeans experienced an impressive period of cultural reform, now known as the Renaissance. Such great Humanists as Desiderius

Erasmus of Rotterdam offered suggestions for reform that later were used by Luther, Calvin, Zwingli and other Protestant Reformers. Humanists also influenced reformers in the Catholic Reformation (previously called the "Counter Reformation"}, in such individuals as Johann Eck (1483-1546), the combatant of Luther, and Jacques Lefèvre d'Étaples (1453-1536}.

What then were the roles of women in this millennium? It is clear to historians that the Christian Patriarchal monopoly continues—even accelerates in this era. It may have reached a new extreme when it is erroneously reported that at the Council of Macon (in Frankish territory} in CE 585, the 59 male bishops present voted on the question of whether women even had souls. The affirmative won by one vote! (Taege, p. 7). This fable, like the future fable of "Pope Joan" three centuries later, are common in medieval histories and in later interpretations by anti-Catholic writers. Notwithstanding these fables, there is an element of truth in many such tales. In both of these stories, women were clearly devalued by uncritical writers, just as they seemed to have been by most men of the cloth in this period.

Throughout the early Middle Ages, women had virtually no opportunity for ministry in the local church. But they did have such possibilities in the monastic movement. Only virgins and widows were allowed to be part of the movement, and all who joined were required to take vows of total poverty. But those who entered the convent were free to minister. The Benedictine monasteries and convents were the first to be organized. Around CE 530 Benedict of Nursia, together with his sister, Scholastica, founded a convent near Monte Cassino in central Italy so that they could be close enough to visit. These convents increased rapidly in number, as women took vows of poverty, chastity, and obedience. These groups of women were governed by an abbess. In time, double monasteries were formed, for men and women, and were almost always governed by an abbess. In reality, the monastic life offered women opportunities to teach, to minister, and to lead, if they were willing to forgo married life and the possibility of having children.

The nun also had opportunities of missionary activity, of travel and spreading the gospel. Among the best known was Bridget of Kildare, Ireland, who worked with St. Patrick in extending their faith throughout the Emerald Isle. In the eighth century, another great missionary, Boniface, commissioned the Anglo-Saxon Benedictine nun, Leoba, to aid him in his efforts in Germany. Leoba is especially remembered for her charismatic gifts, bringing healing to many on her journeys. Missionary activity has always been most successful when accompanied by healing ministry.

Occasionally, women were born into privilege, being children of nobility or kings, or becoming their wives. The early Middle Ages has numerous examples of such Christian ladies, including Clotilda (daughter of the King of Burgundy), Theodelinda (Queen of the Lombards), Irene of Athens (Byzantine Empress), and Margaret of Wessex (Queen of the Scots). All of these, and many more, are memorable for their Christian service.

Of course, sthere also were stay-at-home wives who evidenced a life of Christian vitality. Dhuoda, probably from Gascony, married a duke at the Imperial capital in Aachen in 824. He was the second cousin to Emperor Charlemagne (i.e., related to the Carolingian dynasty). In a horribly chaotic period, Dhuoda was left most of her married life by her warring husband, who eventually was killed by his dynastic competition. She had two sons, who also became warriors. Not able to nurture them in person, she chose yet another avenue of influence, namely writing a handbook or manual, detailing what a life of real Christianity required. She had been assigned to her at-home role, but found a way to promote her powerful value set.

Above all, it was required of most married Christian women to stay-at-home in the Medieval world. Perhaps the most notorious scandal of the period comes out of a legend of a young brilliant girl who attempted to rise in the Patriarchal world by dressing in male garb and becoming a "male", accompanying her lover, another male, to Athens to study at male academies. Eventually, it is reported that she graduated, came to Rome and eventually rose to the top of the male hierarchy, namely becoming Pope Joan (officially John VII, 855-57). Eventually, she was discovered and clubbed to death. Instead of "staying in her place" she assumed the impossible, to be equal to a man and to rise to the male pinnacle. Of course, this was probably a fable, but it had its impact for centuries.

Gratefully, there were women of great intellect and conviction that did rise because of their virtues. At a time when the Christian West was lagging behind Islam in the East and the Byzantine Empire in between, in virtually all cultural domains, a brilliant Benedictine abbess and writer, Hildegard of Bingen (1098-1175) emerged, stunning the Christian world with her universal genius. Like so many other women of the period, she was a visionary mystic. Unlike the rest, however, she painted her visions! She composed music that is still sold commercially today. She wrote continuously, and much of this was revelatory, for she can be counted as a prophetess. She influenced popes, kings and all of Christendom. Once again, she proved that great women could lead with their lives, their brains, and their wisdom, at a time when most females were considered inferior.

Perhaps the most important group of Christian women in the Middle Ages were the mystics. In addition to Hildegard of Bingen, the lives and messages of such mystics as Gertrude of Helfta, Mechtild of Magdeburg, Catherine of Siena, Brigitta of Sweden, Julian of Norwich, and Margery Kempe are leading examples of memorable Christian women in the mid to late Medieval period.

Often forgotten (for that has been the institutional church's intent) are the women in sects, usually called heretics. Of the few that we can still identify is Esclarmonde of Foix, one of the leaders of the Cathars or radical dualists. These perfectionists required their *perfect* to live sinlessly after have been given the rite of *consolamentum* (baptism in the Holy Spirit and fire). They reappeared throughout the Middle Ages beginning with the Paulicians, then the Bogomils, and finally the Cathars (sometimes called the Albigensians because of the crusade by that name that attempted to exterminate them from 1215ff).

Finally, our Medieval story would be incomplete without remembering a young girl who demonstrated great courage and skill in battle, and great piety and devotion to God in death. Of course, this is the legendary Joan of Arc, burned at the stake in Rouen, Normandy, on May 30, 1431 at the age of nineteen years.

BIBLIOGRAPHY

Burgess, Stanley M. *Johann Eck and Humanism.* Ann Arbor, Ml: University of Michigan Microfilms, 1971.

Clark, Elizabeth and Herbert Richardson, eds. *Women and Religion: A Feminist Sourcebook of Christian Thought.* New York: Harper and Rowe, 1977.

Nauert, Charles G. "Rethinking Christian Humanism," in Angelo Mazzocco, ed. *Interpretations of Renaissance Humanism.* Leiden and Boston: Brill, 2006.

Oden, Amy, ed. *In Her Words: Women's Writings in the History of Christian Thought.* Nashville, TN: Abingdon Press, 1994.

Schulenburg, Jane. *Forgetful of their Sex: Female Sanctity and Society ca 500-1100.* Chicago, IL: University of Chicago Press, 1998.

Taege, Marlys. *And God Gave Women Talents!* St. Louis: Concordia, 1978.

Tucker, Ruth A., and Walter L. Liefeld. *Daughters of the Church: Women and Ministry from New Testament Times to the Present.* Grand Rapids, Ml: Academie Books, Zondervan Publishing House, 1987.

Wemple, Suzanne. "Women from the Fifth to the Tenth Century," in Christiane Klapisch-Zuber, ed. *A History of Women: Silences of the Middle Ages.* Cambridge, MA: Harvard University Press, 1992.

Stanley M. Burgess

Scholastica

According to the *Dialogues* of Gregory the Great (Book 11, Chapters 33-34), Scholastica was born c. 340 in Nursia, Umbria, Italy to a wealthy couple. Our sources differ on whether she was a twin to St. Benedict or simply his sister. According to Gregory, she was dedicated to God from the beginning. She and Benedict were brought up together until the time he left to pursue studies in Rome.

A young Roman woman of Scholastica's class and time would probably have remained in her father's house until her marriage or her entry into religious life. Benedictine tradition relates that Scholastica established a hermitage about five miles from Monte Cassino (where her brother founded and lived in the famed monastery). However, an alternate version, proposed by Ruth Clifford Engs, is that Scholastica actually lived in her father's house with other religious women until her father's death when she moved nearer to Benedict.

Perhaps the most interesting story told about Scholastica is that she would, once a year, go and visit her brother at a farmhouse near his abbey, and that they would spend the day, worshipping together and discussing religious matters. One day they had supper and continued their conversation until it was time for Benedict to leave. As he prepared to depart, Scholastica pleaded with him to stay with her overnight. He was aware that this would violate his own rule (the Benedictine rule, which became standard for virtually all western monasteries). At this point, Scholastica folded her hands in prayer. Immediately thereafter a fierce storm arose, which made it impossible for Benedict to leave until the morning following, after spending the night in discussion.

Three days later (February 10, 543), from his cell, Benedict saw his sister's soul leaving the earth and soaring into the heavens as a shining white dove. Benedict brought her body to his monastery, and buried it in the tomb which had prepared for himself. Scholastica is the patron saint of nuns, education, and convulsive children. She is venerated in the Roman Catholic Church, the Eastern Orthodox Church, and the Episcopal Church.

BIBLIOGRAPHY

Adrienne von Speyr. *Book of All Saints: Scholastica.* San Francisco: Ignatius Press, 2008.

Goo, Mary Richard and Joan M. Braun. "Emerging from the Shadows: St. Scholastica," in *Medieval Women Monastics,* Miriam Schmitt, Linda Kulzer, eds. Collegeville, MN: Liturgical Press, 1996.

Engs, Ruth Clifford. *St. Scholastica: Finding Meaning in her Story.* St. Meinrad, IN: Abbey Press, 2003.

Stanley M. Burgess

Mary of Egypt

From Saint Sophronius, the Patriarch of Jerusalem (634-638), we gain most of our information about Mary of Egypt, also known as Maria Aegyptiaca (c. 344-c. 421). When she came to the age of twelve she ran away from her parents to the city of Alexandria. There she lived an extremely sinful life. Sophronius even states that she often refused the prostitute monies offered to her because she was so driven by passion. She also lived by begging, as well as spinning flax.

After seventeen years of this lifestyle, she traveled to Jerusalem for the Feasts of the Exaltation of the Holy Cross. She paid for her trip and her early time in the Holy City as a prostitute. When she attempted to enter the Church of the Holy Sepulchre for the celebration, she was barred from entry by an unseen force. Suddenly realizing that this was because of her impurities, she prayed for forgiveness and promised to give up her lifestyle. Instead, she pledged to become an ascetic. Again, she attempted to enter the church and was permitted in. After venerating a relic of the true cross, she heard a voice telling her to cross the Jordan River, where she would find "glorious rest."

This she did, and reportedly stayed in ascetic lifestyle until her death. She became famous for her transformed lifestyle, and is venerated as patron Saint of penitents by Eastern Orthodox, Oriental Orthodox, Roman Catholic and Anglican churches. Her feast is on April 1st.

BIBLIOGRAPHY

Chisholm, Hugh. "Sophronius", *Encyclopedia Britannica* 28/429. Cambridge, UK: Cambridge University Press, 1911.

MacRory, Joseph. "St. Mary of Egypt," *Catholic Encyclopedia,* Vol. 9. New York: Robert Appleton Company, 1910.

Ward, Sr. Benedicta. "St. Mary of Egypt: Ascent From Prostitution to Sanctity", in *Harlots of the Desert: A Study of Repentance in Early Monastic Sources.* Kalamazoo, Ml: Cistercian Publications, 1987.

Stanley M. Burgess

Brigid of Kidare, Ireland

Along with Saint Patrick and Saint Columba, Brigid of Ireland or Brigid of Kidare (c. 451-525) is one of Ireland's patron saints. She is remembered as a Christian ascetic, an abbess, and the founder of several convents, including that of Kildare in Ireland, which was among the most revered. At least two Latin lives had been composed by the end of the seventh century describing her as a nobleman's daughter who chose to consecrate herself to God, and became the leader of a community of women (or perhaps men and women) at Kildare. By the seventh century she was the leader of a major double monastery at Kildare that regarded her as its founder.

Although accounts of her early life are often conflicting, it seems clear that she was born to a Christian Pict slave named Brocca, who had been baptized by Saint Patrick. Her father was Dubhthach, a chieftan of Leinaster. Her mother was sold to a pagan druid when she became pregnant with Brigid, and so she was born a slave. Because of his own impurity, Brigid became ill whenever her father tried to feed her.

As she grew older, Brigid performed miracles, including healing and feeding the poor. At one time it is said that she gave away her mother's butter supply, only to replenish it miraculously. Brigid is also credited with founding a school of art (illumination and metalwork).

Brigid and Patrick worked together efficiently and in harmony. We are told in the *Acta Triadis Thaumaturgae* (the "Three Wonderworkers") that they achieved many great works and are known as the "pillars of the Irish people." We are told in our primary sources that these great works included turning water into beer, stilling the wind and the rain, predicting the future, various healings, and the preservation of a nun's chastity in difficult circumstances.

Brigid died on February 1, 525, of natural causes and she was buried to the right of the high altar of Kildare Cathedral. She is venerated in Eastern Orthodox, Roman Catholic, and Anglican churches. February 1 is her feast day.

BIBLIOGRAPHY

Acta Triadis Thaumaturgae seu divorum Patricii, Columbae, et Brigidae, trium et majoris Scotiaae, seu Hiberniae. In *Acta Sanctorvm Veteris Et Maioris Schotiae* II. Apud Cornelivm Coenestenivm, 1647.

Herbermann, Charles, ed. "St. Brigid of Ireland," *Catholic Encyclopedia.* New York: Robert Appleton, 1913.

Selinor, Edward. *Wisdom of the Celtic Saints.* Notre Dame, IN: Ave Maria Press, 1993.

Stanley M. Burgess

Clotilda of France

Clotilda (470-545) was the daughter of Chilperic, King of Burgundy in what later became a province in France. She lived in the turbulent period when the Germanic nations were invading the weakened Roman Empire and destroying what was left of Roman political power.

The tribal force that invaded Burgundy was the Franks, who swept over the Rhine River into Roman Gaul. Eventually, they would give the area their name: Frankland or France. The leader of the Franks was Clovis, a brutal and shrewd young leader who combined the Frankish clans into a united army and in 486 defeated the Roman governor, Syagrius, at Scissons in northeast France.

Some of these invading Germanic tribes were already Christian, but belonged to heretical Arian Christianity, which denied the Roman Catholic teaching that Jesus was co-equal with the divine Father. The Arians insisted that Jesus was begotten within time by God the Father rather than being co-eternal with the Father. The orthodox teaching is called Trinitarianism or homoousianism.

The real solution to this problem was not the work of a synod or council. Rather, it was the marriage in 492 of Clovis to Clotilda, a devout Catholic Christian. Apparently, this doctrinal problem was a significant issue between the two until Clovis yielded to Clotilda when he permitted her to have two of their newly born sons baptized as Christians. In addition, he was losing a battle to the German Alemanni when he vowed to "Clotilda's God" that he would embrace the Christian faith if granted a victory. He won the battle and then followed through on his vow.

On Christmas Day 499, Clovis was baptized by the Bishop of Rheims, and his people followed him to the baptismal font. Clovis and his queen later founded in Paris the church of the Apostles Peter and Paul.

Unfortunately, after Clovis' death in 511, the queen mother was shocked by the feuding of her three sons. Clotilda eventually left Paris to get away from this violence. She went to the shrine city of Tours where she passed her remaining years serving the poor.

Clotilda is venerated in Eastern Orthodox and Roman Catholic churches. Her feast is on June 3 (June 4 in France).

BIBLIOGRAPHY

Asimlov, Isaac. *The Dark Ages.* Boston: Houghton Mifflin, 1968.

Chisholm, Hugh. "Clotilda, Saint", *Encyclopedia Britannica* 6 (11th edition), p. 557. Cambridge, UK: Cambridge University Press, 1911.

Farmer, David Hugh. *The Oxford Dictionary of Saints* (4th edition). Oxford: Oxford University Press, 1997.

Stanley M. Burgess

Theodelinda

T heodelinda (c. 570-628 AD) was queen of the Lombards by marriage to two consecutive Lomband rulers, Authari and then Agilulf, and regent of Lombardia during the minority of her son Adaloald, and co-regent when he reached majority, from 616-626. She was born a Bavarian princess to King Garbald I and his wife, Walderada, who was from the royal line of the previous Bavarian ruler, Waco.

She was married for approximately two years to Authari, who suddenly died in 590. She then had the right to choose his successor, Agilulf, and they were wed, with Theodelinda remaining in power throughout the transition. She exerted much influence in restoring Nicene Christianity (Roman Catholic) to a position of primacy in Italy against its rival, Arian Christianity.

Theodelinda was both an excellent queen and a very devout woman. She encouraged agriculture and instituted policies to increase Lombardy's economic stability. She also had built numerous churches, monasteries and convents. The most famous of her churches is in Monza, a suburb of Milan-the Duomo di Monza, which houses one of the very earliest holy relics in Christendom. It is the Iron Crown and a piece of the True Cross and one nail from Jesus' crucifixion. The crown has been used for the crowning of all Italian kings from the seventh through the nineteenth centuries (the last time was to crown Ferdinand I of Austria the King of Lombardy-Venetia in 1838).

Theodelinda was known for her charitable work, and gained such a reputation for intelligence and faith that Pope Gregory I the Great dedicated one of his works, the *Dialogues* to her. Paul the Deacon, who typically points out the flaws and political antagonism of queens and duchesses throughout his historical texts, depicts Theodelinda in a very favorable light, making her into a heroine.

BIBLIOGRAPHY

Dunbar, Agnes. *Dictionary of Saintly Women*. 2 vols. London: G. Bell & Sons, 1904.

O'Donnell, James. *The Ruin of the Roman Empire*. New York: Harper Collins, 2006.

Wallace-Hadrill, J. M. *The Barbarian West, 400-1000*. Oxford and Malden, MA: Wiley-Blackwell, 2004.

Wickham, Chris. *The Inheritance of Rome: Illuminating the Dark Ages, 400-1000*. New York: Viking, 2009.

Stanley M. Burgess

Leoba

L eoba (710-782 AD) was an Anglo-Saxon Benedictine nun, whose mother, Aebbe, received a dream that her child still to be born was "the chosen/beloved" child of Christ. In the dream, Aebbe was told that her offspring would lead a spiritual life, and would serve the church. The parents named her Leoba ("greatly loved").

Deeply religious, Leoba entered the doublt monastery of Wimbourne Minster as an oblate, and later as a nun. She attended the lectures of St. Winifred and St. Boniface at Nhutscelle, near Wimbourne. Boniface maintained communication with a number of British religious houses. Leoba asked Boniface for prayer for her aged parents. Several years later, Boniface invited Abbess Tetta to send Leoba and others to assist him in spreading Christianity in Germany. In 748 Leoba traveled to Germany to aid Boniface.

It is reported that Leoba was involved in numerous miracles. We must recognize that tales of this type, particularly during the Dark Ages (400-1000) are often best classified as hagiographic, i.e., portraying a saint in a more favorable light than critical historians would accept. This often occurs when a man or woman is being considered for sainthood. In any event, Leoba was credited for a wide variety of miracles, including saving a village from fire, saving a town from a terrible storm, saving the life of a dying nun-all accomplished through her prayers. It also is reported that many miracles occurred at her gravesite. These incidents are recorded by numerous sources, especially Rudolf of Fulda (David Farmer, "Lioba").

Leoba is venerated by Roman Catholic and Eastern Orthodox churches. Her feast is on September 28.

BIBLIOGRAPHY

Hollis, Stephanie. *Anglo-Saxon Women and the Church.* Durham, NC: Boydell Press, 1992.

McNamara, Jo Ann, et al., eds. *Sainted Women of the Dark Ages.* Durham, NC: Duke University Press, 1992.

Rudolf of Fulda, "The Life of Leoba, Abbess of Bischofsheim" (c. 836), in *Monumenta Germaniae Historica, Scriptores,* XV/**1,** ed. Waitz. Hanover, Germany: 1887. Translated into English by Dorothy Whitelock in *English Historical Documents.* Second Edition. London: Methuen, 1955, pp. 719-722.

Stanley M. Burgess

Irene of Athens
Byzantine Empress

L ittle is known of the young Irene except that she was an extraordinarily beautiful orphan girl from Athens. She was born c. 752 CE and was an orphan in 768 when she was brought to Constantinople by Emperor Constantine V and was married to his son Leo IV. We are told that she was chosen to be his wife as a result of a bride-show, in which eligible young women were paraded before the bridegroom until one was finally selected.

On January 14, 771, Irene gave birth to a son, the future Constantine VI, named after his grandfather, Irene's father-in-law, Constantine V. When Constantine V died in 775, Leo IV ascended to the throne at the age of twenty-five years, with Irene as his empress consort.

The struggle over whether the Byzantine church should permit the veneration of icons became front and center in the reign of Leo IV and Irene. We have a report that Irene had been caught with two sacred icons under her pillow. Leo, influenced by his military leaders, thereafter refused to have marital relations with his wife.

Irene intervened in religious affairs on several occasions. First in 784 CE she made her former secretary Tarasios the Patriarch (Bishop) of Constantinople, despite knowing that he had never been ordained. Then she convened a Church council in Constantinople in 786 to put an official end to the destruction of icons (iconoclasm). Influential members of the army opposed this move and organized a riot which forced the council to close. Irene was not to be deterred, however, and quickly stationed the troublemakers to Asia Minor (Turkey) under the guise of preparations for a new military campaign. They were shortly disbanded and their positions in Constantinople were given to men more loyal to Irene.

With opposition quelled, Irene went to the Seventh Ecumenical Council at Nicaea in September 787 CE. There Irene and 350 invited bishops finally ruled to restore the orthodoxy of the veneration of icons in the Christian church and thereby ended iconoclasm. For this alone Irene came to be venerated as a saint. She certainly was not known for her Christian character or her asceticism.

It is reported that Irene ordered that her son, Constantine's eyes be gouged out. Shortly thereafter, he died of his wounds. Irene ruled from 797 to 802 CE as emperor in her own right. Near the end of her reign, she attempted to negotiate a marriage with the western Roman Emperor, the great Charlemagne, but this maneuver failed.

One could argue that there should be no place in this tome for Irene. None of the memorable women included herein was perfect, however. She is included because she successfully defended the inclusion of icons in the Christian churches, and that has great significance. The Seventh Ecumenical Council at Nicaea ended the iconoclastic controversy and reunited the Eastern church with that of Rome.

BIBLIOGRAPHY

Barbe, Dominique. *Irene de Byzance: La femme empereur.* Paris: Perrin, 1990.

Garland, Lynda. "Irene (769-802}", *Byzantine Empresses: Women and Power in Byzantium, AD 527-1204.* New York and London: Routledge, 1999.

Kazhdan, Alexanderk ed. *The Oxford Dictionary of Byzantium.* Oxford and New York: Oxford University Press, 1991.

Stanley M. Burgess

Dhuoda

Dhuoda (c. 800-844) is one of the outstanding women of the ninth century, a period of great turmoil in the Christian West, with the Roman Empire long expired, the Christian East, or Byzantium holding on, and Islam on the rise. This was one of the darkest periods of the so-called Dark Ages. We are not sure who Dhuoda's parents were, but it is thought that her father might have been Sancho I, Duke of Gascony. The first certainty is that Dhuoda married Bernard, Duke of Septimania, at Aachen (in western-most Germany) on June 24, 824. Bernard was the son of William of Gellone, Emperor Charlemagne's cousin. In brief, Dhuoda was probably wealthy.

On November 29, 826, Dhuoda and Bernard's first son, William of Septimania, was born. The second son, Bernard Plantapilosa, followed on March 22, 841. In the interim, Dhuoda and Bernard lived apart most of the time, she in the Rhone Valley in Southern France, and he at the imperial court in Aachen. What little we know of Dhuoda's life thereafter comes from her book, the *Liber Manualis,* or *Manual,* which she wrote for her eldest son, William, between 841 and 843. In 843 she sent the *Manual* to William. By this time Dhuoda had been separated from both of her sons, due to the conflicting ambitions of Charlemagne's descendants. Eventually, politics caught up with her family. Her husband, Bernard was condemned for rebellion and executed in 844. The two sons also were killed, William in 850, Bernard in 885.

Dhuoda is a memorable Christian woman because she stood up for what she considered to be Christian principles for living in a decadent and chaotic period of warfare. Her *Manual* attempted to establish a moral compass for both William and young Bernard. The book deals with such topics as loving God, the mystery of the Trinity, social order, moral living,

God's chastisement of those he loves, the usefulness of the beatitudes, the deaths of body and spirit, interpreting numbers, and the usefulness of reciting the Psalms.

The *Manual* provides insights into the education of well-to-to women in the Carolingian period, as well as the raising of children, the order of society, the importance of fathers (noteworthy: it does not really address that of mothers), and how Christianity impacted the lives of nobility in early French society.

This tome is a rare look into the life and values of a devout Christian woman who employed all of her talents to help her children, but who did not attempt to reach beyond the subordinate role expected of all women of the period. As such, it is in sharp contrast to the legend of another eighth century woman, specifically Ioannes Angelicus ("Pope Joan") who allegedly reigned as pope for a few years (855-857) during the same period. According to the tale, Joan was born John Anglicus of Mainz. The young girl followed her lover into ecclesiastical service, attending a training program for clergy in Athens, Greece, and then, because of her excellence in seminary studies was elevated into the priesthood, and eventually to Rome, where she finally reached the Papal level (as Pope John VIII).

The legend continues that "Pope" Joan's sex is finally revealed when she delivered a baby during a procession through Rome. An attendant declared it to be a "miracle", but to no avail. She is said to have passed away, either that day, at the hands of an angry mob of the faithful, or shortly thereafter from natural causes. This legend was clearly believed by the pontifical hierarchy for they avoided processing through the very spot of the birth, and to this day it is said that they created a vetting ritual to assure that future popes were male.

The legend of Pope Joan was believed until the 16th century, when both Catholic and Protestant scholars called the story into question. The story. Is now widely considered fictional, though the legend remains influential in cultural depictions of the ninth century in Roman Catholic history.

It also provides a striking contrast when contrasted with the steady and godly devotion of Dhuoda, who played out her role as a woman who never attempted to exceed her gender roles, and the legendary Pope Joan, who took advantage of her "intelligence" to rise to the papacy through deception.

BIBLIOGRAPHY

Dronke, Peter. *Women Writers of the Middle Ages.* Cambridge: Cambridge University Press, 1984.

Jean de Mailly. *Chronica Universalis Mettensis.* 1254.

Oden, Amy, ed. *In Her Words: Women's Writings in the History of Christian Thought.* Nashville: TN: Abingdon Press, 1994. (The latest translation of Dhuoda's *Manual.*)

Stanford, Peter. *The She-Pope. A Quest for the Truth behind the mystery of Pope Joan.* London: Heineman, 1998.

Wilson, Catherine M. *Medieval Women Writers.* Athens, GA: University of Georgia Press, 1984.

Stanley M. Burgess

Princess Olga of Kiev (c.890-969)

There is little information about the life of Princess Olga of Kiev that is free from folkloristic embellishments and accepted as credible by scholars. She was the wife of Prince Igor (r. 912-945), the ruler of Kievan Rus'. In 945 Igor was killed and Olga assumed power as regent of the Kievan state on behalf of their son Svyatoslav, then a minor. Thus, she became the first female ruler of Russia. Even after Svyatoslav reached maturity (c. 963), Olga continued to be in charge of the internal policies of Kievan Rus'. Also known as "Vesheii" (wise), she had the full support of the army, which was a testimony to the great respect she held among the people.

Princess Olga played a considerable role in the centralization of power and unification of the country by establishing national boundaries, towns, trading posts, which also served as administrative centers controlled by her agents. She is also credited with establishing the first legal tax system in Kievan Rus'. Her biggest accomplishment, however, was her role in paving the way for the Christianization of the Kievan state in 988. Olga was a devout Christian herself and was one of the first to bring this new religion to the pagan Kievan society. She realized that the act of accepting Christianity would provide new opportunities for internal development of the country, as well as for its international recognition. The Princess visited Constantinople after the death of her husband and it is highly probable that she sought the sending of a mission headed by a bishop to Kiev. She may have received some promises by the Byzantine Emperor Constantine VII (r. 913-959), but such missionaries were never sent to Kiev. Then Olga turned to the Holy Roman Emperor Otto I (r. 962-973) with a request that a bishop and priests were sent to administer the new Russian church. The Emperor's envoy, Adalbert of Trier, arrived in Kiev most probably in the summer of 961, where, however, he was met with hostility by the new ruler Svyatoslav I and his allies. Unable to accomplish his mission, Adalbert returned to Germany in 962. Thus, Olga failed in her attempts to establish Christianity as an official religion in the country, neither did she succeed in persuading her son to accept the new religion. It was her grandson, Prince Vladimir the Great (r. 980-1015), raised and influenced by Princess Olga, who adopted Christianity as an official religion for the Russians in 988. In 1547 the Russian Orthodox Church declared Princess Olga to be a saint and equal-to-the apostles. She became one of only five women to be honored with this status in the history of Christianity.

Three main issues related to Olga of Kiev, however, have long been and remain the subject of scholarly debate: her place of birth, her name, and the time and place of her baptism. One reason for the divergences in the existing views on these issues is the discrepancies in the main source of the medieval history of Kievan Rus', *The Tale of Bygone Years* or the *Primary Chronicle,* also known as the *Russian Primary Chronicle.* The manuscript was compiled in Kiev around 1113 and has survived in several later editions and codices, each one displaying variations in the content. Its reliability has been called into serious question after chronological errors, questionable style, differences in handwritings, deletions, missing and interpolated pages, and logical incongruities have been pointed out by historians over the years. On the other hand, toward the end of the nineteenth century two significant publications dedicated to Princess Olga appeared in Russia, which shed considerable light on these three contested issues. They were written by some of the most prominent researchers of the old Russian literature and history - Prince Mikhail Obolensky (1805-1873) and Archimandrite Leonid (Lev Kavelin) (1822-1891). Mikhail Obolenski proved, for example, that the original source of the *Primary Chronicle* was a manuscript that was brought to Kievan Rus' by a missionary from the First Bulgarian Kingdom, a representative of the Bulgarian King Petar (r. 927-969) around the middle of the tenth century. The document was deliberately destroyed at some point after 1039 when a Byzantine metropolitan bishop was installed as a head of the Russian Orthodox Church. Archimandrite Leonid provided new information based on a manuscript dated from the 15th century that had preserved a much older tradition from the 13th and 11th centuries. His assertions contradicted the official version of the then

Russian historiography and Orthodox Church, which continues to be upheld until today, that Olga was born in the Russian town of Pleskov / Pskov and was of Varyag (Varangian), or Viking (Scandinavian) origin. According to the manuscript cited by Archimandrite Leonid, Princess Olga's birth city was Pl'skova or Pliska- the name of the first capital of the First Bulgarian Kingdom. Olga's Bulgarian origin was also confirmed by a statement in this document that Oleg, Igor's custodian, brought to him a wife from Bulgaria. Upon her arrival in Kiev she was given the new name of Olga, also transcribed as Helga (an Old Norse name). The name Olga/ Helga is one of the main arguments of the researchers who support the thesis that Olga was of Varangian origin, which has been contested. Had she been of local or Varangian origin, there would not have been the need to change her name, as the historian Asen Chilingirov has argued. Leonid further stated that at the beginning of the 10111 century there was only one city in Europe bearing the name of Pl'skova/Pliska and that was the first capital of Bulgaria. By contrast, archeological excavations evince that the first stone buildings in the Russian town of Pskov date to mid 12th century.

There are hardly more disputed questions concerning the early Russian medieval history than the place and time of the baptism of Princess Olga. Scholars' interpretations of the historical sources and their conclusions differ considerably. Regarding the place, the majority holds the view that Olga was baptized in Constantinople, while some scholars argue that her baptism may have occurred in Kiev or even in Bulgaria before she was brought to Kievan Rus'. With respect to time, the official Russian historiographers adhere to the year 955 mainly because it is the year given directly or indirectly in three of the relatively early sources about Olga's life- *The Primary Chronicle* (12th century), *'Eulogy' of Princess Olga* (c. 11th century) in *Memory and Eulogy of the Rus 'ian Prince Vladimir* (13th century), as well as in the *Synopsis historiarum* of John Skylitzes (11th century). Other international and some Russian scholars, however, have challenged the reliability of these documents and have suggested other likely years of her baptism: 946, 957, 959, 960. Some of these scholars go even further and question, or categorically deny the assertion that Olga was baptized during her visit at the imperial court of the Byzantine Emperor Constantine VII, which supposedly occurred in 957. This group of scholars finds a strong evidence for their claims in the fact that the only first-hand account of Princess Olga's visit to Constantinople- *The Book of Ceremonies*, written or at least commissioned by the Emperor Constantine VII Porphyrogenitus, makes no mention of such baptism; neither does it state directly whether the Princess was already a Christian at the time, nor does it give any year of her visit. If Olga's conversion had transpired during her visit, the event would have been recorded on account of its great significance not only for Kievan Rus', but also for the Byzantine Orthodox Church. Some indirect conclusions, however, have been drawn based on the description of the visit, which shed additional light on the status of the Kievan Princess. The fact that she appears in *The Book of Ceremonies* under her pagan name (Elga) rather than her Christian name (Helena/Elena), does not prove anything. Based on the names used for other baptized foreign rulers and princes in the same book, it appears that baptismal names were used for more private occasions, whereas the usage of dynastic ("pagan") names was the norm in public and diplomatic contexts. Regarding Olga's Christian name, Helena/Elena, historians are also divided- some are of the opinion that she received her name in honor of the Empress Helen, the wife of Constantine VII, which would have acknowledged that she was the spiritual daughter of the imperial couple, whereas others argue that Olga assumed the name of the mother of the Emperor Constantine the Great, Saint Helena, which underscores Olga's awareness of her role in spreading the Christianity in the land of Rus'. Far more significant in Constantine VII's account are the details that demonstrate the honor with which the Kievan Princess was treated: the seating position she held during the ceremonial banquet in the midst of the imperial family, the opportunity she was given to converse freely with the Emperor, and her ceremonial garments. All these elements indicate that Olga was not a pagan princess, rather a Christian one at the time of her visit in Constantinople and that her baptism must have occurred prior to her visit. One more factor that supports such a standpoint was the presence of a Christian priest by the name of Grigorii (Gregory) in Olga's suite, the only member of her suite recorded with his title, *papas* (a priest of high rank), in the document. It was Mikhail Obolenski who identified this priest with one of the most prominent literary agents of the Preslav Literary School (893-972) founded by the Bulgarian King Simeon I (r.893-927) - *prezviter* Grigorii- the same priest who was sent as missionary to

Kievan Rus' by King Petar. Subsequently the title of Bishop of Mizia was added to Grigorii's name in several later Russian ecclesiastical manuscripts. Mizia (Lat., Moesia), being the name of a province of the Roman Empire, was, in fact, used by the Byzantine authors to denote the Bulgarian land. Grigorri was canonized as a Saint by the Russian Orthodox Church for his enormous contribution to the development of the medieval Russian literature, literacy and the culture of Kievan Rus'. On the one hand, the documented information that Grigorii accompanied Princess Olga in her trip to Constantinople, that he remained with her, in the highly likely capacity as her mentor in the Christian religion, until the end of her life, and conducted a Christian funeral for her as she·had requested, and on the other hand, Olga's remarkable diplomatic skills, forward-looking, wise economic and political policies and activities as a governing regent, as well as her acute sense of her Christian mission, provide strong arguments in favor of the Kievan Princess' links with the ruling Bulgarian dynasty and her royal origin, possibly the daughter of King Simeon I, an elder sister of King Petar, and a granddaughter of Saint co-apostolic King Boris-Mikhail (r. 852-889), the baptizer of the Bulgarian people.

For about two hundred and fifty years the official Russian historiography has ignored and/or manipulated data concerning essential aspects of the two main issues connected with the great Princess Olga of Kiev- her birth place and religious adherence, which are also at the core of the Russian national political doctrine stating that Russia is the sole legitimate successor of the Byzantine tradition and culture. Despite the manipulations of the historical sources and their intentionally incorrect interpretation, the few preserved authentic documents that have not been counterfeited, alongside the results of archeological excavations, make it possible to uncover the historical truth.

BIBLIOGRAPHY

In Latin:

Constantini Porphyrogeniti Imperatoris. De Cerimoniis Aulae Byzantinae libri duo [The Book of Ceremonies}. Bonnae, 1829-1830, vol. 1-2, archive. org/details/bub_gb_OFpFAAAAYAAJ. Accessed 16 May 2020.

Obolensky, Dimitri. "The Baptism of Princess Olga of Kiev: The Problem of the Sources." *Philadelphie et autres etudes*. Paris: Editions de la Sorbonne, 1984, pp. 159-176, books.openedition.org/psorbonne/2159?lang=en#ftn50. Accessed 16 May 2020.

"Olga (c. 890-969)." *Women in World History: A Biographical Encyclopedia. Encyclopedia.com*, 23 Apr. 2020, www.encyclopedia.com/women/encyclopedias-almanacs transcripts-and-maps/olga-c-890-969. Accessed 14 May 2020.

Poppe, Andrzej. "Once Again Concerning the Baptism of Olga, Archontissa of Rus'". *Dumbarton Oaks Papers, Vol. 46, Homo Byzantinus: Papers in Honor of Alexander Kazhdan*, 1992, pp. 271-277. *JSTOR*, doi: 10.2307/1291660. Accessed 2 May 2020.

"Primary Chronicle." *Wikipedia*, Wikimedia Foundation, 11 May 2020, en.wikipedia.org/wiki/Primary_Chronicle. Accessed 15 May 2020.

"Prominent Russians: Princess Olga of Kiev." *Russiapedia*, RT, 2005-2020, russiapedia.rt.com/prominent-russians/history-and-mythology/princess-alga-of-kiev. Accessed 15 May 2020.

Runciman, Steven. "Emperor of the Bulgars and the Romans". *The First Bulgarian Empire*. London: George Bell & Sons, 1930, p.182, www.promacedonia.org/en/sr/sr_3_l.htm#157_1. Accessed 16 May 2020.

"Simeon I of Bulgaria." *Wikipedia*, Wikimedia Foundation, 5 May 2020, en.wikipedia.org/wiki/Simeon_I_of_Bulgaria#cite_note-106. Accessed 16 May 2020.

In Cyrillic:

Chilingirov, Asen. *Tsar Simeonoviyat Sbornik at X Vek: Izsledvaniya [King Simeon's Collection From the I0lh Century: Studies]*. 2nd extended ed. Berlin, 2011, www.ivanstamenov.com/files2011/cssabornikla.pdf. Accessed 11 May 2020.

Chilingirov, Asen. *Bulgaria i Pokrastvaneto na Rusite [Bulgaria and the Conversion <?lthe Russians]*. Sofia: Alfagraf, 2011, www.docdroid.net/8GHONwU/pokrstvaneto-na-rusite-i blgariya-izsledvaniya-asen-cilingirov-pdf. Accessed 15 May 2020.

Gorina, Lyudmila. "Istoriya Bolgarii v Trudah Knyaza M.A. Obolenskogo" ["The History of Bulgaria in the Works of Prince M.A. Obolenski"]. *Russia-Bulgaria: Vektory Vzaimoponimaniya. XVIII-XXI vv. Rosiisko-Bulgarskie Nauchnye Diskusii [Russia-Bulgaria: Vectors of Understanding. XVIII-XXI centuries. Russian-Bulgarian Scholarly Discussions]*, ed. Ritta Grishina. Moskva: Institut Slavyanovedeniya RAN, 2010, pp. 107-112, www.promacedonia.org/rbvv/rbvv_1_7.htm. Accessed 16 May 2020.

lvanova, KL, and Sv. Nikolova, editors. "Bulgarskata Literature ot Kraya na IX do Srcdata na *X* Vek" ["Bulgarian Literature from the End of the IX to the Middle of the X century"]. *Turzheslvo na Slovoto. Zlatn(vat Vek and Bulgarskata Knizhnina [Celebration t?/the lif/ord. The Golden Age (/Bulgarian Literature]*. Sofia: Agata-A, 1995, maccdonia.kroraina. com/zv/zv uvod.html. Accessed 16 May 2010.

Leonid, Archimandrite. "Otkuda Rodom Byla Sv. Velikaya Knyaginya Russkaya Ol'ga?" ["Where was the Saint Great Russian Princess Olga Born?"]. *Russkaya Starina*, XIX/59, July 1888, pp. 215-224.

Obolenski, Mikhail. *Nieskol'ko Slav o Pervonachal'noi Russkoi Lietopisi [A Few Words About the Russian Primary Chronicle]*. Moskva, 1870, http:// www.promacedonia.org/mons/index.htm. Accessed 16 May 2020.

Rumyana Hristova

Saint Petka-Paraskeva
10th-11thcenturies

T he Eastern Orthodox Church recognizes three saints called Paraskeva (froin Greek, *paraskevi,* "Friday"): the great martyr Paraskeva the Roman (feast day 26 July), who was beheaded during the second century A.D.; the great martyr Paraskeva of Ikonion (feast day 28 October), a hermit and missionary who was decapitated in the third or fourth century A.D.; and Paraskeva of Epivat/Epibatos (present day Turkey) (feast day October 14), a hermit, who lived at the end of the tenth, or the beginning of the eleventh century. The last mentioned Paraskeva is one of the most venerated female saints in the Balkan countries (Bulgaria, Serbia, Montenegro, Bosnia, Macedonia, Albania, Greece, Rumania), as well as in Russia, Ukraine, Moldova, Lithuania, Poland. Thus, she can be rightfully regarded as a general Balkan saint. To all Slavic speakers she is also known as Sveta ("Holy") Petka *(petak,* masculine *I petka,* feminine, "Friday").

St. Petka-Paraskeva was born in the village of Epivat, Thrace, on the shores of the Sea of Marmara, near Constantinople, to wealthy, noble, pious parents. Researchers determine the time of her life in accordance with the documented information on the Saint's brother, Euthymius, Bishop of Madita, who was canonized and died around 989-996 A.D. St. Petka-Paraskeva claimed that at the age of ten, she heard the words, "whoever wants to be my disciple must deny themselves and take up their cross and follow me" (Mark 8:34) while attending a church service. These words had a profound effect on the girl. She started giving away her clothes to the poor people despite her parents' objections. Following her calling Petka left her wealth and status and went to Constantinople. There she spent her time in prayer, fasting and meditating on Christ's words. Having received a vision of the Virgin Mary and her instruction, Petka made a pilgrimage to Jerusalem. After spending some time there, she joined a convent in the Jordanian desert leading an ascetic life in solitude and prayer, striving to regain that likeness to God which was lost after Adam's fall. One night she received a vision of an angel who ordered her to return to her native land where she would ascend with her soul to the Lord. At the age of twenty-five Petka moved back to Kalikratia where she lived at the Church of the Holy Apostles for two more years. She was given a Christian burial, but because no one knew who she was she was buried in an unmarked grave. Legend says that many years later Petka appeared in a dream to two local people and demanded that her relics be taken away from a stinky corpse who was buried near her. The Saint's remains were found incorrupt and emitting a spiritual fragrance. They were interred in the church where she had spent the last two years of her life. From that point on St. Petka-Paraskeva's relics became famous for their healing power. Many people were healed of various diseases and the blind received their sight. Thus the cult of St. Petka emerged. It is assumed that the canonization of the Saint was carried out in the middle of the 12111 twelfth century by Patriarch Nicholas IV Muzalon (1147-1151). However, due to the Crusades and the military expansion of the Ottoman Empire, St. Petka's relics did not remain in Kalikratia for too long. The history of their transfer from one country to another is worthy of mentioning. The Bulgarian king Ivan Asen II (r.1218-1241) moved her relics from Epivat to Tarnovo, the capital of the Second Bulgarian Kingdom, in 1234. After the fall of Tarnovo under Ottoman rule, they were transferred to the Vidin Kingdom on the Danube River in 1393. After the Ottomans conquered this area, the relics were transferred to Belgrade in 1396. In 1521 Sulleyman II conquered Belgrade and moved St. Petka's remains to Constantinople. The relics were received with great respect there. Numerous miracles were reported, which caused the Holy Petka-Paraskeva to be worshipped by Muslims as well. In 1641, with the permission of the Constantinople's Patriarch, Vasili Lupu, the ruler of Moldova brought St. Petka's relics to Moldova's capital, Iasi (present day Rumania), where they remain to this day. All these events account for the existence of the alternate forms of the Saint's name: Petka Tarnovska, Petka Beogradska, Petka of Serbia, Petka the New of Bulgaria, Petka Iashka, Paraskeva Pyatnitsa, and more.

Numerous sources (original manuscripts, copies, ecclesiastical texts, hymnographic compositions) have been preserved about Saint Petka's life, which can be found in libraries and archives in Bulgaria, Serbia, Rumania, Russia, Poland, Venice, Athens, Mount Athas. The most influential of these sources is the extensive hagiography of St. Petka written by the Bulgarian Patriarch Evtimiy Tarnovski (1325- c.1404) in 1385 and reprinted in Venice in 1538. It is a magnificent example of the life-panegyric style. It served as a literary model and historical source of a number of late Bulgarian, Serbian, Rumanian and Greek works about St. Petka. Some of the typical elements *(tapai)* of the hagiography genre are observed in Patriarch Evtimiy's work; they also show the stages through which a human being can attain holiness: *imitatia Christi, imitatia angeli,* an austere life, giving away of wealth to the poor, abandoning of the secular life and withdrawal in the desert, a masculine behavior in a female body, fasting, contemplation and meditation on God, prayers, struggles with demons and evil spirits, visions, catharsis, tears, an "immaculate bride of Christ", a ladder to the heavenly realm, wisdom, the miracle workings of the relics. Patriarch Evtimiy also uses universal *tapai* and biblical symbols, representing sanctity, to depict St. Petka who was canonized as Reverend Saint: "luminary," "sun," "lily," "bee," "dove," "cedar tree," "holy vessel" (her body), "imperishable treasure" (her relics). Another essential element in St. Petka's apotheosis is using the archetypal Christian cult of *Theotokos* ("God-bearer" or the Mother of God) as a model. Virgin Mary is not only a symbol of motherhood, but also a miraculous healer, merciful protector, guardian of the human race, mediator and intercessor for people before God. Thus, we can see St. Petka performing similar functions.

Folklore, legends, and songs have proved to be a very fertile medium of transmission for the St. Petka's story. They further developed and enriched her image. For example, in popular religion the veneration of St. Petka among the Slavic people, is closely related to the day of the same name. The Orthodox Church has proclaimed Friday, the crucifixion day of Jesus Christ, to be a weekly fasting holy day. According to a belief in Serbia nothing should start or end on Friday; women should not weave, spin, or sow. In Bulgaria St. Petka is the patron of the home, family, women, and women who give birth; and she punishes those who violate the ban for some type of activities on Friday. St. Petka is also related to St. Nedelya (i.e., "Sunday," the day of

Christ's resurrection), who is her sister, and to St. Dimitar (the herald of the beginning of winter), who is their nephew. Thus, the calendar time between the feast days of St. Petka (14 October) and St. Dimitar (26 October) has a sacred meaning, it is the end of the agricultural work, a transition between the seasons. St. Petka is also honored in Bulgaria as a mediator between the worlds. Together with Archangel Michael she mediates the passage of the souls to the Other World. And together with her sister, St. Nedelya, she builds a bridge between this and the Other World, which can be crossed only by the virtuous souls. In Greece St. Petka is depicted as a warrior against cholera and against a dragon. The slaying of the dragon symbolizes in Christian terms the victory over the devil and sin. The cult of St. Petka is also connected with water, particularly with healing water that flows out of the coffin with her relics, or from a spring with holy healing water in close proximity to her relics. This connection is observed in both Slavic and Byzantine sources. Moreover, recent archeological excavations in the Belgrade Bishopric have revealed the existence of a complex system for the transfer of water from the spring of St. Petka to a cistern in the archbishopric complex where probably her relics were kept. An intriguing supposition has been made that the references in the hymns to healing waters streaming from her relics are not just a literary *tapas,* but are based on real facts and circumstances related to the cult of the Saint.

An enduring testimony to the enormous popularity of St. Petka and her place in the history of Slavic and European medieval culture is the numerous churches built and named after her in the Balkan countries, Russia and elsewhere, as well as the medieval art of the South and Eastern Slavs - icons and murals portraying the image of St. Petka-Paraskeva and her miraculous powers.

BIBLIOGRAPHY

In Latin:
Detelic, Mirjana. "St Paraskeve in the Balkan Context." *Folklore,* vol. 121, no. 1, 2010, pp. 94-105. *JSTOR,* www.jstor.org/stable/29534110. Accessed 26 May 2020.

"Life of Saint Petka." *St. Petka Serbian Orthodox Church,* Orlando, Florida, 2006-2020, http://www.svetapetka.org/english/zivot.html. Accessed 27 May 2020.

"Paraskevi." *Religion Wiki,* 2020, https://religion.wikia.org/wiki/Paraskevi. Accessed 28 May 2020.

In Cyrillic:

Bezovska, Albena. "Narodni Predaniya za Sveta Petka" ["Folk Tales About Saint Petka"]. *Istoriya i Vyara [History and Faith],* Bulgarian National Radio, 5 October 2011, https://bnr.bg/radiobulgaria/post/100230844/narodni-predaniya-za-sveta-petka. Accessed May 28, 2020.

Mineva, Evelina. "Sluzhbata za Sv. Petka Tarnovska v Prepis ot Rakopis na Plovdivskata Mitropoliya" ["The Liturgy of St. Petka of Tarnovo in a Copy of Manuscript from the Plovdiv Bishopric"]. *Bulgaria Mediaevalis,* vol. 5, no. 1, 2014, pp. 257-265, https://www.ceeol.com/search/article-detail?id=513299. Accessed 28 May 2020.

Stankova, Radoslava. "Bibleiski Toposi za Izobrazyavane na Zheni-Svetitsi v Yuzhnoslavyanskite Literaturi prez Srednovekovieto" ["Biblical Topoi in the Representation of Female Saints in Medieval South Slavonic Literatures"]. *Slavia Meridiana/is,* vol. 16, 2016, pp. 238-261, doi: https://doi.org/10.11649/sm.2016.014. Accessed 28 May 2020.

Stankova, Radoslava, eta!. "Sv. Petka (Paraskeva) Tarnovska." ["St. Petka (Paraskeva) of Tarnovo"] *Encyclopaedia Slavica Sanctorum,* Sofia University "St. Kliment Ohridski", 2010-2020, http://eslavsanct.net/viewobject.php?id=1855&lang=bg. Accessed 25 May 2020.

"Sv. Prepodobna Paraskeva-Petka Epivatska (Tarnovska)" ["St. Reverend Paraskeva-Petka of Epivat (of Tarnovo)"]. *Pravoslavie [Orthodoxy],* The Bulgarian Orthodox Church in Norway, 1999-September 2014, http://www.pravoslavieto.com/life/10.14_sv_Petka_Epivatska_Bulgarska.htm. Accessed May 28 2020.

Rumyana Hristova

Clare of Assisi

Clare of Assisi (1194-1253) is an Italian saint and one of the first followers of Saint Francis of Assisi. She was born in Assisi during the Crusades era to Favarone Sciffi, Count of Sasso-Rosso and his wife Ortolana. According to our sources, the father was a wealthy representative of an ancient Roman family. Her mother was a devout Christian who had undertaken pilgrimages to Rome, the Holy Land, and other religious sites. Late in her life, Ortolana entered Clare's convent, as well as her two sisters.

We have no reason to assume that Clare's father did not have marriage plans for her. As a teenager, however, she heard Francis of Assisi preach at the church of San Giorgio at Assisi and asked him to help her to live "the manner of the Gospel." On March 20, 1212, she left her father's home and proceed to the chapel of the Porziuncula to meet with Francis. There her hair was cut and she put on a plain robe and veil. Francis placed her in the convent of the Benedictine nuns of San Paulo, near Bastia. Her father attempted to force her to come back to his home, but she resisted by clinging to the altar of the church and showing him her cropped hair. She declared that she would have no other husband than Jesus.

A few days later, Francis sent her to Sant' Angelo in Panzo, another Benedictine convent nearby, providing her greater solitude. Clare was soon joined by one of her sisters, Catarina, who took the name Agnes. They stayed there until Francis prepared a small dwelling next to the church of San Daminao, which became the center of Clare's new religious order. They were known originally as the "Poor Ladies of San Damiano." They lived a simple life of poverty, austerity and seclusion from the world, according to a Rule given to them by Francis as a Second Order (Poor Clares). By 1263, just shortly after Clare's death, they became known as the Order of Saint Clare. According to an act of Gregory IX, they were granted the *Privilegium Pauperitatis,* namely, that nobody could oblige them to accept any possession.

The Poor Clares were not allowed to itinerate or move around the country to preach (unlike the Franciscan friars). They lived in enclosure, engaged in manual labor and prayer, went barefoot, slept on the ground, ate no meat, and observed almost complete silence.

Meanwhile, Clare sought to imitate Francis' virtues and way of life. She played a significant role in encouraging and aiding Francis, and took care of him in his final illness. In her own last days, Clare endured an extended period of poor health. She died on August 11, 1253 at the age of 59. She was canonized on September 26, 1255 by Pope Alexander IV. Clare of Assisi is venerated in the Roman Catholic Church, the Anglican Communion, and the Lutheran Church.

Many places, including churches, convents, schools, hospitals, towns, and counties are named for St. Clare. Lake Saint Clair between Ontario and Michigan was named on her feast day in 1679. The Saint Clair River, St. Clair Shores, Michigan, and St. Clair County, Michigan were later named for her. Similar honors have been granted in California, New Mexico, and around the world.

BIBLIOGRAPHY

Armstrong, Regis J. and Ignatius C. Brady, translators and editors. *Francis and Clare: The Complete Works. The Classics of Western Christianity.* New York, Ramsey, NJ, and Toronto: Paulist Press, 1982.

Oden, Amy, ed. *In Her Words: Women's Writings in the History of Christian Thought.* Nashville, TN: Abingdon Press, 1988.

Thomas of Celano (trans. Raschal Robinson). *The Life of Saint Clara.* Philadelphia, PA: Dolphin Press, 1910 (original c. 1258).

Stanley M. Burgess

Margaret of Scotland

M argaret of Scotland (also known as Margaret of Wessex; c. 1045-November 16, 1093) was both an English princess and a Scottish queen. She was born in exile in the Kingdom of Hungary, as the sister of Edgar Aetheling, the uncrowned Anglo-Saxon King of England. When she was twelve years of age, Margaret and her family returned to England, but was forced to flee, this time to Scotland, when William the Conqueror came across the English Channel to seize the throne of England in 1066. By the end of 1070, Margaret had married King Malcolm Ill of Scotland, becoming Queen of Scots.

Sometimes called "The Pearl of Scotland", Margaret was a very pious Roman Catholic. This resulted from her being raised in the very religious environment of the Hungarian court. Her husband, Malcolm, was illiterate and uncouth, and had two sons by an earlier marriage. Margaret and Malcolm had eight children, six sons and two daughters. Three of their sons, Edgar, Alexander 1, and David 1, ruled Scotland between 1097 and 1153, and one daughter, Edith (also named Matilda) became Queen Consort of England, the wife of English monarch Henry 1.

Margaret is credited by her chronicler/biographer Turgot of Durham as having a civilizing effect on King Malcolm. This was especially true on matters ecclesiastical. Because of her influence, a change was made on the period of celebrating Lent, and the weekly day of rest for this Christian community was changed from Saturday to Sunday. Margaret served orphans and the poor every day before she ate, and washed the feet of the poor, imitating Jesus. She invited the Benedictine Order to establish a monastery in Dunfermline, Fife in 1072. She established ferry service at Queensferry and North Berwick to assist pilgrims journeying from the Firth of Forth to St. Andrew's in Fife. She also instigated the restoration of Iona Abbey in Scotland, and interceded for the release of fellow English exiles who had been forced into serfdom by the Norman conquest of England. While her husband King was not overly religious, he allowed her to facilitate many good works.

Malcolm Ill and their eldest son, Edward, were killed in the Battle of Alnwick against the English on November 13, 1093. Margaret died three days later, reportedly from grief. She was buried before the high altar in Dunfermline Abbey in Fife, Scotland. In 1250 she was canonized by Pope Innocent IV for her personal holiness, her fidelity to the Roman Catholic Church, her work of ecclesiastical reform, and her charity. She is venerated as a saint by the Roman Catholics as well in the Anglican Church. Her feast day in June 10.

BIBLIOGRAPHY

Bangley, Bernard, Ed. *Butler's Lives of the Saints.* Brewster, MA: Paraclete Press, 1989/2005.

Keene, Catherine. *Saint Margaret, Queen of the Scots: A Life in Perspective.* New York: Palgrave Macmillan, 2013. (Includes Turgot of Durham, *Vita S. Margaritae Scotorum Reginae)*

Stanley M. Burgess

Hildegard of Bingen Universal Genius

Hildegard of Bingen (1098-September 17, 1179L also known as the Sibyl of the Rhine, was perhaps the greatest female mystic of the Middle Ages. She was a German Benedictine abbess, writer, composer, philosopher, Christian mystic, visionary and polymath. She is one of the best known composers of sacred monophony, and, incidently, the most recorded in modern history. She also stands as the greatest woman in the Twelfth Century Renaissance. She was truly a universal genius.

Her parents were Mechtild of Merxheim-Nahet and Hildebert of Sermersheim, a family of free lower nobility. Sickly from birth, by tradition she is considered the youngest of ten children (some scholars insist that there were only eight). Details of precisely when she first entered monastic life are somewhat contradictory, but we do know that she was enclosed in a community at the age of fourteen under the direction and instruction of a nun, Jutta. When Jutta died in 1136, Hildegard was elevated to be head of that Benedictine community. Twelve years later she founded her own convent near Bingen.

Hildegard reports first having had visions at the age of five but not revealing them to others. At the age of forty-two she experienced a calling to proclaim God's words in the Spirit. She proceeded to describe his *Scivias* (short for *Scito vias Domini* or "Know the ways of the Lord") and to draw a self-portrait of her experience in which, like the original Pentecost event, she was crowned by parted tongues of fire.

Encouraged by Bernard of Clairvaux and other church leaders to accept her divine calling by publishing all she had learned from the Holy Spirit, she also was taken seriously as a prophetess by everyone from popes to humble serfs. At the synod in Trier (1147-8) Pope Eugenius heard about

Hildegard's writings and gave her Papal approval to document her visions as revelations from the Holy Spirit, giving her instant credence.

She wrote to many prominent people, never mincing words when she considered their behavior unworthy of their calling. She went on numerous preaching missions, delivering fiery apocalyptic sermons-an exceptional role for a woman in those days. In addition, she wrote seventy-seven hymns of divine praise (her own poetry, which she set to music) a history of the universe, numerous theological commentaries, a book on natural history, and a book on medicine. She also drew thirty-six multicolored "illuminations" in which her visions are vividly captured.

Hildegard placed great emphasis on the creative and re-creative work of the Holy Spirit. She also insisted that those who have experienced a personal Pentecost by being touched by the fiery tongues of the Spirit will be virtuous, with overflowing grace and an ability to discern good from evil. For Hildegard, God's "elect" are those who have been touched by the Holy Spirit, and the reception of the gift of the Holy Spirit is necessarily accompanied by the production of divine fruits. The Divine Spirit also gives gifts in abundance to those born of water and of the Spirit (these include those enumerated in Isaiah 11:1-3 and I Corinthians 12), as well as tears and compunction from which the fruit of holiness must grow.

Her biographers, Godfrey of Disabod, Dietrich of Echternach, and Theodoric of Echternach, provide insights into Hildegard's spiritual life. She is remembered for her unknown language *(Lingua Ignota)* perhaps glossolalia, her "concerts" or singing in the Spirit, her ecstatic visions and resulting prophecies, and her numerous miracles. Perhaps most significantly, she is remembered for the transparency with which she portrays her own spiritual experiences through artistic and written media.

Hildegard died September 17, 1179 (aged 81) in Bingen. She is venerated in the Roman Catholic Church, and the Anglican and Lutheran Communities. Her feast day is September 17.

BIBLIOGRAPHY

Flanagan, Sabina. *Hildegard of Bingen, 1098-1179: A Visionary Life.* London: Routledge, 1989.

Fox, Matthew, ed. *Hildegard of Bingen's Book of Divine Works with Letters and Songs.* Santa Fe, NM: Bear and Co., 1987.

Hart, Mother Columba Hart and Jane Bishop, eds. *Hildegard of Bingen: Scivias.* Classics of Western Spirituality Series. New York: Mahwah: Paulist Press, 1990.

Higley, Sarah L. *Hildegard of Bingen's Unknown Language. Translation and Discussion.* New York: Palgrave Macmillian, 2007.

Moulinier, L., ed. *Beate Hildegardus Cause et cure.* Berlin: Akademie Verlag, 2003.

Pfau, Marianne Richert. *Hildegard von Bingen: Symphonia* 8 vols. Complete edition of the Symphonia chants. Bryn Mawr: Hildegard Publishing Company, 1990.

Stanley M. Burgess

Esclarmonde of Foix

E sclarmonde of Foix (Esclarmonda de Fois in Occitan language) was born after 1151 AD in Occitania, France to Roger Bernard I, Count of Foix, and Cecile Trencavel. The name Esclarmonde means "light of the world" in the Occitan language. In 1175, she married Jourdain, lord of L'Isle Jourdain, with whom they had six children. In October 1200 Escarmonde was widowed. Sometime thereafter, she adopted Catharism, an alternate form of Christianity prevalent in southern France at that time. It was considered to be heresy by the Roman Catholic church.

The Cathars were a group of dissenters in twelfth and thirteenth century France who claimed to be restoring the purity of the Church. They were radical dualists, teaching that God was totally pure, and humans un-mediated by Catharist doctrines and practice were essentially evil. They rejected Church sacraments, priestly leadership, marriage (to them, sin was a sexually transmitted disease!), and the doctrines of bodily resurrection, hell, and purgatory. In place of the sacraments, they instituted the *consolamentum,* a baptism of the Holy Spirit by the laying on of hands. After receiving this sacrament, the recipient became one of the *Perfecti (Parfaits),* who were expected to live perfected lives without sin. This, coupled with their rejection of the physical world, which they claimed was inherently evil, led to excesses, including starving themselves even to the point of death. The Cathars were persecuted to extinction by the Inquisition, led by Pope Innocent Ill, who instituted the Albigensian Crusade 1208-1229}, which many historians consider a horrible act of genocide.

Radically dualist groups had existed in medieval Europe from about 653 when Constantine Silvanus brought a copy of the Gospels to Armenia. This resulted in the emergence of the radical dualist groups, the Paulicians in Armenia, the Bogomils from Bulgaria and the Balkans, and the Cathars.

Esclarmonde was a woman of great strength and courage, fighting against injustice wherever she found it. When the papal legate, Henri de Marcy, took the Cathar town, Lavaur in 1181, she rushed to the castle and helped all the *parfaits* to escape, leading them over the mountains to safety in her county of Foix. Now a widow, Esclarmonde proceeded to give all her riches to her children, and to live out her life for the betterment of Cathar communities. She started hospitals, workshops and schools. She constantly met with local nobles, trying to stop their incessant feuding. In April 1206 she participated in a debate between Catholic prelates and the Cathars —Esclarmonde and three of her followers. A monk, Etienne (Stephen) commanded her to go to her womanly duties, spinning, and not to do an unwomanly debate. Clearly, Esclarmonde won the debate. Because of this, Pope Innocent Ill decided to begin the Albigensian Crusade in 1208. Esclarmonde proved to be unstoppable, despite frequent appearances in the area of Foix, papal forces could not capture her.

For more than thirty years, Esclarmonde lived as a fugitive on the run, sleeping sometimes in caves and keeping a hair's breadth ahead of her inquisitors and bounty hunters. We only know of one mention of her in 1232 when she was 78 years old when she attended the marriage of her nephew Roger-Bernard. But that was the only appearance, and she vanished until her death, probably in one of her caves.

As a heretic, Esclarmonde is not remembered by orthodox religious communities as a saint. She is celebrated by others as "la Grande Esclarmonde" for her establishment of hospitals and schools in medieval France. She also is remembered as the "Fox of Foix" for her ability to escape authorities of the Church.

BIBLIOGRAPHY

Martin, Sean. *The Cathars: The Most Successful Heresy of the Middle Ages.* Chartwell Books, 2006.

Roquebert, Michel. *The epopee cathare. 1198-1212: The invasion.* Toulouse: Privat, 1970.

Stanley M. Burgess

Gertrude of Helfta

Gertrude of Helfta (1256-1301/2) was born on Epiphany, the Feast of Lights (January 6th) to a family, about which we have no information, not even the names of her parents. Committed at the age of five to the care of the nuns of the cloister school at Helfta, Gertrude soon developed a strong devotion to the sacred heart of Jesus. This seems to be the result of her association with Mechtild von Hackeborn, the chantress of the abbey.

At the age of twenty-six, Gertrude began to receive a series of visions which continued until her death. On January 27, 1281, without warning, she had a vision of Jesus-who told her that he would help her to lead a more fervent life. She now realized that she had become too attached to secular studies, and that she was depriving herself of true spiritual understanding. With diligence she studied the Scriptures, compiling explanations and simplifications of difficult passages. She also collected several books full of the sayings of the saints. All of this led to a spirituality so intense that she was often insensible to what was happening around her.

It would be a mistake to characterize Gertrude's theology merely as Christocentric. In reality, she was devoted to the entire divine Trinity. She developed a relationship to each member of the Godhead, characterizing the Father as wisdom, the Son as power, and the Holy Spirit as goodness or love. The goodness of the divine Spirit continually came to her despite her unworthiness, ministering with ineffable sweetness and providing for her a precious nuptial alliance with the Trinity. The Spirit's breath quickens, attracts, draws, and consumes the faithful. It also breaks down human boundaries to God's will.

Gertrude taught that the Christian may be baptized in the power of the Holy Spirit, and thus be free from the wiles of the enemy. Gertrude asked Christ that she be given four virtues-purity of heart, humility, tranquility and concord-in order to prepare a place for the Holy Spirit. Then she saw a vision of honey, flowing from the sacred heart of Jesus, which entirely filled her heart. This she recognized as the grace of the Holy Spirit, purifying her from every stain.

Of all Christian saints, Gertrude used the most encompassing definition of spiritual gifts, drawing from lists found in Isaiah 11:1-3; Rom. 5:1-5, 12:6-8; 1 Cor. 12:8-10; Gal. 5:22-23; Eph. 4:8, 11-12; and 2 Tim. 1:6-7.

In addition to her visions and prophecies, Gertrude is credited with a variety of miracles, including the ending of a severe winter, and later for the cessation of excessive rains. In addition, she was frequently graced with extreme compunction and divinely induced weeping. But above all, she was given fervency in love, patience in tribulation, and a desire to be among the wise maids as she waited for the heavenly Bridegroom.

Gertrude died at Helfta, near Eisleben, Saxony, around 1302. Her feast day is November 16. She was never officially canonized, although she is venerated throughout the Catholic world.

BIBLIOGRAPHY

Burgess, Stanley M. *The Holy Spirit: Medieval Roman Catholic and Reformation Traditions.* Peabody, MA: Hendrickson, 1997.

Gertrude of Helfa. *Exercises.* Trans. a Benedictine nun of Regina Laudis. Westminister, MD: Newman, 1956.

The Herald of Divine Love. Trans. and ed. M. Winkworth. New York/ Mahweh: Paulist, 1993.

The Life and Revelations of St. Gertrude. Westminster, MD: Christian Classics, 1992.

Tucker, Ruth A., and Walter Liefeld. *Daughters of the Church: Women and Ministry from New Testament times to the present.* Grand Rapids, Ml: Zondervan Academic, 1987.

Stanley M. Burgess

Elizabeth of Hungary

E lizabeth of Hungary (Heilige Elisabeth von Thuringen, July 7, 1207-
1231) was a princess of the Kingdom of Hungary, Landgravine of
Thuringia, Germany, and the daughter of King Andrew II of Hungary
and Gertrude of Merania. She was married at the age of fourteen (having
been betrothed at the age of four) to Louis IV of Thuringia.

In 1223, Franciscan friars came to Thuringia, and the teenage
Elizabeth not only learned about the ideals of Francis of Assisi, but started
to live them. Louis was not worried about his wife's charitable efforts,
believing that the distribution of his wealth to the poor would bring eternal
reward in heaven. Elizabeth then assumed control of affairs at home and
distributed alms in all parts of their territory, giving away state robes and
ornaments to the poor. Just below the Wartburg Castle, she built a hospital
with twenty-eight beds and visited the patients daily to care for them.

On September 11, 1227, Louis, on route to join the Sixth Crusade, was
struck down by a fever and died. Elizabeth is reported to have stated that
her entire life vanished on that day. She sent her children away, but retained
her dowry, using the funds to support her newly constructed hospital. She
took solemn vows to celibacy, and refused all efforts on the part of suitors
to re marry. It is reported that she even threatened to cut off her own nose
so that no man would find her attractive enough to marry!

Meanwhile, Elizabeth had moved from Thuringia to Marburg in
Hesse, where she also built a hospital for the poor. Once again, she and
her companions cared for the patients. In 1231, Elizabeth died in Marburg
at the age of twenty-four. She was buried in the chapel at the hospital in
Marburg. Numerous miracles were reported at her shrine there. As a result
of her piety and concern for the needy, and her building of hospitals, she

received quick canonization, which occurred on May 24, 1235 by Pope Gregory IX.

Elizabeth is venerated by Roman Catholics, Anglicans, and Lutherans. Her feast days are November 17 and 19.

BIBLIOGRAPHY

De Robeck, Nesta. *Saint Elizabeth of Hungary: A Story of Twenty-Four Years.* Milwaukee, WI: Bruce Publishing *Co.,* 1954.

Seesholtz, Anne. *Saint Elizabeth: Her Brother's Keeper.* New York: Philosophical Library, 1948. Wolf, Kenneth Baxter, ed.*The Life and Afterlife of St. Elizabeth of Hungary: Testimony from her Canonization Hearings.* Oxford, UK: Oxford University Press, 2010.

Stanley M. Burgess

Brigitta of Sweden

The most celebrated saint of Sweden, Brigitta (or Bridget) Birgersdotter (c. 1303-July 23, 1373) was born to Birger Persson of the family of Finsta, governor and lawspeaker of Uppland, one of the richest landowners of the country, and his wife Ingeborg Bengtsdotter, related to the Swedish kings of her time. At the age of fourteen she married Ulf Gudmarsson of the family of Ulvasa, Lord of Narke. They had eight children, four daughters and four sons. Their second daughter is now honored as St. Catherine of Sweden.

Bridget became known for her works of charity, particularly toward unwed mothers and their children. She also became chief lady-in-waiting to the new Queen of Sweden, Blanche of Namur. She and her husband went on a pilgrimage to Santiago de Compostela (the famous Christian pilgrimage site in Northwestern Spain which was known as a place of resistance against Islamic invaders). In 1344, just after their return, Ulf died. Bridget became a member of the Third Order of St. Francis and devoted herself to a life of prayer and caring for the sick and the poor.

She also developed the idea of establishing a religious community known as the Order of the Most Holy Savior, or the Brigittines. It had double monasteries, with both men and women forming a single community, though with separate cloisters. They were to live simply, with excess money given to the poor. Significantly, they were allowed to have as many books as they desired.

During the Jubilee Year 1350, Bridget made a pilgrimage to Rome accompanied by her daughter, Catherine, and a small party of priests and disciples. This was during a period of plague throughout the continent. Their trip was intended to seek Papal authorization for her new order, as well as to elevate the moral tone of the period, which was scandalized by the so-called Babylonian Captivity of the church, the move of the papacy from Rome to Avignon in southern France. Waiting in Rome for the return of the prelate, she persistently agitated for that moment.

As she waited, Bridget became universally beloved for her kindness and wood works. When Pope Urban V arrived to Rome, he confirmed her new order. She established a center for hospitality for pilgrims from the north. Except for occasional pilgrimages (including to Jerusalem and Bethlehem) she remained in Rome for the rest of her life, which came to an end on July 23, 1373.

Bridget is also remembered for her many visions, especially that of the nativity and of Jesus' passion on the cross. Her story is recorded in the *Vita* by her two confessors, and in the *Revelations,* telling her story in Sweden, Rome, and the Holy Land. She was canonized on October 7, 1391 by Pope Boniface IX. Venerated by Roman Catholics, Anglicans, and Lutherans, her feast is on July 23.

BIBLIOGRAPHY

Harris, Marguerite Tjader. *Birgitta of Sweden: Life and Selected Revelations.* The Classics of Western Spirituality. New York, Mahweh: Paulist Press, 1990.

Jönsson, Arne. *St. Bridget's Revelations to the Popes: an edition of the so-called Tractatus de summis pontificibus.* Lund: Lund University Press, 1997.

Stanley M. Burgess

Julian of Norwich

The life of Julian of Norwich (c. 1342-after 1416), the famed fourteenth century English mystic, is shrouded in mystery. What we do know comes from her account of her visions, *The Revelations of Divine Love* or *Showings,* together with a few bequests in her fourteenth and fifteenth century wills and a description of her encounter with another mystic in *The Book of Margery Kempe.*

What we can determine is that she lived as an anchoress in a cell adjoining the parish Church of St. Julian in Conisford at Norwich, England, opposite the house of the Augustinian friars. She had a maidservant to tend to her needs. Her mother was present with others at her bedside at a time when she seemed to be near death, but her mother's presence caused considerable controversy.

Julian received her revelations on May 13, 1373, when she was thirty and a half years old. She claimed that at this time that she was ignorant (lewd) and "knew no letter." People came to her for spiritual counseling. This we know from *The Book of Margery Kempe,* written by a person who sought her help. Julian produced the first book in English by a woman that has survived, namely the *Showings*. She deserved the title "first English woman of letters."

Her work is based on a series of sixteen visions she received at a time that she was thought to be dying. She suddenly saw Christ bleeding in front of her. She became acutely aware of his sufferings and his love for us. Her message remains one of hope and trust in God, whose compassionate love is always given to us. There can be no element of wrath in this all-gracious God. The wrath is in us, not in God. God's saving work in Jesus of Nazareth and in the gift of the Holy Spirit is to overcome our wrath in the power of his merciful and compassionate love. Julian did not perceive that God is judging or blaming us, but rather is enfolding us in love. Julian also used women's experience of motherhood to explore how God loves us, referring to Jesus as our Mother.

Julian died after 1416 but before 1423. Modern interest in Julian's writings has grown over recent decades. Her shrine is in Norwich and her feast days are on May 8 and May 13.

BIBLIOGRAPHY

Clark, Elizabeth and Herbert Richardson. *The Book of Margery Kempe.* In *Women and Religion: A Feminist Sourcebook of Christian Thought.* New York: Harper and Row, 1977.

Colledge, Edmund, and James Walsh. *Julian of Norwich: Showings.* The Classics of Western Spirituality. New York, Ramsey, Toronto: Paulist Press, 1978.

Pelphrey, Brant. *Christ our Mother: Julian of Norwich.* Wilmington, DE: Glazier, 1989.

Ramirez, Janina. *Julian of Norwich: A very brief history.* London: SPCK, 2016.

Stanley M. Burgess

Catherine of Siena

Catherine di Giacomo di Benincasa (March 25, 1347-April 29, 1380), better known as Catherine of Siena, was born to a family of cloth dyers. The 23rd child of her mother, Lapa (who eventually had 25}, Catherine became one of the greatest mystics of the church, and an author who had significant influence on Italian literature.

Early in life, Catherine decided to devote herself to God, against the will of her parents. According to her biographer and confessor, Raymond of Capua, she is said to have had her first vision of Christ in glory with the apostles Peter, Paul, and John at the age of five. Two years later, she vowed to give her entire life to God.

When she was sixteen, Catherine lost an older sister, Bonaventura, in childbirth. Shortly thereafter, she completely rejected her parents' demands that she marry the new widower. She decided to fast and to cut her long hair. At eighteen, she received the Dominican habit (the third Order of St. Dominic).

At first Catherine gave herself to solitary contemplation. In 1368, however, she came to believe that she had been mystically espoused to Christ-at which time she gave herself to the service of the poor and the sick. Her mysticism became more intense as she lived without much food or sleep. This resulted in a wide following, including many of noble rank.

Catherine lived in a period of great uncertainly, with the Black Plague ravishing Europe and the Popes of Rome moving to Avignon (the so-called "Babylonian Captivity of the church"). Her efforts to return the papacy to Rome resulted in large part from Pope Gregory Xi's belief in prophetic visions. Catherine's spiritual life included exceptional charismatic gifts.

She recognized that in the beginning God created humans in the image and likeness of God (Gen. 1:26-27). After humans then lost their innocence, God the Trinity reclothed humanity with the innocence with the presence of the Son of God, restoring the divine image and likeness. In the Eucharist, she believed that she received "the whole of God"-the warmth and light of the Spirit, the light and wisdom of the Son, and the power and strength of the Father.

Heeding her Dominican call, Catherine preached to crowds often exceeding 1,000 people. Her words burned with such effectiveness that the very person of the Holy Spirit seemed to speak through her. She taught that the Spirit intended that individuals enlarge their love for the poor, as a result distribute their wealth to the needy. She personally demonstrated gifts of seeing into the future, preaching, and healing the sick.

She died in 1380, exhausted by her penances. Pope Urban VI celebrated her funeral. She was canonized in 1461, declared patron saint of Rome in 1866, and of Italy (together with Francis of Assisi) in 1939. Along with Teresa of Avila, she was declared the first female "doctor of the Church" by Pope Paul VI on October 4, 1970. Finally, she was named patron saint of Europe by Pope John Paul II in 1999. She is venerated by Roman Catholics, Lutherans, and Anglicans. Her feast days are April 29 and 30.

BIBLIOGRAPHY

Noffke, Suzanne, trans. and ed. *Catherine of Siena: The Dialogue.* The Classics of Western Spirituality Series. New York, Ramsey, Toronto: Paulist Press, 1980.

_____ trans. and ed. *The Letters of Catherine of Siena.* 4 vols. Binghamton, NY: Center for Medieval and Early Renaissance Studies. State University of New York at Binghamton, 1988.

_____,trans. and ed. *The Prayers of Catherine of Siena.* New York: Authors Choice Press, 2001.

Raymond of Capua. *The Life of Catherine of Siena.* Conleth Kearns, ed. Wilmington, DE: Glazier, 1980.

Stanley M. Burgess

Margery Kempe, 1373-1438

W ritten in 1436, *The Book of Margery Kempe* is the earliest surviving autobiography in English. According to its proem, clerics who witnessed Kempe's spiritual revelations as inspired by the Holy Ghost instructed her to have a book written. Some offered to write it for her, but Kempe refused until after twenty years of communing with Christ, her Lord commanded her to seek a writer. An English-born layman living in Germany returned to England and wrote her narrative, but it was so poorly crafted that the priest whom Margery approached next had difficulty reading the script. After deferring to write her book for four or more years, not only because of the inferior draft but also because the community criticized Kempe's spiritual acts, the priest was troubled because he had promised to write the book, so he began listening to Kempe and rewriting her story (Kempe 35-37). Though the book claims Kempe is illiterate so that she could not write the book herself, contemporary feminist scholarship suggests that Kempe may not have been wholly illiterate, citing a passage where Christ said to Margery that he is pleased whether she reads or hears readings (Finke 178). Considering Kempe's garrulous nature as well as her keen observations of religious visuals associated with the voice of Christ or of Scripture, she may have naturally discerned script-audio connections that would enable her to read to an extent. The proem, though, is in the priest's voice as he shares how he came to write her story, supported by Kempe's prayers and encouragement. He does not manipulate the text into chronological order, but says he writes situations as they came to Kempe's mind in her oral storytelling of the twenty years since her first spiritual revelations (Kempe 36). Although Kempe was a contemporary of Julian of Norwich and visited the anchoress, who lived about 40 miles from Kempe's home in Bishop's Lynn, they lived disparate lives (Finke 176). Julian's writing is more contemplative, from one who did not have a family and who lived in an enclosure, though she could still give religious instruction and converse with visitors who sought spiritual wisdom. Kempe, on the other hand, was married to a burgess and had fourteen children. Her speech was more dramatic and widespread as she traveled to Jerusalem, Palestinian sites, Venice, and Santiago de Compostela. Kempe's initial assurance of Christ speaking within her happened after the birth of her first child, which was followed by months of great mental and physical suffering. After hearing Christ, her spirit calmed, her mind and body were restored, and she was able to perform daily responsibilities (Kempe 42-43). When Kempe was about forty, she distinguished her desire for a holy life by negotiating with her husband to take a vow of celibacy. Living in chastity, her body would be wholly God's. ·

With this vow settled, Kempe was freer to travel to holy sites, and her public spiritual expressions intensified. Her loud weeping especially provoked strong reactions from other pilgrims, some who marveled at this evidence of grace and others who were annoyed. Before her journey, Christ spoke within Kempe's mind, calling her daughter and assuring her that tears of contrition, compassion, and devotion were gifts sent by God, and Julian of Norwich confirmed that tears were evidence of the Holy Ghost working in her soul (78). When Kempe went to the Church of the Holy Sepulchre in Jerusalem, she was so stirred by compassion for Christ, as she envisioned him suffering before her, that her intense, loud weeping amazed others. Conscious that her high-volume weeping could be annoying, she tried to suppress it, but her face turned the color of lead, and overcome by the love of Christ in her soul, the cries loudly burst from her. Kempe's weeping episodes were frequent, and while some were moved with compassion and awe, others said she had an evil spirit (104-105). Her narrative cycles through scenes where Kempe is slandered and accused of being a heretic or wicked, and these accusations are usually disproved by a respected person who is convinced of Kempe's authentic spiritual experience. The priest of St. John Lateran, for instance, decided to prove whether Kempe's tears were a pretense to impress the audience for Sunday mass or really a gift of God. One Sunday he served her communion in another church with no one else but himself and a clerk, and when Kempe copiously wept without the usual audience, he was convinced that her tears were the work of the Holy Ghost (119-120). Her community's reproof is one measure of Kempe assuring herself and her audience that Christ loves her. Ongoing criticism for Christ's sake does not threaten but rather confirm the righteousness of her speech acts (Windeatt 13).

On her Jerusalem journey, Kempe irritated pilgrims because she was too pious and would not eat meat, so they mocked her by cutting her gown to a little below the knee and made her wear a white canvas apron. Friars and yeoman near Beverly asked her why she did not spin and card wool like other women (Kempe 168). The Archbishop of York told Kempe not to teach or attempt or rebuke others in his diocese (164). Others saw her white clothing as a false claim to virginity, whereas Kempe wore it because she heard Christ ask her to, probably because it externally represented her internal chastity (Finke 186). Kempe's acts distinguished her from community expectations, and the narrative justifies her behavior because of her special intimacy with Christ, which is a full sensory experience.

Although Kempe confessed to priests, Christ also spoke into her mind, without mediation, saying he would wash her from all her sin with his blood. When God invited her to be wedded to the Godhead, he took her by the hand in her soul before Christ, the Holy Ghost, Mary, the apostles, saints, and angels and said the marriage vows before them. In the context of this experience, Kempe described smelling fragrances sweeter than anything on earth and of hearing melodies with her physical ears that no one else could hear. Another sound was like the wind from bellows in her ear, which Christ told her was the Holy Ghost, and gradually the sound decrescendoed into a dove's voice and ended with a robin's song as expressions of Christ's love for her. During cold weather, she felt a flame of love burning in her heart like a person would feel a real fire with his hand, and Christ told her this heat of the Holy Ghost was a flaming love that would burn away her sins. Like a wife would show love to her husband, Christ said Kempe may take him into the arms of her soul and kiss him (Kempe 123-127). Therefore, Kempe touched and was touched by Christ, heard the Holy Ghost, smelled unearthly sweetness, tasted Christ through the sacrament, and was warmed in the cold by a burning baptism of love. Her spiritual life moved through each of her senses so that she was never forsaken or abandoned by Christ, and these inner workings were her support of grace when she was outwardly attacked.

Kempe's inner spiritual life, combined with her travels, sharp tongue, teaching, and weeping, granted her an exceptional power of life. Pushing the limitations of community expectations for a burgess's wife, she explored the full potential of her voice: its wailing, prophecy, and discernment in her community but also its quieter contemplation within her soul as she articulated the voice of Christ in her mind.

BIBLIOGRAPHY

Finke, Laurie A. *Women's Writing in English: Medieval England.* Longman, 1999.

Kempe, Margery. *The Book of Margery Kempe.* Translated by B.A. Windeatt. Penguin Books, 1985.

Windeatt, B.A. Introduction. *The Book of Margery Kempe.* Translated by B.A. Windeatt. Penguin Books, 1985, pp. 9-28.

LaDonna Friesen

Joan of Arc

Joan of Arc (Jeanne d'Arc) was born c. 1412 to Jacques d'Arc and Isabelle Romee, who lived in Domremy, a village in northeastern France. Her parents owned about 50 acres of land, and her father supplemented farm income with minor village jobs, such as collecting taxes. They remained loyal to the French crown, although their home was surrounded by competing pro Burgundian lands. They lived in the period of the Hundred Years War (1337-1453).

Joan was illiterate and her letters were probably dictated by her to scribes. She also signed her letters with the help of others. In 1425 at the age of 13, while she was in her "father's garden", Joan reported experiencing visions of figures she identified as Saint Michael, Saint Catherine, and Saint Margaret, who told her to drive out the English and to take the Dauphin (heir to the French throne) to Reims for his consecration.

At the age of 16 she petitioned her garrison commander to provide an armed escort to take her to the French Royal Court at Chinon. After being rebuffed at the Court, she persisted in her efforts to assist the Dauphin, arguing that God intended that she help him (against the English). In addition, she apparently prophesied about the outcome of a battle before messengers arrived to report it. As a result, she was taken to the Dauphin, disguised as a male soldier to avoid hostile Burgundians.

Joan made a positive impression on Charles the Dauphin (later to be King Charles VII), to the extent that she was allowed to accompany him in full armor to Orleans, which was besieged by the English. Her advice, rather than any military strength, won the day. The French came to believe that she was divinely inspired. When the English were forced to give up the siege and retreated away from Orleans, the ability of a peasant girl to defeat their armies was regarded as proof that she was possessed by the devil.

The victory of the "Maid of Orleans" was followed by a series of French successes as they moved towards Reims, where the Dauphin was consecrated Charles VII on July 17, 1429. In the various campaigns what led to this glorious moment, Joan suffered an arrow wound in her neck, and after the coronation, she experienced a wound to the leg from a crossbow bolt. Notwithstanding, she continued on with her pro-French endeavors. It is interesting to note that she also chose to struggle against the Hussites, followers of John Hus, who had broken with the Catholic Church on a number of doctrinal points. Joan was an ardent Catholic who hated all forms of heresy, as well as Islam. She even offered to join the hated English if they would go with her to Bohemia to fight the Hussites. This was rejected by the English.

Ironically, Joan was headed for the same terminal fate as John Hus had only recently experienced. He was burned at the stake in Constance on July 6, 1415. Joan suffered a similar execution in Rouen, Normandy, on May 30, 1431, at the age of 19 years. Joan's demise resulted from her capture on May 23, 1439, by the Burgundians, allies of the English, at the Battle of Compiegne. She was handed over to the English, put on trial by the pro-English bishop Pierre Cauchon on a variety of charges. After Cauchon declared her guilty, she was burned at the stake.

The charges against Joan included heresy (declaring that she was certain of being in God's grace), and cross-dressing (dressing like a man). The latter charge was based on her tendency to wear military clothing, because it gave her the ability to fasten her pants, boots and tunic together into one piece, which deterred rape by making it difficult to pull her pants off.

After Joan died, the English raked back the coals to expose her charred body so that no one could claim she had escaped alive. Then they burned the body twice more, to reduce it to ashes and prevent any collection of relics, and cast her remains into the Seine River.

In 1456, an inquisitional court authorized by Pope Callixtus Ill examined the trial. They debunked the charges against her, pronouncing her innocent and declaring her a Catholic martyr. In 1803 she was declared a national symbol of France by Emperor Napoleon Bonaparte. She was beatified in 1909 and canonized in 1920. She is venerated in the Roman Catholic Church and in the Anglican Communion.

BIBLIOGRAPHY

Allmand, C. *The Hundred Years War: England and France at War* c. *1300-1450*. Cambridge: Cambridge University Press, 1988.

Beaune, Colette. *Jeanne d'Arc* (in French). Paris: Perrin, 2004.

Fraioli, Deborah. *Joan of Arc: The Early Debate*. London: Boydell Press, 2002.

Joan of Arc Archive (http://archive.ioan-of-arc/) Online collection of Joan of Arc related materials, including biographies and translations.

Stanley M. Burgess

Introduction

Reformation Era and Early Modern Era

R eformation scholars recognize that there were three separate reform movements operating during the sixteenth and early seventeenth centuries in Europe. Obviously, virtually all of us recognize the Protestant Reformation and its long-term effects. Increasingly, we have come to recognize the Radical Reformation, including that of Thomas Muntzer, the Anabaptists and of the Mennonites. Finally, we have come to acknowledge the presence of a very powerful Catholic Reformation (previously called the "Counter Reformation") known for its new religious orders, such as Ignatius of Loyola's Jesuit movement and the great Catholic mystics, such as Teresa of Avila and her student, John of the Cross.

On October 31, 1517, as a professor of history, indeed a specialist on the Renaissance Reformation Era, I used to say to my students that this was a day that changed everything. Yes, it was the beginning of the Protestant reform movement, the day that Martin Luther nailed the 95 Theses on the Castle Church door at Wittenberg and mailed them to Archbishop Albert of Brandenberg, attacking the indulgence teaching of the Roman Catholic Church. Yes, it did mark a schism in the Church. But did it change everything?

While Luther and other Protestant reformers did not set out to define women's role in the church, they fleshed out their theological convictions of Sola Scriptura and the priesthood of all believers. Luther's study of

Scripture and his resulting conviction of the equality of all believers led him to initiate changes in the way education, the church, family, and societal structures were conceived. As a result, women were given new opportunities to be educated, to participate in the church and in the family, and to share the Gospel.

By all believers, Luther meant women as well as men. No longer were women to be considered "defective and misbegotten" as Thomas Aquinas had argued, but created in the image of God and of infinite value. Luther also encouraged men to love their wives selflessly and sacrificially, as Christ loves the church. He insisted that men could not do without women.

Notwithstanding these advances, women were still to be submissive to their husbands and had limited options outside the home. Ironically, when Luther closed convents and found husbands for the released nuns, many lost their chance to enjoy higher education, and thus to pursue a calling in the church's ministries. John Calvin actually opened the doors for the young men and women to be educated, but he was no egalitarian. He continued to believe that a woman's place was in the home, although it is known that he contacted several noblewomen to learn their opinions on certain religious topics.

In following pages the reader will meet the wives of Luther, Calvin, Zwingli, and Zell. These remarkable women certainly opened the door to a married priesthood and to the positive effects of having pastors' wives. But these women, with the exception of Katharina Zell did not preach, following the Pauline injunction in 1 Timothy 2:11-15. In fact, only the Anabaptists could preach in church or publish their theological/religious messages. The Zells ministered in the free city of Strasbourg, which was one of the centers of Anabaptism in southern Germany.

Later Baptists, such as theologian Dr. John Gill (1690-1771) would differ, basing their rejection of women in pulpit ministry on Genesis 3:16, which speaks to a setting after the "fall" when the woman was to desire her husband, while he ruled over her. This is direct contrast with the Genesis 1: 26-27 passage which states that God created humans, men and women he created in his image and likeness.

Methodist founder John Wesley (1703-1781) upheld male headship, but allowed women to speak in church meetings if they are under the "extraordinary impulse of the Spirit" (Wesley's notes on I Corinthians

14:34-35). This would have profound repercussions, especially in the nineteenth century Holiness movement (See Phoebe Palmer) and in the larger Pentecostal/Charismatic renewal of the twentieth century (see numerous individuals, such as Amy Semple McPherson and Marie Burgess Brown).

The early eighteenth century was the time of the First Great Awakening or the Evangelical Revival. In addition to John Wesley, George Whitefield and Jonathan Edwards articulated a theology of revival and of salvation, as well as an emphasis on providential outpourings of the Holy Spirit.

The Awakening played a significant role in the lives of women, although they were still not allowed to preach or assume leadership roles. They began to analyze their feelings, to share them with other women, and to write about them. They had more freedom to come to their own decisions, including whom they would marry. Caucasians began to welcome dark-skinned people into their churches, taken their spiritualities seriously. Black Americans were also welcomed into roles as exhorters, deacons, and, to a lesser extent, as preachers.

Of course, there were women who based their entire ministries on hearing the voice of God. Such a person was Sister Ann Lee (1730-1784) a Quaker who founded the Shaker movement. Again, she treated men and women identically, although she rejected physical union between the genders, thus leading to a rejection of sex and marriage, and to eventual elimination of the movement.

The reader should notice that this introduction about women in the Reformation period and the Early Modern era also is structured about the more famous men, whose lives and activities dominated the period. We are still attempting to re-balance the emphasis between the genders. An examination of the bibliographies in the books listed below reveal this problem. The older tomes, unless they specifically address women in their titles, do not even have the word "women" listed in their indexes!

BIBLIOGRAPHY

Bainton, Roland H. *Women of the Reformation in England and France.* Boston, MA: Beacon Press, 1974.

_____. *Women of the Reformation in Germany and Italy.* Boston, MA: Beacon Press, 1971.

Griffith, R. Marie, and David G. Roebuck. "Women, Role of/' in Stanley M. Burgess and Ed van der Maas, eds. *The New International Dictionary of Pentecostal and Charismatic Movements.* Grand Rapids, Ml: Zondervan, 2002.

Knox, Ronald. *Enthusiasm: A Chapter in the History of Religion, with Special Reference to the XVII and XVIII Centuries.* Oxford, UK: Oxford University Press, 1950.

Stetina, Karin. What the Reformation Did and Didn't Do for Women. La Mirada, CA: The Great Book Blog-Biola University, 2017.

Wesley, John. *The Works of John Wesley.* Third Edition. 14 vols. Grand Rapids, Ml: 2007.

Wesley, Susanna. *The Complete Writings.* Ed. Charles Wallace, Jr. Oxford, UK: Oxford University Press, 1997.

Whitson, Robley Edward, ed. *The Shakers: Two Centuries of Spiritual Reflection.* New York: Paulist Press, 1983.

Williams, George Hunston. *The Radical Reformation.* Philadelphia, PA: Westminster Press, 1963.

Stanley M. Burgess

Teresa of Avila

Saint Teresa of Avila (also known as Teresa Sanchez de Cepeda y Ahimada and Teresa of Jesus) was born on March 28, 1515 and died on October 4 or 15, 1582. Her parents were both devoted Catholics who inspired her to pursue a life of prayer. She was especially close to her mother who provided a warm environment, in contrast to her father whose strictness resisted her personal impulses. When the mother passed away, she was judged harshly by her father for her social life and came to look on herself as a "miserable sinner." At the age of sixteen, she was sent by her father to a convent school to be educated. Shortly thereafter, Teresa decided to become a nun in the Carmelite Order.

Carmelites in the early sixteenth century had declined into having very loose rules, with overcrowded conditions and highly materialistic motives. As part of a very strong Catholic reform movement, Teresa moved to transform the Carmelite order, both for women and men. She is especially known for introducing her order to discalced, or shoe-less, service. Barefooted in the cold Spanish weather, even in summer months, the reformed Carmelites broke from the older, less severe sisters and brothers. This split was approved by the papacy in 1580.

Teresa's zeal for mortification of the flesh led to severe illnesses, and with that of virtually constant readings on contemplative prayer. She began to experience instances of religious ecstasy. Shortly thereafter, she began to levitate (to rise above the ground without support). She was embarrassed by the levitation, asking her companion nuns to sit on her to hold her down!

She devoted much of the rest of her life to travelling around Spain setting up new convents. Her work evoked both admiration by some and radical criticism by others. At one point, the Spanish Inquisition chose to discredit her, resulting in her writing *The Life of St. Teresa of*

Avila, which Professor Carlos Eire of Princeton University considers to be less an autobiography than a defense. She continued to have other critics, including the famed psychologist, Sigmund Freud (1836-1939), who pronounced her the patron saint of hysterics!

Her seminal spiritual writing, *The Interior Castle,* written in 1577, remains one of the most significant tomes in Spanish Renaissance Literature. In all of her works, she emphasizes the soul's rise to God through four steps. The first, devotion of the heart, involves mental prayer and contemplation, especially devout meditation on the passion of Christ. The second, devotion of peace, is where human will is surrendered to God. The third, devotion of union, is essentially an ecstatic state, in which reason is surrendered to God, and one is enraptured by the love of God. The final stage is devotion to ecstasy, where one loses consciousness of being in the body while in a trans-like state. For Teresa, the fourth stage also involved the gift of tears and of levitation, especially during Mass.

Teresa died in 1582 as she travelled from Burgos to Alba de Tormes, and was buried in the latter town in the convent there. Some forty years later, she was canonized by Pope Gregory XV. She was finally declared a Doctor of the Church by Pope Paul in 1970, together with Saint Catherine of Siena, marking the first women to be awarded that distinction.

BIBLIOGRAPHY

Abiven, Jean. *15 Days of Prayer with Saint Teresa of Avila.* Hyde Park, NY: New City Press, 2011.

Eire, Carlos. *The Life of Saint Teresa of Avila.* Princeton, NJ: Princeton University Press, 2019.

Oden, Amy. *In Her Words: Women's Writings in the History of Christian Thought.* Nashville, TN: Abingdon, 1994.

Peers, E. Allison, trans. and ed. *The Complete Works of St. Teresa of Jesus.* 5 vols. London: Sheed and Ward, 1982.

Stanley M. Burgess

Katherine Von Bora

Katharina von Bora (January 29, 1499-December 20, 1552), after marriage to the great German reformer, Martin Luther, has been referred to as Katharina or Catherine Luther or "the Lutheress." Catherine was born to a family of Saxon petty nobility. When she was five, her father sent her to a Benedictine cloister in Brehna for education. At the age of ten she was placed in a nunnery at Nimschen when her father remarried. She took her vows at the age of sixteen.

Meanwhile, Luther's writings were infiltrating even monastic houses. Nine of the sisters of Nimschen became disquieted in spirit, i.e., dissatisfied with their lives in the convent. They wrote to Luther, asking for his counsel. He suggested escape and proceeded to make arrangements. They made their escape in a covered wagon among herring barrels, and fled to Wittenberg.

Within two years, Martin Luther was able to arrange homes, marriages, or employment for all of the escaped nuns except Catherine. Luther had long resolved not to marry, but that intent began to soften. Encouraged by his own father to marry and to provide him with progeny, and the willingness of "Kate", Martin made quick arrangements for the wedding. This occurred on June 13, 1525, when Martin was 41 and Catherine was 26. The following morning they held a wedding breakfast for close friends. The couple took up residence in the "Black Cloister" (Augusteum), a former dormitory and school for Augustinian Friars studying in Wittenberg-a wedding gift from John, Elector of Saxony.

In addition to taking responsibility for the lands and grounds of the monastery, Catherine eventually bore six children for Luther. The couple also raised four orphan children. She was very responsible, rising at 4 a.m. each summer morning, and at 5 a.m. in the winter. For this Martin called her the "morning star of Wittenberg." In turn, she showed her respect for her husband by calling him formally, "Sir Doctor."

Perhaps of greatest importance was the effect of their marriage and life together in the development of the Protestant Church, particularly regarding its stance on marriage and the role each spouse might take in that marriage.

When Martin died in 1546, after 21 years of marriage, Katie was left with the financial difficulties most widows of that era faced. She remained in Wittenberg in poverty until 1552, when she was forced from the town by the ravages of the Black Plague and a harvest failure. She fled to Torgau where she was thrown from her cart into a watery ditch near the city gates. For three months she lingered, in and out of consciousness. She died on December 20, 1552 at the age of 53.

Katerina von Bora is commemorated in the Calendar of Saints of some Lutheran churches in the United States. Her feast day is December 20.

BIBLIOGRAPHY

Bainton, Roland H. *Here I Stand: A Life of Martin Luther.* New York: Penguin, 1950, 1995.

_____*Women of the Reformation in Germany and Italy.* Minneapolis, MN: Augsburg, 1971.

Karant-Nunn, Susan C., and Merry E. Wiesner. *Luther on Women: A Sourcebook.* Cambridge, UIK: Cambridge University Press, 2014.

Stanley M. Burgess

Idelette Calvin

Idelette Stordeur de Bure Calvin {1500-1549) was the wife of the famous French reformer, John Calvin (Jean Cauvin). Idelette came from Flanders and early married John Stordeur from Liege. They apparently moved to Strassburg, where they were known to be Anabaptists. They had two children, Charles and Judith, before John Stordeur died after a brief illness. Idelette was left a widow.

John Calvin (July 10, 1509-May 27, 1564} was so involved in his labors in the French Reformation that he did not seem to consider marriage until the age of thirty. At that time he asked friends to find a woman who would meet his needs: to be chaste, agreeable, not hard to please, economical, patient, and careful of his health. He considered marriage to a woman of noble class, on condition that she learn French. This union never materialized. Then his friend and fellow reformer, Martin Bucer recommended an acquaintance, Idelette to Calvin. They were married in August 1540.

Idelette bore Calvin one son and possibly a few daughters, all of whom died in infancy. When Catholics suggested that these deaths resulted as a judgment on them for being heretics, Calvin replied that he was satisfied with his many sons in the faith. Calvin suffered numerous illnesses, with Idelette caring for him diligently. She provided a home that was open to refugees, fleeing for their lives and faith.

The couple survived the plague when it ravaged Geneva, but Idelette died after a long illness in 1549. Calvin commented at that time that he had lost the best companion of his life, that she was never troublesome during her illness and cared for her children. In his last 15 years, he remained a widower.

BIBLIOGRAPHY

Backus, Irena, and Philip Benedict, eds. *Calvin and His Influence. 1509-2009.* Oxford, UK: Oxford University Press, 2011.

Bainton, Roland H. *Women of the Reformation: In England and France.* Boston: Beacon Press, 1974.

Good, James I. *Famous Women of the Reformed Church.* Birmingham, AL: Solid Ground Christian Books, 1901, 2007.

Stanley M. Burgess

Anna Reinhart Zwingli

Anna Reinhart Zwingli (c. 1484-1538) was the first woman to become a Reformer's wife. Ulrich Zwingli was actually her second husband. Before meeting Zwingli, Anna, who was reported to be beautiful, met and married a young local nobleman, John von Knonau. John's family opposed the marriage, and so Anna and John were wed in secret. When the news broke, John's father disowned him. As a result, he was obliged to join the Swiss army in order to support his bride. After several campaigns, he returned home, wounded in battle and in broken health, and died in 1517, leaving Anna a widow with three children.

It was one of these children, a son, Gerold, who brought his mother and Ulrich Zwingli together. Zwingli came to Zurich in late 1518, at a time when Anna was struggling to support and train her family. Her home was in his parish and she was among his most attentive listeners. Zwingli began to tutor Gerold, which created a relationship with Anna. Before long, the pastor fell in love with his parishioner.

Because priests were not allowed to marry, Zwingli and Anna were secretly married in 1522, keeping the news from all but their closest friends until 1524. Roman Catholics charged him with breaking his vows and marrying Anna for her beauty and her money. Zwingli retorted that she had little money, but never refuted his attraction to her beauty. He, along with several other clergy, petitioned the Bishop of Constance to be freed from his vow of celibacy.

Anna took good care of her new husband. He called her his dearest housewife, a useful helpmeet to him. She worried that he did not have enough rest because he was so absorbed in his pastoral work. He began translating the Scriptures, and reading his proof sheets in the evenings to

Anna. When the complete Bible was completed and published in 1529, Ulrich gave her a copy. This proved to be her favorite book.

Zwingli was constantly under the threat of assassination. Anna arranged for guards to protect him when he was on pastoral duties. But she could not protect him from the Roman Catholic army which approached to Zurich in October, 1531. After the battle, Ulrich, together with her son, Gerold, a brother and a cousin lay dead on the field. Once again, Anna became a widow.

During her final years, Ann only went to church. She remained very sick for years, and finally died on December 6, 1538. The esteemed modern historian, Roland H. Bainton, reports that another historian, Kenneth Scott Latourette, when questioned about his unmarried estate, said that he did not know what was worse, the enforced celibacy of the Catholic clergy or the enforced matrimony of the Protestants (Bainton, 162).

BIBLIOGRAPHY

Bainton, Roland H. *Women of the Reformation in Germany and Italy.* Minneapolis, MN: Augsburg, 1971.

Good, James. *Famous Women of the Reformed Church.* Birmingham, AL: 1901, 2007.

Zwingli, Ulrich. *The Latin Works and the Correspondence of Huldreich Zwingli Together with Selections from his German Works.* New York: G. P. Putnam's Sons, 1912.

Stanley M. Burgess

Katharina Zell

Katharina Schultz Zell (1497/8-September 5, 1562) was a Protestant clergy woman and writer during the sixteenth century Reformation. She was the daughter of Elisabeth Gerster and Jacob Schultz in Strasbourg. Katharina was the fifth child often. Her family, although not wealthy, lived comfortably, and consigned a significant part of their resources to education. Katharina was fluent in German, and to a lesser extent, in Latin.

At the same time as Katharina was growing up, the Protestant Reformation was taking shape. The writings and teachings of Martin Luther were spreading across Western Europe, and clearly lnfuencing Strasbourg, which was situated at that time in the Holy Roman Empire, and today in eastern France near the German border. Luther's teachings were communicated by numerous followers, including Matthew Zell, who became a pastor in Strasbourg in 1518.

On December 12, 1523, five years after Matthew Zell came to Strasbourg, he married Katharina. The ceremony was performed by Martin Butzer, another evangelical pastor who was already married. Martin Luther immediately sent her a letter of congratulations. Shortly thereafter, both Butzer and Zell were excommunicated by the area Catholic bishop, who would not tolerate clerical marriage. Until 1529, both Catholic and Reformed services were conducted in the same church building in Strasbourg. The Catholic bishop's appointees administered the sacraments from a high altar, while Matthew Zell, often speaking to an audience of 3,000, spoke from an improvised lower altar.

Katharina had two children with Matthew, although both children died at an early age. Mathew died on January 9, 1548, and Katharina dealt with her grief and did not become ill (with dropsy) until 1561, dying the following year. Katharina wrote a hymn book, as well as numerous pamphlets, which became basic tools of the Reformation. She articulated her concept of the role of the pastor's wife, to be a "helfer" {helper) to her husband, to spin and care for the poor, but not to overshadow his leadership. While she never ascended to the pulpit, she actually preached her own funeral at the cemetery, shortly before her passing.

BIBLIOGRAPHY

Bainton, Roland H. *Women of the Reformation in Germany and Italy.* Boston, MA: Beacon, 1971.

McKee, Elsie Anne. *Katharina Schultz Zell:: the Life and Thought of a Sixteenth-century Reformer.* Vol. 1. Leiden: Brill, 1999.

Reforming Popular Piety in Sixteenth Century Strasbourg: Katherina Schultz Zell and Her Hymnbook. Princeton, NJ: Princeton Theological Seminary, 1994.

Stanley M. Burgess

Pocahontas
Rebecca Rolfe

Pocahontas (c. 1596-March 1617), born Matoaka, also known as Amonute, was a native American, living in the Tidewater area of Virginia, near the colonial settlement of Jamestown. She was the daughter of Powhatan, chief of a network of tributary tribes living in that area. She was captured and held for ransom by the new Colonists in 1613. The English conquerors encouraged her to convert to Christianity and she was baptized under the name of Rebecca. In April of the following year she married tobacco planter John Rolfe, who had lost his first wife and child enroute to Virginia. Pocohantas/Rebecca was 17 years of age. In January 1615 she bore their son Thomas Rolfe.

In 1616 the Rolfes sailed to London where Pocahontas was presented to English society as an example of the "civilized savage." Obviously, this was done to stimulate investment in the Jamestown colony. She became a celebrity and was elegantly feted by high society, even to the point of attending a ball at Whitehall Palace with King James 1 in attendance. In 1617 the Rolfes began their trip back to Virginia, but Pocahontas died of unknown causes and was buried in St. George's Church in Gravesend, on the river Thames in Kent. At that time, she was either 20 or 21.

After returning to Virginia, Thomas Rolfe and his son, Thomas Rolfe II began a family which have been known as among the First Families of Virginia. Among these is the famous wife of President Woodrow Wilson, first lady Edith Bolling Wilson, who is remembered for unofficially taking charge of the presidency when her husband proved incapable of fulfilling presidential duties. Also among the Thomas Rolfe descendants have been performer Wayne Newton and astronomer Percival Lowell.

Pocahontas is also remembered for her relationship with Captain John Smith, who survived death by clubbing when Pocahontas stepped between the Captain and his native American attackers.

BIBLIOGRAPHY

Brown, Stuart E. Jr., and Lorraine F. Myers. *Pocahontas' Descendants: A Revision, Enlargement and Extension of the List as Set Out by Wyndham Robertson in His Book Pocahontas and Her Descendants {1887}*. Third Corrections and Additions. Baltimore, MD: Genealogical Publishing Co., 1997.

Burgess, Ruth L. *Burgess family archives: Bolling family documents and history.*

Kuppeman, Karen Ordahl. *Indians and English: Facing Off in Early America*. Ithaca, NY: Cornell University Press, 2000.

Lemay, J. A. Leo. *Did Pocahontas Save Captain John Smith?* Athens, GA: University Georgia Press, 1992.

Roundtree, Helen C. *Pocahontas, Powhatan, Opechancanough: Three Indian Lives Changed by Jamestown*. Charlottesville and London: University of Virginia Press, 2005.

Woodward, Grace Steele. *Pocahontas*. Norman, OK: University of Oklahoma Press, 1969.

Ruth Vassar Burgess

Susanna Annesley Wesley

S usanna Wesley (nee Annesley; January 20, 1669-July 23, 1742) was the daughter of Dr. Samuel Annesley and Mary White. She was the 25th of 25 children. Dr. Samuel Annesley was a dissenter of the established Church of England. At the age of 13, Susanna joined the official Church of England, thereby demonstrating her independent nature.

Susanna married Samuel Wesley on November 11, 1688. Among their 19 children were John and Charles Wesley. For this she is best remembered as the Mother of Methodism, this despite the fact that she never preached a sermon or published a book or founded a church. Clearly, John and Charles, whether consciously or unconsciously, applied the example, the teachings, and the circumstances of their home life. Susanna was the primary source of her children's education.

Susanna is especially remembered for her powerful prayer life, for leaving marks on her wooden floor, made by her knees in prayer. She had much to pray about because she faced many hardships throughout her life. Her husband left her and the children for over a year because of a dispute. He spent time in jail twice due to his poor financial condition, and their lack of money was a continual struggle for Susanna. Their house was burned down twice. During one of these fires, her famous son, John, nearly died, finally being rescued from a second story window.

After two fires had decimated their rectory, Susanna was forced to place her children into different homes for nearly two years while the home was rebuilt. She was mortified that her children were using improper speech and playing more than studying. While in their own home, with Susanna in charge, their children learned for a minimum of six hours daily, eventually all of them (including the girls) learning Latin and Greek, as well as classical studies, which prepared John and Charles for their future success at Oxford University.

Dissatisfied with services at the local church, and at a time that father Samuel was out of town defending a friend against charges of heresy, Susanna assembled her children Sunday afternoon for family services. They would sing a psalm and then Susanna would read one of her husband's or her father's sermons, finally finishing with another psalm. The power of these services prompted local people to ask whether they also could attend. At one point, there were over 200 people who would attend Susanna's Sunday afternoon services, while the Sunday morning service at the local church dwindled to nearly nothing.

In addition to letters, Susanna Wesley wrote meditations and scriptural commentaries, including those on the Apostles Creed, the Lord's Prayer, and the Ten Commandments. Charles Wallace has provided the best study and edition of her writings.

In London, on July 23, 1742 at the age of 73, Susanna Wesley died. She was buried in Bunhill Fields burial ground in London.

She is remembered as a great mother, a woman that influenced Christian history, and as a person who both loved and served her Master.

BIBLIOGRAPHY

McMullen, Michael. *Prayers and Meditations of Susanna Wesley.* Peterborough: Methodist Publishing House, 2000.

Wesley, John. *The Works of John Wesley.* Third edition. 14 vols. Grand Rapids, Ml: Baker, 2007.

Wesley, Susanna. *Susanna Wesley: The Complete Writings.* Ed. Charles Wallace, Jr. Oxford, UK: Oxford University Press, 1997.

Stanley M. Burgess

Ann Lee

Ann Lee (February 29, 1730-September 8, 1784) was the founding leader of the United Society of Believers in Christ's Second Appearance, also known as the Shakers. She was born in Manchester, England. Her parents were members of a group in the Society of Friends (Quakers), and were too poor to afford their children, with virtually no educational opportunities. Her father, John Lees, was a blacksmith and a tailor. Her mother, whose name is unknown, was a very religious woman.

In 1758, Ann joined an English sect founded by Jane Wardley and her preacher husband, James. This was a precursor to the Shaker sect, teaching that it was possible to attain perfect holiness by giving up all sexual relations. Like the Wardleys, she taught that their shaking and trembling were caused by sin being purged from the body by the Holy Spirit, who was purifying the worshipper.

It appears that Ann had been uncomfortable with all sexuality, especially her own. She repeatedly attempted to avoid marriage and remain single. Despite these signals, her father forced her to marry Abraham Stanley on January 5, 1761. She became pregnant four times, all with difficulties, and with each child dying in infancy. The experiences increased her dislike of sexual relations. She soon began to advocate complete celibacy and even the abandonment of marriage. She added these beliefs to her existing pursuit of perfection. In her denial of sex and marriage, she differed from the Quakers, who did not believe in forbidding sexuality within marriage.

Ann began to reveal visions and messages from God, including the message that celibacy and confession of sin were the only true roads to salvation. Her extremism resulted in frequent arrests for dancing on the Sabbath, for her shouting and other disturbances she caused during church services. By 1770 her followers began to call her "Ann the Word" and

"Mother Ann." She exercised the gift of tongues and is reported to have performed a number of miracles, including healing the sick.

By 1774 Ann decided to leave England for America to escape her persecutors. Following her to America was her husband, who shortly deserted her, and several followers. They arrived in New York City, where they worked for nearly five years. In 1779 the Shakers settled in Niskayuna, Watervliet, near Albany. They carefully avoided sides in the American Revolution against England, maintaining that they were pacifists.

From 1780 onwards, Ann and her followers went on missionary journeys to find converts in Massachusetts and Connecticut. Her fellow Shakers began to claim that Mother Ann embodied all the perfections of God in female form, and was, actually the "second coming of Christ." Because of these extreme doctrines and practices, the Shakers were subjected to violence similar to that which they experienced in England.

Because of this new violence, Ann became frail. She died at the age of 48 on September 8, 1784, and was buried in the Shaker cemetery in Watervliet Shaker Historic District. She is remembered, not only for her extremism, but also for treating men and women equally. Because the Shakers also separated men and women, they eventually lost their following, having robbed their movement of children. While they reached approximately 16,500 adherents in their history, by 2017 there were only two Shakers alive worldwide.

BIBLIOGRAPHY

Campion, Nardi Reeder. *Mother Ann Lee: Morning Star of the Shakers.* Hanover, NH: University Press of North America, 1990.

Francis, Richard. *Ann the Word: The Story of Ann Lee, Female Messiah, Mother of the Shakers, the Woman Clothed with the Sun.* New York: Arcade Publishing, 2000.

Hall, Roger Lee. *Invitation to Zion: A Shaker Music Guide.* Skyland, NC: Pine Tree Press, 2017.

Muir, Elizabeth Gillan. *A Woman's History of the Christian Church.* Toronto: University of Toronto Press, 2019.

Stanley M Burgess

Soeur (Sister) Françoise and Seour Marie: Jansenist Girls

wo Christian girls nailed to crosses. Nailed to crosses by other Christians. How can this be? How can anyone explain this horrible situation? And it was caused by other Christians?

It turns out that the girls suffered this fate for the sole purpose of proving the truth of the theological positions of radical Catholic Augustinians in the late seventeenth and early eighteenth centuries in France. The Jansenists first emerged in France, with emigrants in Italy, Holland, and England. The group was named after their founder, Cornelis Otto Jansen (1585-1638}, who captured the essentials of the Jansenist faith in his famous work, *Augustinus* (1640}, published just after his death. It contains five propositions: (1} that it is impossible to fulfil the commands of God without special grace; (2) that grace is irresistible; (3} for merit and demerit man does not need freedom from compulsion; (4} that the Semipelagians are heretical because they held that human will could resist grace or correspond to it; and (5) it is Semipelagian to teach that Christ died for all men (note: no word about women).

These conclusions drew radical criticism from the catholic church. Jansenists argued that the sacraments of the church were efficacious only when God had already transformed the inner nature of the recipient by his grace. With divine grace limited to the elect, it was not necessary to attempt the conversion of humans still outside the church, but should rather purify itself by severe discipline and rigorous asceticism. Those who received the sacraments had by their moral discipline been qualified to receive them.

The mortal enemies of the Jansenists were the Jesuits, who resented the publication of Jansen's *Augustinus* after the author's death. Jansenism was condemned by two popes, Innocent X and Alexander VII, and many of the community were expelled from France. The headquarters of the Jansenists at Port-Royal was destroyed.

Having exhausted all efforts to defend their theological and canonical arguments, some of the Jansenists attempted to invoke in their behalf the direct testimony of God Himself, namely, through miracles. They suggested that marvelous cures took placed at the tomb of the deacon François de Paris in the little cemetery of Saint-Medard. Soon the sick and the curious flocked to the cemetery. The sick are reported to have experienced strange agitations, nervous commotions, either real or simulated. They fell into violent transports 11 of the Spirit." The cemetery was closed by order of the court in 1732.

The Convulsionaries continued their displays in private houses. Young girls were seized by such fits, while claiming a divine gift of healing. Their bodies seemed insensible and invulnerable, even though wounded by the sharpest instruments or bruised by enormous weights or blows. R. A. Knox *(Enthusiasm,* 384} provides two examples of girls who were nailed to crosses for periods of up to three and a half hours. Secour Françoise was nailed by both her hands and feet, and her ribs pierced with a kind of spear. To be sure, the cross never was raised to its full height, so her full weight was not on the nails. The other girl, Secour Marie, could not stand it for more than twenty-five minutes, and then begged to be released.

All of this to prove the Jansenist claim to miracles, and thus to their theological correctness. Of course, it was two young girls who were chosen to make the painful sacrifice to make the point.

BIBLIOGRAPHY

Knox, R. A. *Enthusiasm: A Chapter in the History of Religion.* Oxford, UK: Clarendon, 1950.

Radner, Ephraim. *Spirit and Nature: The Saint-Medard Miracles in 18th century Jansenism.* New York: Herder and Herder, 2002.

Strayer, Brian E. *Suffering Saints: Jansenists and Convulsionaires in France, 1640-1799.* Portland, OR: Sussex Academic, 2008.

Stanley M. Burgess

Introduction
Nineteenth Century

In the early nineteenth century, white males enjoyed almost universal suffrage, while women of all colors were continually refused by patriarchal forces, including their husbands, politicians, and men of the cloth, to vote or to hold political office. Women had limited education and usually could not attend college. They were considered physically and intellectually inferior to men. They faced unfair working conditions, and were usually unable to control their own property. Beginning in the mid-1850s, however, women began to battle for their rights, especially the right to vote.

The Second Great Awakening in large part facilitated, even generated this battle. This was a religious revival movement during the nineteenth century that was challenging women's roles in religion. It fueled the women's rights movement, the abolitionist movement, and the temperance movement—three movements closely tied together. Women came to believe that the Bible taught their potential for progress, as well as encouraged their faith in social reform.

In July 1848 (a revolutionary year by all counts) the first women's rights convention was held in Seneca Falls, New York. Elizabeth Cady Stanton drew up a Declaration of Sentiments, based on the Declaration of Independence. The document declared that all men *and women* were created equal (Genesis 1:26-27). Two years later, the first annual National Women's Rights Convention was convened. This continued to occur each year until 1860. They dealt with equal wages, expanded education, property rights, marriage reform, and temperance. After the Civil War (1861-65} was over, Susan B. Anthony, together with former slave, Sojourner Truth, led the way towards women's rights. But the women's rights movement would have only limited success until 1920 when the 19th Amendment was passed, granting women the vote.

A strong new Holiness movement emerged in the early nineteenth century, led by Phoebe Palmer (1807-1874}, that would defend the role of women in ministry in Protestantism. Palmer would greatly influence Catherine Booth, as well as the temperance movement.

In England, a new revivalist movement emerged during the early nineteenth century. The Salvation Army, under the leadership of a former Methodist Reform Church minister, William Booth, and his wife, Catherine, has become the single largest non-governmental social relief agency in the world. It was founded to meet the needs of the poor, destitute and hungry by meeting their physical and spiritual needs. It has developed hospitals and other relief and welfare institutions in 131 countries world-wide.

It has been argued by several scholars that a Third Great Awakening took place after the American Civil War, lasting until early in the 20th Century. (Note that the eminent scholar, Kenneth Scott Latourette, has insisted that this never came to America.). Regardless, in this period, Evangelical leaders, such as Dwight L. Moody, advanced the revivalist movement by founding Moody Bible Institute in Chicago, Illinois. Other leaders include hymnists Ira Sankey and the famed Fanny Crosby, who composed over 8,000 hymns and spiritual songs, despite being blind! The late nineteenth century also saw increased missionary activity around the world. Among the most notable was Anglican Amy Beatrice Carmichael, who championed the cause of women and orphans in Southern India.

While the nineteenth century has been called the "Protestant Century," Roman Catholic women also made significant contributions. Bernadette Soubirous {1844-1879}, a malnourished and uneducated girl saw a series of eighteen visions of the Virgin Mary near Lourdes, France. Remarkably, Lourdes became the largest center of Christian faith-healing in Europe. A Catholic medical center popped up next door to test the veracity of miraculous cures. It is important to note that this is also the time {December 8, 1854) when the dogma of the Immaculate Conception of the Virgin Mary in the womb of her mother, Anne, was declared by Pope Pius IX.

BIBLIOGRAPHY

Cerillo, Augustus. "The Beginnings of American Pentecostalism: A Historiographic Overview," in Edith Blumhofer, Russell Spittler, and Grant A. Wacker, eds. *Pentecostal Currents in American Protestantism.* Urbana, IL: University of Illinois Press, 1999.

Muir, Elizabeth Gillan. *A Women's History of the Christian Church.* Toronto: University of Toronto Press, 2019.

Oden, Amy, ed. *In Her Words: Women's Writings in History of Christian Thought.* Nashville, TN: Abingdon, 1998.

Stanley M. Burgess

Bernadette Soubirous of Lourdes

B ernadette Soubirous or Bernadette of Lourdes (January 7, 1844-April 16, 1879) was the eldest daughter (of nine children) of François Soubirous, a miller, and Louise (nee Casterot), a laundress. She was born on January 7, 1844, and baptized two days later, on her parents' wedding anniversary.

The family was poor and Bernadette was a weak, sickly child, suffering from cholera as a toddler and from asthma throughout her life. She never grew above 4ft 7in. She spoke the language of Occitan, which was popular in the Pyrenees region at that time. After age 13 she studied French in school, although she was frequently ill and a poor learner. By the time of her first vision, the family was in terrible financial and social condition. They lived in a one-room basement lodging, formerly used as a jail, called "the dungeon" ("*le cachot*").

On February 11, 1858, Bernadette, aged 14, had the first of eighteen visions that transformed her life, and for which she is remembered. While gathering firewood near a local grotto, a white figure in a dazzling light appeared to her. At the time of her third vision, Bernadette revealed that "the vision" asked her to return to the grotto each day for two weeks. No one accompanying her saw any of the visions.

Bernadette never claimed the vision to be the Virgin Mary until the seventeenth vision, although townspeople who believed her reports, assumed that she had seen the Queen of Heaven. The conversations that accompanied these visions emphasized the need for prayer and penance, and to drink of the water of the spring, to wash in it and to eat the herb that grew there-all acts of penance. Bernadette also stated that "the Lady" told her to build a chapel and to form a procession. In the sixteenth vision, the Lady told Bernadette that she was "the immaculate Conception."

Bernadette Soubirous of Lourdes was rigorously interviewed by the Catholic Church and the French government. She stuck to her story. By 1862 the Church confirmed the authenticity of the apparitions. Subsequently, miraculous cures began to take place at the grotto. The Lourdes Medical Bureau insisted that there was no other explanation for the healings that continued to multiply as Catholic pilgrims came to Lourdes to drink of the water at the grotto. At present, nearly five million pilgrims come from all over the world each year to seek healing at Lourdes.

All of this attention caused Bernadette to be uncomfortable. She followed the development of Lourdes as a pilgrimage shrine while she lived at Lourdes, but afterwards stayed away. She was not present when the Basilica of the Immaculate Conception was consecrated in 1870. She retreated to the motherhouse of St. Bernard at Nevers, where she died from asthma at the age of 35 in 1879. She was canonized by Pope Pius XI on December 8, 1933. Her feast day is April 16.

BIBLIOGRAPHY

Laurentin, Rene. *Bernadette Speaks: A Life of Saint Bernadette in Her Own Words.* Toronto, ON: Pauline Books and Media, 2000.

Taylor, Therese. *Bernadette of Lourdes.* London: Burns and Oates, 2003.

Stanley M. Burgess

Florence Nightingale

Florence Nightingale (May 12, 1820-August 13, 1910) was one of the great English social reformers in the Victorian era. She also is recognized as the founder of modern nursing. She was born in Florence, Italy, while her parents were on an extended vacation there. When she returned to Britain, she experienced the first of several experiences that she believed were from God, prompting her to devote her life to the service of others.

Her family, which was wealthy, reacted negatively to her decision to work as a nurse, seeing this as uncomely to a woman of her rank. This also caused her to spend most of her time with patients and with young male intellectuals. She remained close friends with the politician and poet Richard Monckton Milnes over a period of nine years, before rejecting his proposals of marriage. She feared that marriage would interfere with her ability to follow her calling to nursing.

In Rome in 1847, she met Sidney Herbert, on his honeymoon there. Herbert had been Secretary of War (1845-46). He and Nightingale became close friends. He became Secretary of War again during the Crimean War (1853-56), when he and his wife facilitated Nightingale's nursing career in the Crimea. At this time, her emphasis was on relieving the horrific conditions of the wounded. In October 1854 she and her staff of 38 women volunteer nurses that she trained, and 15 Catholic nuns were sent under the authorization of Sidney Herbert to the Ottoman Empire.

It has been reported by Stephen Paget (Dictionary of National Biography) that Nightingale reduced the death rate from 42% to 2%, by making improvements in hygiene. We also know that ten times more soldiers died from illnesses such as typhoid, typhus, cholera and dysentery than from battle wounds. Upon return to England, she was enabled to create nursing programs, including the Nightingale Training School at

Saint Thomas' Hospital in 1860, now a part of King's College, London. In 1859, Florence wrote *Notes on Nursing*. It was the first of its kind ever to be written. Some scholars believe that she remained chaste for her entire life, perhaps because she felt a religious calling to her career. She was a lifelong member of the Anglican Church, although she was committed to a theology of universal reconciliation (in this she closely resembled the ancient Origin of Alexandria).

Florence Nightingale died peacefully in her sleep on August 13, 1910, and was buried in the graveyard at St. Margaret's Church in East Wellow, Hampshire, near Embley Park, near one of her family's home. This location, despite numerous efforts to inter her at Westminster Abbey.

BIBLIOGRAPHY

Bostridge, Mark. *Florence Nightingale: The Woman and Her Legend.* London: Viking, 2008.
Widham Smith, Cecil. *Florence Nightingale.* Penguin UK, 1951.

Stanley M, Burgess

Phoebe Palmer

Phoebe Palmer (December 18, 1807-November 2, 1874), a Methodist evangelist and writer who is recognized as one of the founders of the Holiness movement within Methodism. She was born Phoebe Worrall in New York City to Henry Worrall and Dorothea Wade Worrall. Henry Worrall had experienced a religious conversion in England during the Wesleyan Revival, before immigrating to the United States.

Phoebe married Walter Palmer, a homeopathic physician who also was a devout Methodist. The couple became interested in the life and work of John Wesley, the founder of Methodism. Specifically, they concentrated on his doctrine of perfectionism, the belief that a Christian can live a life free from sin. On July 26, 1837, Phoebe Palmer experienced what John Wesley called "entire sanctification." Acknowledging that the first spiritual blessing was conversion, the perfectionists insisted that complete dedication to Christ would bring a second spiritual blessing, namely, that of complete sanctification. Phoebe taught others about this experience, and how to receive it and have it for themselves.

Phoebe Palmer and her husband Walter became itinerant preachers, speaking at conferences, camp meetings, and other events. Phoebe wrote several books, including *The Way of Holiness,* which became a primary book in the Holiness movement (see Amy Oden for a portion of these writings). She influenced Catherine Booth, the co-founder of the Salvation Army, and Frances Willard, the temperance leader, among many others. Another of Phoebe's books, *The Promise of the Father,* defended the idea of women in Christian ministry. Because of these and other achievements, she had been acknowledged to be the "mother of the holiness movement."

Today, Phoebe Palmer is considered a link between Wesleyan Methodism and modern Pentecostalism, as well as a root in the emergence of the Salvation Army, the Church of the Nazarene, and the Church of God (non-Pentecostal). Phoebe's daughter, Phoebe Knapp, wrote several hymns, including the melody for Fanny Crosby's "Blessed Assurance."

Phoebe Palmer died on November 2, 1874, at the age of 66.

BIBLIOGRAPHY

Burgess, Stanley M., ed. *Reaching Beyond: Studies in the History of Perfectionism.* Peabody, MA: Hendrickson, 1986.

Heath, Elaine A. *Naked faith: the mystical theology of Phoebe Palmer.* Eugene, OR: Pickwick Publications, 2009.

Oden, Amy, ed. *In Her Words: Women's Writings in the History of Christian Thought.* Nashville, TN: Abingdon, 1998.

Reuther, Rosemary Radford, and Rosemary Skinner Keller. *Women and Religion in America: The Nineteenth Century.* San Francisco: Harper and Row, 1981.

Stanley M. Burgess

Fanny Crosby

Frances Jane van Alstyne Crosby (March 24, 1820-February 12, 1915L better known as Fanny Crosby, was one of the greatest hymnist in history, writing more than 8,000 hymns and gospel songs. This incredible accomplishment, despite losing her eyesight shortly after birth. She is also known for her rescue mission work and for her poetry and teaching.

Crosby was known as the "Queen of Gospel Song Writers" and the "Mother of modern congregational singing in America." Her music was featured in a wide range of revival campaigns, including those of Ira Sankey and Dwight L. Moody. Among the favorites were:

"All the Way My Savior Leads Me"
"Blessed Assurance"
"Close to Thee"
"Eye Hath Not Seen"
"He Hideth My Soul"
"More Like Jesus"
"I Am Thine, 0 Lord (Draw Me Nearer)"
"Jesus is Tenderly Calling Me Home"
"My Savior First of All"
"Near the Cross"
"Pass Me Not, 0 Gentle Saviour"
"Praise Him, Praise Him"
"Redeemed, How I Love to Proclaim It"
"Rescue the Perishing"
"Safe in the Arms of Jesus"
"Saved by Grace"
"Savior, More Than Life to Me"

"Take the World, But Give Me Jesus"
"Tell Me the Story of Jesus"
"To God Be the Glory"

Her hymns were so popular that some publishers were hesitant to have so many by one person in their hymnals, so Crosby used nearly 200 different pseudonyms during her career.

Crosby also wrote more than one thousand secular poems and had four books of poetry published, in addition to two autobiographies and several cantatas of biblical and patriotic songs. She was extremely commited to Christian rescue missions and was a popular public speaker. Fanny Crosby died in 1915 at the age of 94 in Bridgeport, Connecticut.

BIBLIOGRAPHY

Blumhofer, Edith L. "Fanny Crosby, William Doane, and the Making of Gospel Hymns in the Late Nineteenth Century/' in Noll, Mark A., and Edith Blumhofer L, eds. *Sing Them Over Again to Me: Hymns and Hymnbooks in America*. Tuscaloosa, AL: University of Alabama Press, 2006.

Her Heart Can See: The Hymns and Life of Fanny Crosby. Grand Rapids, Ml: Eerdmans, 2005.

Commire, Anne, and Deborah Kiezmer. *Women in World History: A Biographical Encyclopedia*. Waterford, CN: 2000.

Stanley M. Burgess

Catherine Mumford Booth

atherine Mumford Booth (January 17, 1929-October 4, 1890} was born to a Methodist family in Ashbourne, Derbyshire, England. Her father, John Mumford, was an occasional lay preacher and carriage maker. Her mother was Sarah Milward Mumford. Catherine became one of the greatest women of the Victorian era.

Catherine's parents were ardent members of a Wesleyan Methodist chapel. Catherine spent much of her childhood confined to bed, suffering from spine, lung and heart troubles. As a result, she was home schooled by her devoted mother who encouraged her to read her Bible. By the time she was twelve she had read Sacred Scriptures through eight times. She also read about church history, especially being influenced by the life and work of John Wesley.

In 1834 the Mumfords moved to Boston, Lincolnshire, her father's native town. Unfortunately, her father became an alcoholic and lost his faith. Catherine took up the cause of the temperance movement, writing letters to a variety of magazines and serving as a secretary of a Juvenile Temperance Society. In 1844 the Mumfords moved to Brixton in south London, where Catherine joined a Wesleyan congregation as well as joining the temperance movement. She taught a girls' Sunday School class in Clapham. She also wrote a diary between 1847 and 1848, and a series of spiritual letters to her friends and associates. Before long, she became dissatisfied with the Wesleyans and became a member of another congregation led by the Reformers.

Most significantly, in 1852, she met William Booth, with whom she fell in love. They were married on June 16, 1855. Despite her physical weaknesses, she bore eight children. Meanwhile, she developed strong Christian feminist views. While her husband gradually accepted her arguments in favor of female equality, he was reluctant to allow female preaching. Never challenging the accepted Victorian notions of the appropriate roles of women at home, she quickly became a co-pastor to William after he accepted his Methodist New Connection pastorate. In 1860 Catherine began to preach herself with the full approval of her husband. She was convinced that women were not intellectually inferior to men and had every right to preach.

Catherine Booth soon proved to be an exceptional orator in and out of the pulpit, as she began to significantly influence moral and social reform. She preached in South London and in Bermondsey. While her husband was away on evangelistic tours, she shared his pastoral work. She discovered a model in Phoebe Palmer, the American Wesleyan revivalist. With her husband's encouragement, she wrote a pamphlet, *Female Ministry: Women's Right to Preach the Gospel* (1859}. She argued that the Holy Spirit had ordained and blessed women in ministry and so the practice must be justified.

She also began to speak to people in their homes, especially to alcoholics, whom she helped to make a new start in life. She eventually began to hold her own campaign revival services. In December, 1859 she also published the pamphlet, *Female Teaching*. Catherine was eloquent and compelling in speech and in writing, for twenty-five years defending the right of women to preach the gospel on the same terms as men. She was especially effective among the well-to-do population. She actually lobbied Queen Victoria to promote legislation that safeguarded females—the so-called "Parliamentary Bill for the protection of girls."

In London's East End, William Booth preaching to the poor and oppressed, while Catherine spoke to the wealthy, raising funds for their expanding ministry. In the emergent Salvation Army, women were expected to help run the corps, and eventually became leaders in the internationalization of the movement.

Catherine Booth died of breast cancer at age 61, and was buried with her husband in Abney Park Cemetery, London. She is to be remembered for the great movement of social work that she co founded. Catherine also help to open up Christian pulpits to talented and anointed women. Among the most lasting legacies of the Booths was the Catherine Booth Hospital and nursing school in Nagercoil, India. A personal note: On November 27,

1937, Stanley M. Burgess, the co editor of this book, was born in Nagercoil, Madras State, S. India, at the Catherine Booth Memorial Hospital.

BIBLIOGRAPHY

Booth-Tucker, Frederick St. George. *The life of Catherine Booth, the Mother of The Salvation Army.* Whitefish, MO: Kessinger Publishing, 2004.

Eason, Andrew M. and Roger J. Green, eds. *Settled Views: The Shorter Writings of Catherine Booth.* Lanham, MD: Lexington Books, 2017.

Green, Roger J. *Catherine Booth: A Biography of the Cofounder of the Salvation Army.* Grand Rapids, Ml: Baker Books, 1996.

Mayne Kienzle, Beverly, and Pamela J. Walker, eds.*Women Preachers and Prophets Through Two Millennia of Christianity.* Berkley and Los Angeles: University of California Press, 1998.

Murdoch, Norman H. *Origins of the Salvation Army.* Knoxville: University of Tennessee Press, 1996.

_____. "Female Ministry in the Thought and Work of Catherine Booth," *Church History,* Vol 53 (3) 1984, 348-362.

Stanley M. Burgess

Harriet Ross Tubman

arriet Tubman, granddaughter of an enslaved African woman, was born in Cambridge, Maryland c. 1820 as Araminta ('Minty') Ross. Her father, Benjamin Ross, received his freedom in 1840 but worked on a neighboring plantation. Minty lived with her mother, Harriet Green Ross, a cook on the Brodess plantation, from where Minty was hired out at age six to work for white families. In addition to suffering hard labor and mistreatment, Harriet persistently feared being sold away from her family, as two of her sisters had been. As a young teen, Harriet received a traumatic head injury from a heavy weight thrown by an overseer as she intervened to protect another slave. This debilitating injury caused 'somnolence' and resulted in headaches, seizures, dreams, and powerful visions.

By the time she married John Tubman, a free man, in 1844, Araminta had taken the name Harriet, after her mother. Harriet began to dream of her own freedom. In 1849, fearing she would be sold, she escaped and made the dangerous 100-rnile trek north to Pennsylvania and freedom. After finding work and networking with anti-slavery activists, Harriet soon began working for the Underground Railroad. She was determined to return and free her family, feeling a sense of mission from God, guided by visions she felt He sent to help on her many journeys of liberation. On one trip, to bring her husband north, she discovered he had remarried. Overcoming that trauma, Harriet then focused her attention on her work of saving other slaves, returning numerous times to lead dozens to freedom throughout the next decade.

After the 1850 Fugitive Slave Act made abolitionist work increasingly difficult, Harriet and her brothers established a base in St. Catharines, Canada in 1851 for several years before eventually settling in Auburn, New York in 1859. Throughout the 1850s Harriet continued to befriend and network with notable activists in the abolitionist and women's suffrage movements and was in demand as a public speaker.

In 1858 she befriended abolitionist John Brown, who dubbed Harriet "General Tubman." She helped Brown prepare for his attack on Harper's Ferry by putting him in contact with possible African Canadian recruits. Soon, given Harriet's expert knowledge, skills as a strategist, and remarkable physical strength, she was found serving in the Civil War-as a nurse, scout, spy and then notably as the first woman to lead an armed U.S. military raid. In 1863 she and 150 black soldiers led 750 enslaved people off plantations to freedom. Though hailed as "Moses," while returning home on a government train pass, Harriet suffered racial abuse and physical assault. It also took her until 1899 to receive her war pay after petitioning the government.

After the murder of her first husband by a white man in 1867, Harriet married Nelson Davis in 1869 (the year of her first biography, done as a fundraiser for her ongoing projects). Her work from Auburn included providing a home for her parents and family, opening a shelter for elderly former slaves (the Harriet Tubman Horne), helping with schools for freed slaves in South Carolina, and speaking for women's suffrage. She was involved in the Central Presbyterian Church there and later the African Methodist Episcopal Zion Church. Brought up by devout Christian parents who attended church and fasted, Harriet's ecstatic spirituality was characterized by God's guidance and empowerment through dreams, waking visions, prophetic foresight, and even out-of-body experiences. Her stories depict a life of spiritual transformation that included a strong prayer life, faith and courage for endurance, a deep sense of justice based in biblical truth, and themes of obedience, God's goodness, forgiveness, and deliverance.

Harriet Ross Tubman-Davis died on March 10, 1913 and was buried with military honors.

BIBLIOGRAPHY

Bradford, Sarah Hopkins. *Harriet, the Moses of Her People.* Auburn, NY: W. J. Moses, 1869 (Rev. ed. 1886).

Clinton, Catherine. *Harriet Tubman: The Road to Freedom.* New York: Little, Brown and Company, 2004.

Conrad, Earl. *Harriet Tubman: Negro Soldier and Abolitionist.* Washington, DC: The Associated Publishers, 1943. (New York: International Publishers, 1976).

Larson, Kate Clifford. *Bound for the Promised Land: Harriet Tubman: Portrait of an American Hero.* New York: Ballantine Books, 2003.

Humez, Jean M. *Harriet Tubman: The Life and the Life Stories.* Wisconsin Studies in Autobiography. Madison, WI: University of Wisconsin Press, 2004.

_____. "Search of Harriet Tubman's Spiritual Autobiography." In *This Far sby Faith: Readings in African-American Women's Religious Biography,* edited by Judith Weisenfeld and Richard Newman, 240-261. New York: Routledge, 1996.

Sernett, Milton C. *Harriet Tubman: Myth, Memory and History.* Durham, NC: Duke University Press Books, 2007.

Lois E. Olena

Elizabeth Cady Stanton

E lizabeth Cady Stanton (November 12, 1815-October 26, 1902} was born in New York City to Daniel Cady and Margaret Livingston Cady. She married Henry Brewster Stanton in 1840 and enjoyed many years of married life, bearing seven children. She became an American suffragist, social activist, abolitionist, and leading figure in the earthly women's rights movement. Her Declaration of Sentiments, presented to the Seneca Falls Convention of 1848 in Seneca Falls, New York, was a major step in organizing women's rights and women's suffrage movements in the United States.

Before Elizabeth Stanton turned her attention almost exclusively to women's rights, she was an active abolitionist, together with her husband, Henry, who co-founded the Republican party. Stanton was particularly concerned with the right to vote, to own and control property, parental rights, issues of employment as well of divorce, birth control, the economic health of the family, and the temperance movement. Following the American Civil War (1861-65}, along with Susan B. Anthony, she refused to support the Fourteenth and Fifteenth Amendments to the United States Constitution. She reasoned that women's rights must go before racial equality. This led to a division in the women's rights movement which lasted about twenty years. When the two sides finally joined back together, she was elected President of the National American Woman Suffrage Association (1890-92}.

In 1895 and 1898, Elizabeth Stanton produced the two-part *Women's Bible.* In this work, she rejected traditional Christianity as inherently patriarchal and oppressive. In its place she called for a more rational religion embodying her revisionist principles. She refused to accept the Bibles of the Christian traditions as sacred texts. This brought considerable criticism, as did her acceptance of interracial marriages. She publicly congratulated Frederick Douglass on his marriage to Helen Pitts, a white woman, in 1884.

In her late years, Stanton wrote many pieces and contributed to several significant books, including a six-volume *History of Women's Suffrage,* completed by Ida Harper in 1922. She wrote her autobiography, *Eighty Years & More: Reminiscences 1815-1897.* Elizabeth Cady Stanton died of heart failure at her home in New York City in 1902, eighteen years before women were granted the right to vote in the United States. She was inducted into the National Woman's Hall of Fame in 1973. She is celebrated as a saint of the Episcopal Church; her feast day in July 20.

BIBLIOGRAPHY

Ginzberg, Lori D. *Elizabeth Cady Stanton: An American Life.* New York: Farrar, Strauss, Giroux, 2009.

Oden, Amy, ed. *In Her Words: Women's Writings in the History of Christian Thought.* Nashville, TN: Abingdon, 1994.

Stanley M. Burgess

Amy Beatrice Carmichael

A my Beatrice Carmichael (1867-1951) was born in a small village in Ireland, her parents being David Carmichael, a miller, and his wife Catherine. She was the eldest of 7 children in a family of devout Presbyterians. They eventually settled in Belfast where they founded the Welcome Evangelical Church. Amy developed a strong ministry among the mill girls of Rosemary Street Presbyterian Church to the point that they raised money to fund a larger meeting hall. In 1889, she received a call to work among the mill girls in Manchester, England.

Amy was sickly throughout her life, suffering from neuralgia, which made her weak and constantly in pain. Notwithstanding, she continued to serve her Master whenever doors seemed to open. In 1887, she attended the annual Keswick Convention, known for launching many Christian careers at home and abroad, and heard the famed Hudson Taylor, founder of the China Inland Mission, speak of his life on the mission field. Amy was powerfully moved, and was convinced of her own missionary calling. She joined the China Inland Mission and lived for a short period at the CIM training facility in London. However, it was determined that she was too sickly to pursue her chosen calling. She eventually left the CIM and joined the Church Missionary Society, which sponsored her overseas call.

Ms. Carmichael initially went to Japan, but fell ill and returned home. Again, she went back to Asia, serving in Ceylon (now Sri Lanka), until poor health forced her to Bangalore, South India, where she found her ultimate vocation. She again found ministry among girls and young women, especially those who lived out their lives as prostitutes in Hindu Temples. Beginning with just one, then two girls, her ministry grew rapidly. Her followers often commented that it was love that drew them to "Amma"

("Mother" Amy). She had decided that she would give her life for her girls. She once commented that missionary life was simply a chance to die.

In 1901 Amy founded the Dohnavur Fellowship to continue her work. Dohnavur was situated in Madras Presidency (now Tamil NaduL thirty miles north of Cape Comeran (KanyakumariL India's southernmost tip. In 1912 England's Queen Mary recognized Amy's work and helped fund a hospital in Dohnavur. By this time, the Fellowship was serving 130 girls. By 1918 they added a home for young boys, many of them born to former temple prostitutes. Amy Carmichael also formed a Protestant religious order called Sisters of the Common Life (1916).

Amy suffered a severe fall in 1931, leaving her bedridden for most of her final years. She then turned to writing books, amounting to between 35 or as many as *72,* although most are out of print today.

Amy died in 1951 at the age of 83. India outlawed temple prostitution in 1948. The Dohnavur Fellowship continues its work, currently supporting ca. 500 women and men, 16 nurseries and a hospital. Amy Carmichael is venerated in the Anglican Communion Evangelical Church. Her feast day is January 18.

BIBLIOGRAPHY

Elliott, Elisabeth. *A Chance to Die: The Life and Legacy of Amy Carmichael.* Grand Rapids, Ml: Fleming H. Revell, 1987.
Wellman, Sam. *Amy Carmichael: A Life Abandoned to God.* Barbour Publishing, 1998.

Stanley M. Burgess

Introduction

Twentieth Century

The twentieth century opened with an explosion of Pentecostal enthusiasm. Even before the well-known Azusa Street Revival (1906-13} came to Los Angeles, a Roman Catholic sister, Elena Guerra, was pleading with Pope Leo XIII to reconsider the role of the Holy Spirit in the Roman Church. On January 1, 1901, he declared the 20th century to be the Century of the Holy Spirit. Elena Guerra was a precursor to the events occurring in 1962 when Pope John XXIII called the Second Vatican Council into session, when he labelled her an "Apostle of the Holy Spirit," and prayed that the Council would be a "New Pentecost." Shortly thereafter, the Catholic Charismatic Movement broke out at Duquesne University in Pittsburg, Pennsylvania (March 1967}, on the very same day as it emerged in Bogota, Columbia. It was later discovered that similar Holy Spirit revivals had occurred even earlier in the Catholic communities, such as the Legion of Mary (Legio Mariae} in Kenya in 1962.

Less known and certainly less understood, was the presence of 901,000 enthusiasts in African Initiated churches by the year 1900. Our best source for this information has been Professor David B. Barrett, who spent a lifetime studying the "Six thousand contemporary Religious Movements" in schism and renewal (1968}. Because of their profoundly different cultures from the Western churches, they have only recently been recognized as truly "Pentecostal."

On the other side of the world, in India another woman named Pandita Ramabai, an upper class Hindui turned Christian, who opened an orphanage at Khedgaon (near Pune, Maharastra State} for girls, experienced a similar outpouring of the Holy Spirit. In January 1905 Ramabai issued a call to prayer, with more than 500 of her women responding. By June 29th of that same year, the Holy Spirit renewal began at her compound called Mukti ("salvation" in Marathi). It affected many other locations around the world, including the United States, where the Azusa Street Revival was about to begin. Pandita Ramabai is one of the greatest women in the history of the Christian Church, and is honored by being featured on the cover of this book.

Better known in the Western world is the story that this same Holy Spirit revival began in Topeka, Kansas on January 1, 1901 (note the exact same date as listed above for Leo XlII's declaration). This Spirit outbreak was at Charles F. Parham's Bethel Bible School. This led to the Azusa Street Revival, which American Pentecostals often claim as the first recurrence of Pentecostalism since the New Testament period. It was a powerful movement, but was not unique, except for its insistence that glossolalia (tongues speech) was the sole proof of the Baptism in/of/with the Holy Spirit.

Actually, there is a continuous history of Pentecostalism in the history of Christianity, whether Apostolic, Roman Catholic, Eastern Orthodox, Protestant, or modern Pentecostal/Charismatic (S. M. Burgess, 1984, 1987, 1995; see especially 2011).

The 20th Century has finally experienced a release in the variety of religious occupations open to women in virtually all Christian groups. In this section, you will meet champions of racial equality, such as Caretta Scott King and Maya Angelo, medical missionaries such as Dr. Ida Scudder, renowned evangelists Aimee Semple McPherson and Kathryn Kuhlmann, prominent pastors such as Marie Burgess Brown, prominent political leaders such as Eleanor Roosevelt and Madam Chiang Kai-shek, and the great humanitarian Mother Teresa of Calcutta. But you also will meet individuals you have never before heard of, such as Lenora Isabel Scott Vassar, a United States pioneer into western and southern states. Education leaders, such as Dr. Billy Davis, Dr. Elizabeth Caspari, and Dr. Marie Montessori, will be featured, as will social activists Helen Adams Keller and Corrie ten Boon.

Demographers Todd Johnson and Gina Zurlo (2019) have recognized that over the period 1900-2020, profound changes have occurred in the global Christian community, of which women number over one-half. In 1900, over 80% of all Christians were North American or European. Now, that percentage has fallen to 33%, while enormous growth has been experienced in Latin America, Asia, and especially in Africa, which leads in 2020, and is expected to lead, followed distantly by Latin America and Asia, in 2050. This certainly is true of Pentecostal/Charismatic Christianity, which in 2020 had 644,260,000 members and adherents, and is expected to have just over one billion (1,031,500,000) by 2050. Because of the growing influence of women in Christianity, Johnson and Zurlo are presently studying their situation worldwide.

Our study of the history of Christian women has led us through the periods of origin, of persecution, of seclusion, of intolerance, and, finally of significance and influence. And the end is yet to come!

BIBLIOGRAPHY

Anderson, Allan, Michael Bergunder, Andre Droogers, and Cornelis Van Der Laan, ed. *Studying Global Pentecostalism: Theories and Methods*. Berkeley, CA: University of California Press, 2010.

Barrett, David B. *Schism and Renewal in Africa: An Analysis of Six Thousand Contemporary Religious Movements*. Oxford, UK: Oxford University Press, 1968.

Burgess, Stanley M., ed. *Christian Peoples of the Spirit: A Documentary History of Pentecostal Spirituality from the Early Church to the Present*. New York and London: New York University Press, 2011.

_____*The Holy Spirit: Ancient Christian Traditions*. Peabody, MA: Hendrickson, 1984, 1994. *The Holy Spirit: Eastern Christian Traditions*. Peabody, MA: Hendrickson, 1989. *The Holy Spirit: Medieval Roman Catholic and Reformation Traditions*. Peabody, MA, Hendrickson, 1997.

Griffith, R. Marie, and David Roebuck. "Women, Role of", in *The New International Dictionary of Pentecostal and Charismatic Movements*, Stanley M. Burgess and Ed van der Maas, eds. Grand Rapids, Ml: Zondervan, 2002.

Hollenweger, Walter J. *The Pentecostals*. London: SCM Press, 1972.

Johnson, Todd M. and Gina A. Zurlo. *World Christian Encyclopedia.* 3rd edition. Edinburgh: Edinburgh University Press, 2019.

Oden, Amy, ed. *In Her Words: Women's Writings in the History of Christian Thought.* Nashville, TN: Abingdon Press, 1994.

Then Peter Stood Up: Collections of the Popes' Addresses to the Catholic Charismatic Renewal from its Origins to the year 2000. Vatican City: ICCRS, 2000.

Stanley M. Burgess

Elena Guerra

E lena Guerra (June 23, 1835-April 11, 1914) was a Roman Catholic nun and precursor to the Catholic Charismatic Renewal. Elena was the founder of the Oblate Sisters of the Holy Spirit in Lucca, Italy. She formed prayer groups, which she called "Pentecost Cenacles/' hoping that "Come Holy Spirit" might become as popular a prayer as the Hail Mary. Elena wanted the Church united in constant prayer as Mary and the apostles, and advocated twenty-four-hour prayer cenacles.

After hesitating for ten years {1885-95) she also wrote twelve confidential letters {1885-1903) to Pope Leo XIII urging a renewed preaching on the Holy Spirit. She asked that the faithful be led to rediscover a life in the Holy Spirit and that the Church be renewed, together with society and the very "face of the earth."

She wrote that Pentecost is not over; that the Holy Spirit desires to give himself to all humans, and all who want him can receive him. If humans will prepare to receive him, he will come to them just as he did on the Day of Pentecost.

Pope Leo (tenure 1878-1903) responded positively to Elena's letters "The Providential Charity of a Mother", asking for a solemn novena between the Ascension and Pentecost throughout the Church. But this was not enough. Sister Elena prodded the pope through her spiritual guide. On May 9, 1897, Pope Leo wrote the famous encyclical on the Holy Spirit, *Divinum illud Munus* ("That Divine Gift"). This encyclical was not greeted with a positive response by the Church as a whole.

Even more significantly, at the insistence of Blessed Elena, he dedicated the twentieth century to the Holy Spirit, invoking on January 1, 1901, the "Veni Creator Spiritus" ("Come Holy Spirit") upon the entire world.

It should be noted that this came on the very same day as the initial Protestant Pentecostal outpouring In Topeka, Kansas.

Elena Guerra died in 1914. Although she did not live to see the fulfillment of her prophetic mission, it was in part realized when Pope John XXVIII called the Second Vatican Council into session, beginning in July 1962. She was the first woman beatified by John XXIII, who called her a modern-day "Apostle of the Holy Spirit." She is venerated in the Roman Catholic Church. Her feast day is April 11.

BIBLIOGRAPHY

Abbrescia, Domenico M. *Elena Guerra, Prophecy and Renewal.* Makati, Philippines: Society of St. Paul, 1982.

Burgess. Ruth Vassar. "Elena Guerra," in Burgess, Stanley M. and Ed van der Maas, eds. *The New International Dictionary of Pentecostal and Charismatic Movements.* Grand Rapids: Zondervan, 2002.

Then Peter Stood Up...Collection of the Popes' Addresses to the Catholic Charismatic Renewal from Its Origins to the Year 2000. Vatican City: ICCRS, 2000.

Stanley M. Burgess

Pandita Ramabai Mary Sarasvati

The youngest of three children born (1858) to a high-caste, or Brahman, family, Ramabai ("bai" means woman) in her early life suffered from a severe and extended famine. Searching for food, Anant Shastri Dongre and his wife, Lakshmibai, and their children began a life of unending pilgrimage. In the meantime, Ramabai learned thousands of Sanskrit verses from the Puranas, the Gita, and the Sanskrit grammar and dictionary. Disease, famine and poverty took their toll on the family. Her father, mother, and older sister died, leaving Ramabai and her older brother to continue wandering (for 4,000 miles!) in search of eternal peace and spiritual enlightenment.

After reaching Calcutta, the highly trained pundits were impressed with Ramabai's mastery of the Hindu Scriptures and grammar. At the age of twenty, she was examined by two European and one Indian scholar, who gave her the name of Sarasvati ("Goddess of Wisdom") and the honorific title of Pandita (meaning "learned master"). Sadly, she witnessed cruel acts and discriminatory attitudes toward women, including poor education, inadequate health care, child marriages, and harsh treatment of widows. She joined the reformers in Calcutta. Her brother died in 1880. In that same year, she broke Hindu tradition by marrying Ditin Vehari Medhdi-a man of lower caste. In July 1881, a daughter, Manorama, was born. The following February 1882, her husband passed, making her a Brahman widow with a seven-month-old infant.

Meanwhile, Ramabai became convinced that Brahman theology was Christian in origin. In the west central city of Pune, she started the Arya Mahila Marmaj, where teachers were trained to teach women. Before the Hunter Commission on Education, in 1882 she made an impassioned plea for women and the training of women doctors in India. Queen Victoria proceeded to adjust her foreign policy in response to this appeal.

Desiring to become a physician, Ramabai, together with Manorama traveled to England. Unfortunately, a severe hearing loss prevented her from achieving that goal. Instead, she was trained as a teacher. Deeply moved by Christian compassion and love extended to unfortunate women and children, she learned to distinguish between institutional Christianity and the "religion of Jesus Christ." She then travelled to the United States, where the Ramabai Association was formed to support her community and school for child widows (later to be founded at Khedgaon).

After six years abroad, Ramabai returned to India on February 1, 1889. Two years later, she became a committed Christian and took the name "Mary." By 1895 she had acquired a 100 acre farm (the Mukti Sada, "Salvation") in the town of Khedgaon. Mukti was an ashram based on the Tolstoyan model of self-sufficient community. Residents included the blind and the mentally and physically disabled. Pandita Ramabai also established other orphanages, as well as a home for former prostitutes.

In January 1905 Pandita Ramabai issued a call for prayer, and more than five hundred women met twice daily for intercessory prayer. On June 29, 1905, there was evidence of an outpouring of the Holy Spirit, when several were "slain in the spirit" (spiritually taken to the ground}, others spoke in unknown languages. Bands of women traveled to surrounding villages to evangelize. Ramabai also compiled a Bible in Marathi, one of the languages spoken in Western India (she finished the translation in 1913}.

The Mukti revival stands as one of the outstanding outpourings of the Holy Spirit in history. In 1989 the government of India released a postage stamp commemorating one hundred years since the beginning of Ramabai's work. Pandita Ramabai died in 1922, and is buried at her Mukti mission in Kedgaon. Her Mukti mission continues into the twenty-first century under Indian leadership.

BIBLIOGRAPHY

Abrams, Minnie. *The Baptism of the Holy Ghost and Fire.* 2nd ed. Khedgaon: Mukti Mission Press, 1906.

Burgess, Ruth V. "Pandita Ramabai Mary Sarasvati/' in Stanley M. Burgess and Ed van der Maas, eds, *The New International Dictionary of Pentecostal and Charismatic Movements.* Grand Rapids, Ml: Zondervan, 2002.

Kosambi, Meera, ed. and trans. *Pandita Ramabai: Through Her Own Words. Selected Works.* New Delhi: Oxford University Press, 2000.

Mair, Jessie H. *Bungalows in Heaven, the Story of Pandita Ramabai.* 3rd ed. Kedgaon: Mukti Mission Press, 1993.

Ramabai, Pandita. *A testimony of Our Inexhaustable Treasure.* Eleventh ed. Bombay: G.L.S. Press, 1992. Includes *Mukti Prayer-Bell,* 1904, 1905, 1906, 1907, 1911, 1913.

Pandita Ramabai's America: Conditions of Life. Grand Rapids, MO: Eerdmans, 2003.

The High Caste Hindu Woman. New York: Fleming H. Revell, 1887.

Ruth Vassar Burgess

Dr. Lilian B. Yeomans

Lilian B. Yeomans (1861-1942), a medical doctor who overcame a morphine addiction, became a noted Pentecostal evangelist, educator, author, and faith-healer. Her speaking and writing made her a household name among Pentecostals in the 1920s and 1930s, and her books became best sellers.

Early Life

Yeomans was born on June 23, 1861, in Madoc, Ontario, Canada, to Augustus A. and Amelia (LeSueur) Yeomans, just a few months after the start of the American Civil War. Her father was of Puritan ancestry, and her mother was of respectable parentage. Lilian's father supported his young family as a surgeon for the United States Army during the Civil War. Little is known about Lilian's childhood and early adolescence; however, in 1863, while the Civil War was still raging, a sister, Charlotte Amelia (Amy), was added to the family. Charlotte would become Lilian's lifelong companion and coworker, first in the medical profession, and then in the soul profession.

Lilian was raised in a nominal Anglican family and recalled learning to keep the Ten Commandments from an early age. However, learning the Law did not make a Christian of Lilian, but merely made her more aware of her spiritual hunger.

As a young adult, Lilian followed in her father's footsteps, furthering her education through medical training at the Toronto Medical School. In 1880, after completing a year of study, her father, Augustus Yeomans, passed away. Plagued by an ailment for many years, his sudden death was medically attributed to an overdose of the chloral he took to relieve his symptoms. Lilian would later struggle with this same drug.

By September 1880, Lilian's mother Amelia had matriculated into the Department of Medicine at the University of Michigan Ann Arbor as a junior at the age of 38. Lilian also transferred to the University of Michigan Ann Arbor in the fall of 1881. As she studied medicine, Lilian distanced herself from her Christian roots and became a functional agnostic. Lilian graduated from the University of Michigan Department of Medicine in 1882.

By September of 1882, Lilian received her license to practice medicine from the Manitoba College of Physicians and Surgeons. She went on to specialize in midwifery and women's and children's health, in the city of Winnipeg, during the Western Canadian economic boom. After her mother joined her, the pair opened up a joint practice in Winnipeg along with Charlotte who was now a trained nurse. All three ladies were active in a local choral society and Mrs. Yeomans was also involved in social and humanitarian work in the city's poorer sections; an activity which probably also involved her daughters. By April 1886, Lilian was also working at a maternity hospital.

Addiction Begins

Between social responsibilities, family obligations, and a growing medical practice, Lilian began to have difficulty sleeping. To manage her daily stress and insomnia she began to dabble with sulphate of morphine and chloral hydrate. Her occasional usage quickly turned into a life controlling habit.

Lilian's abuse of prescription drugs grew so severe that she found herself regularly taking morphine. She later described her addiction in her book, *Healing from Heaven* (1926). She wrote that she took doses up to "fifty times the normal dose for an adult man" combined with chloral hydrate, which she described as "a most deadly drug used by criminals in the concoction of the so-called 'knockout drops.'" Of this, she took up to twenty-four times the recommended dosage. That the dosage alone did not kill her was a miracle. The drugs became so necessary to her existence that giving them up seemed out of the question. The drugs were destroying her and she desperately tried to quit. On numerous occasions she disposed of huge amounts of the deadly narcotics.

Is Help Possible?

At last recognizing that she needed help beyond her own capacity, Lilian turned to God. However, no matter how much she prayed, God did not deliver her. Consulting multiple physicians, she received opinions and suggestions, but none that could free her from the bondage to her addiction. Since quitting on her own wasn't working, Lilian turned to various other cures and treatments, including the then-famous "Keely Gold Cure." This treatment left her so broken mentally and physically that she had to enter a Sanatorium for Nervous Diseases, where for three weeks she was cared for by a specialist as well as her physician mother.

Encountering the Healer

An unsuccessful attempt to wean herself from the drug addiction by gradual reduction resulted in hospitalization, after which Lilian awoke to find the drugs being injected intravenously. It seemed that her body would not allow her to do without them; her heart and lungs would simply shut down when she did not receive her daily dose. Even her friends thought her condition a hopeless one and encouraged her not to attempt to give up the habit again.

Weakened, Lilian spent a great deal of time in bed. Not ready to face eternity in her present spiritual condition, she began to read her Bible again. She did not just read it, but devoured its contents, finding solace and strength in its pages and in the clear small voice of the leading of the Holy Spirit.

She thought that she must try to quit in her own strength, despite her weakened condition and previously failed attempts. On the contrary, the Lord began to show her that to free herself of the addiction was not her job, but God's. Lilian began to tell her friends and family that she was delivered from the narcotics addiction. Though they responded politely, it was clear that they thought she was out of her mind. Even her mother had given up hope of her being cured.

Zion Divine Healing Home

Deliverance came through a noted Australian faith healer, John Alexander Dowie, who had moved to America and established a city based on biblical principles. In the care of her sister Charlotte, the pair moved to Dowie's healing home on Michigan Avenue in Chicago, Illinois, in early January 1898. Her mother did not join the pair on this trip, reportedly because she was engaged in lectures for the Women's Christian Temperance Union in Canada.

The treatment at the healing home did not involve medical treatment. The standards by which it operated were so strict that some questioned the safety of the home. Upon Dr. Yeomans' arrival, all of her medications were confiscated, and she was left to face the ravages of the addiction without any transitional drugs.

At an especially low point, an unnamed individual encouraged Lilian to get up and go to church. Believing the exertion would kill her, she began to make up her mind not to go, when the Holy Spirit spoke to her heart: "I sent him to tell you to go to the church. Arise." With great effort, she stepped out in faith and *walked* to the church service accompanied by her sister, but noticed little change to her feeble condition. Upon her return from the service, however, she began to feel better. It was as if God used that simple act of faith as a catalyst for her healing. In a tract, "Out of the Depths," she later recalled her healing: "From that time perfect victory through faith in the power of the name of Jesus was mine."

Free At Last!

Yeomans was age 36 on January 12, 1898, when she was set free from drug addiction by the power of God. Remarkably, her personal testimony in *Healing from Heaven* makes no mention of the Zion Healing Home. Rather, it places the healing from the point at which she first began to earnestly search the Scriptures on her own. Perhaps Yeomans (or her editors) chose not to include the Dowie reference in an attempt to distance her story from Dowie, who near the end of his life claimed to be Elijah the Restorer and fell into disrepute. Lilian certainly had a different approach to the medical profession than Dowie, who frequently offered a scathing rebuke of doctors. Lilian, on the other hand, celebrated the healing God brought through faith as well as kindly remembering the hard won achievements of physicians.

Next Steps

After she left Dowie's healing home, Yeomans decided to give up the medical profession and make her life's work praying for the sick and sharing the gospel. Lilian and her sister Charlotte became ordained with a Canadian Holiness association. Moving north of Winnipeg to do missionary work among the Cree peoples, Lilian was the only doctor within 500 miles. She began to be called upon to minister to physical needs as well as spiritual ones.

Caring for the needs of Cree peoples as well as those of the Hudson Bay Company, she found herself in possession of the drugs she swore never to use again. When epidemics broke out among the Cree, the Canadian government demanded her services. The intense pressure of being the sole doctor caring for so many, with the all too familiar drugs in her possession, could have been quite a temptation for the former morphine addict. However, God had healed Lilian of the craving so completely that she claimed that she no longer had a desire for the drugs.

During her work among the Cree, Lilian came to adopt a little girl of mixed Cree and Scotch blood named Tanis Anne Miller. Lilian did not write much about her adopted daughter, but records indicate that Tanis stayed connected with the Yeomans family until well into adulthood. By 1900 Lilian was already referring to herself as an "evangelist," however it is likely that the responsibility of a daughter is what prompted the 45-year-old to take Tanis and join her mother and sister in Calgary, Alberta, in 1906. Lilian obtained a Civil Service job and apparently stayed in Calgary for the next 17 years.

Lilian never married, which was not uncommon for influential female Pentecostal leaders of her time. However, she did not have to serve God devoid of emotional and familial support since her mother and sister were both active in the work of the Lord. At times, her mother was called upon to write of the miracles which God wrought by faith in His gracious provision, and her sister frequently accompanied her to Pentecostal meetings.

Spirit Baptism

By 1907, Lilian had completely given up the medical profession and was settled into her job in Calgary, but she had not forgotten what God had done for her. She held meetings in homes, storefront missions, and churches, sharing her story of deliverance. A longtime friend, Mrs. Lockhart of Winnipeg had received the baptism in the Holy Spirit during the first Pentecostal outpouring in Manitoba under the ministry of Andrew H. Argue. She introduced Lilian to the baptism in the Holy Spirit. Lilian became a fixture in the early Pentecostal movement in Calgary. She, along with her mother and sister, joined a small group of Pentecostals who met in homes for meetings. The Pentecostal Tabernacle of Calgary traces its roots to meetings held in Lilian's home in 1918.

From Canada to California

The Yeomans family eventually emigrated to California. In San Francisco, Lilian and Charlotte were both engaged in full time ministry, leading divine healing meetings, praying for the sick, and preaching at Glad Tidings Tabernacle and elsewhere. By 1921 Lilian was also teaching at the Glad Tidings Bible Institute. The pair obtained credentials with the Assemblies of God in 1922 as ordained evangelists.

Lilian did not limit her evangelism to San Francisco, but also ministered at the healing home of Carrie Judd Montgomery, the Home of Peace in Oakland, California. As early as 1912, she had begun writing for Carrie's periodical, *Triumphs of Faith*. Lilian and her family then moved to San Diego, where she likely served at the Berean Bible Institute in 1925. The sojourn in San Diego was not long, for by 1926 she had moved to Manhattan Beach, located in southern Los Angeles County.

By 1927 she had begun teaching at Aimee Semple McPherson's

Angelus Temple and L.I.F.E. Bible School. For the next fourteen years she mentored pastoral and missionary candidates, teaching classes on church history and divine healing. Her ministry connection to McPherson would prove to be both a rewarding teaching platform and a source of tension between Lilian and her local Assemblies of God district.

Golden Years

Though settled in California, Lilian and Charlotte engaged in extensive evangelism across the United States and Canada. Lilian seems to have lessened her ministry activities after the death of her sister, Charlotte, in 1939 but she never officially retired. In 1940, at the age of 79, Lilian Yeomans still claimed to have preached about 100 times in the prior year. Yeomans reported for active duty in heaven on December 10, 1942. She was buried at Forest Lawn Memorial Park in Glendale, California.

Written Work

Yeomans frequently lectured and wrote about the subtleties of addiction. The miraculous power of God to heal and restore was to become the central feature of her written work. In addition to having a regular column in the *Pentecostal Evangel* and numerous articles in *Triumphs of Faith* she also authored six books published by Gospel Publishing House: *Healing From Heaven* (1926); *Resurrection Rays* (1930); *Divine Healing Diamonds* (1933); *Balm of Gilead* (1936); *The Royal Road to Health-Ville* (1938); and *The Hiding Place* (1940), as well as numerous tracts.

Like her periodicals, her books and tracts contain a combination of personal testimony, stories of faith, and theological instruction. Several of her published works, such as *Healing from Heaven,* originated as lectures delivered in the classroom or the pulpit. Lilian noted the connection she saw between sin and sickness. To escape the law of sin and death one must embrace the "natural law" of God. She also saw a relationship between healing and faith, and this became a prominent motif in her writings.

Citing Matthew 9:29 and Hebrews 4:2, she observed that the proper way to take the "remedy" of God's word is to mix it with faith.

Legacy

A morphine addiction brought successful medical doctor Lilian B. Yeomans face to face with her personal limitations. Arriving at the end of her own strength she discovered the freedom and redemption found only though the healing power of God. This experience was so transformational that she could not keep it to herself. Working first bi-vocationally, and then as a full-time minister, Lilian devoted the second half of her life to testifying of the God who delivered her. An ordained evangelist with the Assemblies of God, an inspiring educator, and a gifted author of numerous books and articles, Lilian worked closely with other leading Pentecostals. Though Lilian B. Yeomans has passed into eternity, her legacy lives on through her written work and the countless lives she touched.

BIBLIOGRAPHY

Rodgers, Desiree D. "Encountering the Great Physician: The Life and Ministry of Dr. Lilian B. Yeomans," *Assemblies of God Heritage* (2015/2016): 4-15.

Robeck, C. M. "Yeomans, Lilian Barbara," in S. M. Burgess and Ed van der Maas, eds. *The New International Dictionary of Pentecostal and Charismatic Movements*. Grand Rapids, MI: Zondervan, 2002.

Yeomans, Lilian B. *Healing from Heaven*. Springfield, MO: Gospel Publishing House, 1926.

_____. *The Hiding Place*. Springfield, MO: Gospel Publishing House, 1940.

_____. "Out of the Depths," Evangel Tract No. 917. Springfield, MO: Gospel Publishing House, [1923?].

Desiree D. Rodgers

Lizzie Robinson: Founder of the Church of God in Christ Women's Departmeni

izzie Woods Robinson (1860-1945), born to slaves in Arkansas, was a prominent early female leader in the Church of God in Christ (COGIC}, the largest African-American Pentecostal denomination in the United States. Robinson organized the COGIC Women's Department in 1911, only four years after Charles H. Mason was elected Senior Bishop of the COGIC. Under Robinson's leadership, the Women's Department raised a significant portion of the denomination's early funding, formed auxiliaries, and was instrumental in helping to establish early COGIC missions efforts.

Little is known about Robinson's childhood. Her given name was Elizabeth Isabelle Smith. Her parents, Mose Smith and Elizabeth Jackson, had been born into slavery and may not have been legally married. Lizzie's life was hard, and she had to assume weighty responsibilities at an early age. By the time Lizzie was five years old, her father had died, forcing Lizzie, her mother, and her five siblings to continue doing arduous field work, despite the ostensible freedom brought by the end of the Civil War. When Lizzie was fifteen years old, her mother died, leaving Lizzie to care for her siblings.

In 1880, Lizzie married William Henry Holt. They had one daughter, Ida. Holt died a short time later, and she remarried, this time to William H. Woods. Woods died a year later, leaving Lizzie a double widow.

Lizzie joined the Baptist Church at Pine Bluff, Arkansas, in 1892. In 1901, Lizzie came into contact with the Holiness movement through

Joanna Moore, a white Baptist missionary to African Americans. In 1884, Moore had established what she called a "Bible Band", an organization that encouraged African American women to study, memorize, and teach scripture and to provide Bibles to the destitute. Bible Bands not only spiritually nurtured and discipled countless African American women, it also trained them to be leaders in church ministry. Moore started a monthly periodical, *Hope*, to train and encourage members of Bible Bands.

Over the following decade, Lizzie became very active in Bible Bands and corresponded extensively with Moore. Lizzie sold subscriptions to *Hope*, distributed bibles, and organized Bible Bands across Arkansas. In 1909, Moore convinced the missionary society of the American Baptists to send Lizzie to school for two years at the Baptist Training Academy in Dermott, Arkansas. Lizzie was soon appointed to serve as the academy's matron.

In May 1911, while working at the academy, Lizzie encountered Charles H. Mason, who was holding evangelistic services in town. Mason, like Robison, had roots in the Holiness movement in Black Baptist churches. He had become one of the leading African American Pentecostal leaders in America. Under Mason's ministry, Lizzie experienced the baptism of the Holy Spirit with the evidence of speaking in tongues.

Lizzie's Pentecostal experience caused the Baptists to reject her, so she cast her lot with the COGIC. Mason was busy organizing COGIC congregations, developing denominational structures, and identifying leaders who could help promote the Holiness and Pentecostal message. Mason quickly realized that Lizzie's training and abilities could prove very helpful and, at the 1911 COGIC convocation, he appointed her to serve as General Overseer of the Women's Work. As the first person to serve in this role, Lizzie laid the foundation for what later became the Women's Department.

Robinson parlayed her experience in the Bible Bands in Arkansas to organize women in the COGIC. When Robinson was appointed Overseer (the title was later changed to "National Supervisor"), women had already been meeting in two groups: Prayer Band and Bible Band. The Prayer Band consisted of women who met for corporate prayer. The Bible Band was already well-established-a holdover from the Baptist church-and was reading Joanna Moore's *Hope* newspaper and promoting biblical literacy.

Robinson merged the two groups, forming Prayer and Bible Band. She formalized the role of "church mothers" who were already in place in most congregations-and gave them oversight over local Prayer and Bible Band groups.

The Women's Department played a vital role in the development of the COGIC. In the early decades of the twentieth century, most local congregations had a Women's Department, which provided a platform for women to engage in church planting, fundraising, and missionary work. The Women's Department eventually established its own missions and auxiliaries, appointed its own leadership, and developed a financial base.

Robinson created a structure within the denomination for women that in some ways paralleled the male episcopate. However, she affirmed the Church of God in Christ position that women should not be ordained or serve as pastors. She encouraged women to "teach" (but not to "preach"), a distinction that satisfied those who maintained theological or cultural opposition to women pastors.

Robinson established two auxiliaries of the Women's Department-the Sewing Circle and the Sunshine Band. These auxiliaries allowed church mothers to bring women together in groups that showcased their talents. The Sewing Circle trained women to sew, knit, crochet, and make patterns. Their handiwork would be sold for fundraisers and helped to ensure that church members were properly attired according to the church's holiness standards. The Sunshine Band provided a children's version of Prayer and Bible Band, featuring Sunday school lessons that taught children ages five to twelve to memorize scripture and learn COGIC doctrine. The auxiliaries emphasized practical, family-centered themes and allowed women with little formal training to participate in the structured leadership of the church.

Robinson was also instrumental in the founding of the COGIC Home and Foreign Missions Board, which occurred in 1926 after Robinson encouraged Ed Searcy, a new COGIC member and a member of another missions organization, to meet with Mason. The Home and Foreign Missions Board became an auxiliary of the Women's Department, which provided funding for countless early missionaries.

In 1912, Lizzie married Edward D. Robinson, pastor of a COGIC congregation in Little Rock, Arkansas. In 1916, the Robinsons moved to Omaha, Nebraska, to be close to Lizzie's only child, Ida Baker. The Robinsons founded the first COGIC congregation in Nebraska, with the help of Lucinda Bostic and Nancy Gamble. The Robinsons persevered in ministry despite suffering physical and verbal attacks because of their faith. Robinson continued to lead the national Women's Department, assisted by her daughter, until her death in 1945. In the 1920s, the Women's Department was given a service, called "Women's Day," at the annual COGIC Holy Convocation held in Memphis, Tennessee. At the service, Robinson led in prayer and gave a Bible lesson, after which reports of given of the work done and monies collected. Robinson was forced to cut back her busy travel schedule in the 1930s, due to her age (she was in her 70s) and the declining health of her husband.

Robinson was instrumental in raising funds for construction of Mason Temple, a vast concrete structure in Memphis capable of seating 7,500 people on two levels, that served as the spiritual and administrative headquarters for the COGIC. She attended the 1945 Holy Convocation, during which Mason Temple was dedicated. She died on December 12, 1945, two days before the end of the convocation, and her funeral was held on the last day of the convocation.

The *Associated Negro Press* reported on Robinson's death:

Mother Lizzie Woods Robinson, national supervisor of the Women's Department, Church of God in Christ Inc., who was ranked with Elder Mason, senior bishop[,] in the esteem in which she was held by thousands of followers throughout the country, died Wednesday .... Through her ability to organize, inspire and direct, Mother Robinson left to the church a rich heritage of 20,000 missionaries, 100,000 laymen, and numerous divisions to the women's department.

Lizzie Woods Robinson influenced the course of the COGIC by developing a large women's organization, despite little formal education, funds, or assistance. Over the course of 34 years she developed structures, mentored and appointed leaders, and spearheaded significant fundraising efforts, helping to lay the foundation for what has become the largest African American Pentecostal denomination. Robinson's biographer, Elijah Hill, deposited the archival collection of Lizzie Robinson and her daughter, Ida Baker, at the Flower Pentecostal Heritage Center.

BIBLIOGRAPHY

Butler, Anthea D. *Women in the Church of God in Christ: Making a Sanctified World* Chapel Hill, NC: University of North Carolina Press, 2007.

Goodson, Glenda Williams. *Bishop Charles Harrison Mason and Those Sanctified Women!* Lancaster, TX: HCM Publishing, 2018.

Hill, Elijah L. *Women Come Alive* Arlington, TX: Perfecting the Kingdom International Ministries, 2005.

Darrin J. Rodgers

Dr. Ida Sophia Scudder

I da Sophia Scudder, M.D. (December 9, 1870-May 23, 1960) was a third-generation American medical missionary to India. In 1809 her grandfather, Rev. Dr. John Scudder Sr., was sent out as a member of the Reformed Church in America. He was followed by seven sons, all of whom served as missionaries to India. She was born to Dr. John Scudder Jr and his wife, Sophia (nee Weld). Ida was raised in India, where famine, disease and poverty were experienced on a daily basis. She was invited by the famed evangelist Dwight L. Moody to attend his Northfield Seminary in Massachusetts where she became known for her piety.

After seminary, Ida planned to stay in the United States, to attend Wellesley College and to marry into wealth. She was known for her beauty, with arresting blue eyes and blonde hair, and numerous suitors. However, in 1890 she returned to India, responding to her father's need for help with his ailing wife. Despite her oft repeated claims that she did not want to spend her life in the subcontinent of India, following in the footsteps of her missionary ancestors, she had a life-changing experience which radically altered her plans.

One night, as she was writing letters, she witnessed the death of three Indian women in childbirth, while she was unprepared to help them. These orthodox Hindu women could not go to a male gynecology or even a male general physician, and lacked a female professional to help them. She suddenly became aware that God wanted her to become a female physician to help women in India.

Ida graduated from Cornell Medical College in New York City in 1899, as one of the first class of women who had been accepted into that institution. After receiving a $10,000 grant from a New York Banker, who had recently lost his wife and wished to honor her, Ida returned to India.

With this money, she started a tiny medical dispensary and clinic at her father's bungalow at Vellore, 75 miles north of Madras (now Chennai) on the east coast of South India. Her father died two years after her arrival. In that two years she had treated 5,000 patients.

In 1902 Ida opened the Mary Tabor Schell Hospital in Vellore. She realized that she would need help with the overwhelming demand of women, she decided to open a medical school for girls only. After she agreed to make the school coeducational, it soon gained the support of 40 missions. The Vellore Christian Medical Center became the largest Christian hospital in the world, with 2000 beds, and the medical school is now one of the best medical colleges in India.

In her later years and with the Vellore hospital and medieval school well established, Dr. Ida Scudder settled in the Palni hills, in the lovely town of Kodaikanal, where she became known for her flowering gardens and her support of students at the International School there. She died in Kodai at the age of 89 at her Kodai bungalow.

An interesting note: members of three generations of Scudders spent their lives of ministry and service for over a combined 1,000 years in India (see ##BIBLIOGRAPHY below). This alone makes Dr. Ida Sophia Scudder's life and work memorable.

BIBLIOGRAPHY

Burgess, Ruth L. Burgess family archives: our memories of Ida Scudder and family as students at Highclerc School in Kodaikanal, India, 1947-1952.

Jeffery, M. Pauline. *Ida S. Scudder of Vellore, India*. Mysore City, India: Wesley Press, 1951.

Scudder, Dorothy Jealous. *A Thousand Years in Sight: The Story of the Scudder Missionaries in India*. New York: Vantage Press, 1984.

Wilson, Dorothy Clark. *Dr. Ida*. New York: McGraw-Hill, 1959.

Ruth Vassar Burgess and Stanley M. Burgess

Alice Reynolds "Mother" Flower

he ancient question, "What is the good life? Is it the active or contemplative?" has been reflected in Christianity from its earliest days. Pentecostals have expressed this distinction by identifying the purpose of the baptism of the Holy Spirit as either power for witnessing (a spirituality of action) or as the development of holy character (a spirituality of being). Most North American Pentecostals have emphasized evangelism and missionary activity as primary. A few, however, such as Alice Reynolds Flower, while living a very active life, repeatedly advocated in her writings, sermons, and poetry, the centrality of intense devotion to Jesus Christ.

Flower (nee Reynolds) was born in 1890 a few years after her mother had been miraculously healed on her deathbed following the prayer of a Quaker minister. Throughout more than a century of life, Alice never ceased recalling that her very existence was miraculous, a gift from a gracious God. She published an article on her mother's healing in 1917 and reprinted it in various forms several more times over the years of her life. When she received the Pentecostal experience on Easter Day of 1907, her joyful thanksgiving for both physical and spiritual life overflowed in worship to Jesus. Worship, devotion, became the hallmark of her being for the next 84 years. She wrote in her Diary on her birthday, November 21, 1908: "... how glad I am that I know Jesus-my precious Redeemer! How I do glorify Him tonight. I feel a need for more humility-lack of self-that Christ may be all and in all. My heart is so hungry for more of His Spirit, that a fragrance of Jesus might be breathed from my life."

Through the years, Alice's longings for a deeper surrender and devotion to Christ would mature and increasingly find expression in poetry, moving from the private world of her diaries to the public one of published poems. One piece which was widely circulated revealed her awareness first seen in her Diary entry on her eighteenth birthday that devotion was not wholly separated from witness. The poem published under two titles, "Spent For Jesus" and "Outpoured," weaves together the hunger for a fuller devotion (a spirituality of character) with a faithful testimony (a life of deeds):

> 0, to be spent for Jesus, Living a life outpoured- Doing
> His service holy, Broken before thy Lord;
> Waiting His precious bidding, Listening for His voice,
> Yielded, and still, and steady, Filling the place of His
> choice.
>
> 0, to be spent for Jesus- Never a power reserved; Treasures
> so dear, so costly, Given unto thy Lord.
> Channels that carry His rivers
> Empty must be and clean;
> Wires that send His message have
> No disconnect between.
>
> Lives that give sweetest perfume, Pressure and breaking
> know;
> Would'st thou give forth His fragrance? Thro' garden
> shadows go.
> The 'box alabaster' unbroken, No sweetness can ever give;
> The lives that are spent for Jesus
> Forever in richness live.

Alice's desires for a deeper spiritual life did not dampen her love for the world of learning and nature. She read widely in the English and American poets at home and in high school in Indianapolis, memorizing many poems. After high school she attended Butler College (now University) for the Fall Semester and Winter Term of the 1909-1910 academic year. A course in astronomy proved to be her favorite one. Years later she taught her own children about the constellations and (from literature) their links to myths. Her experiences of nature and the feelings they stimulated sometimes found in poetry an answering sentiment. As a child she listened and sang as a grammar school teacher taught the class a song about the beauty of fall. Forty or more years later as a mother and grandmother, who had known the death of parents and a 21 year old son, she wrote in prose and verse a rich meditation on love, beauty, loss, service, and hope. In "There Have Been Other Octobers" a reader finds a profound awareness of human mutability wedded to an eternal hope anchored in Jesus Christ. The nostalgia of fall reminds of both the sweetness of summer's joys and winter's losses; and its return stirs hope for yet other Octobers.

During the four decades represented by "There Have Been Other Octobers," Alice developed the skills, wisdom, spiritual maturity, and broad experience for which she would come to be known as "Mother Flower." Many early Pentecostals, thinking as they did of Spirit-baptism as an adult experience, essentially ignored children. Some saw no need for Sunday school; their attention was on adult services focused on evangelizing unbelievers and encouraging believers to receive the baptism in the Holy Spirit. Even before the birth of Alice's first child when she was only 22, she began writing outlines for children's Sunday school lessons. Originally published in a magazine (*The Christian Evangel*) she and her husband produced, a local newspaper in Indiana asked for permission to print them weekly. Surely, one aspect of a mother's concerns is for her children to learn early and well the matters one considers of first importance. Alice continued writing literature for children for many years, publishing quarterlies for children and middle schoolers in the 1920s in Springfield, Missouri. Prior to moving to Springfield, the Flowers lived on a farm near Stanton, Missouri; there, during the winters when local children could not travel to their school, Alice converted the living room of their farm house into a make shift school. She gathered the children with hers and taught them not only the Bible stories, but drawing on her high school and college learning, also, laid foundations and strengthened them in the three Rs.

In January of 1926 Alice and her husband moved with their six children to Scranton, Pennsylvania, where J. Roswell became the pastor of a Pentecostal church in a multi-ethnic community of European immigrants, African-Americans, and older white Americans. Flower's two oldest children were approaching their teen years. They attended the local public schools and faced social and educational situations very different than those in Missouri. Alice took this in stride by beginning a special teaching time for the youth of the church on Sunday afternoon just prior to the evening service and by writing a series of devotional pieces for youth under the title "Twilight Chats," which she continued for some years. One collection from those chats bears the title *The Set of Your Sails.* As a wise mother teaching her own children, Alice drew on a broad range of observations to help youth think about living a faithful Christian life. The meditation, "A Systematic God," begins with observations she made in the astronomy class she had taken in college about the order of the universe, its systematic order and movements. Then, she moves to the Bible's account of the order of creation, to Jesus' orderly feeding of thousands in the Gospels, and from Scripture to the practice of order in daily life. "If you hold any office for God, perform your duties systematically, faithfully.... Order your personal affairs in the same manner. Keep your room in order, for God dwells there. Run your private business so no one else suffers through your carelessness.... have sacred, regular trysting times with your Lord each day, following definite lines of Bible study. This is practical, everyday religion and will enhance the power of your life before others, saved and unsaved."

Alice loved youth and came also to love college age young adults. She and the family had moved from Scranton to Lititz, Pennsylvania, in the early 1930s. As the Great Depression deepened and many youth were unable to leave home to attend a Bible institute or college in another state, Alice, along with her husband and another man, designed a summer curriculum to be taught from Memorial Day to Labor Day at the campgrounds owned by the church. She carried the much of the weight of the administrative and teaching responsibilities when classes were in session. The success of that venture can be measured in two ways: first, the summer terms developed into the two terms of an academic year and passing through the stages of a Bible institute to a Bible college is now the University of Valley Forge, a liberal arts Christian university granting both undergraduate and graduate degrees. She was publically honored for her role in the University's founding at a ceremony when she was in her 80s. The life of one man provides a second measure of success. An impoverished youth hitchhiked 90 miles from his home to attend the summer program. Stimulated by Alice Flower's teaching and personal counsel to him, he built a business that became a multi-million dollar company which in the third generation of leaders continues to donate thousands of dollars to educational, religious, and civic organizations.

In her late-80s and early-90s, again living in Springfield, Missouri, she loved addressing and engaging with students at the colleges. She welcomed students into her home and willing gave interviews to those seeking information for assignments, papers, and for personal problems and decisions. She remained to them a mother of wise and practical counsel.

Alice's husband was elected to a national office in the Assemblies of God church at its national meeting in late-1935. He moved to Springfield in January of 1936 to take up the office and Alice and two children remaining at home moved from Lititz following the end of the school year in June. She remained a citizen of Springfield until her death at age 100 in January 1991. Over those nearly 55 years, Alice's ministry grew in depth and extent so that when she died the notice of her death carried in the magazine *Advance* (a denominational publication for ministers) began with the words: "No name, no person has been more a part of the Assemblies of God than Alice Reynolds Flower. Through the years she became affectionately known by the Fellowship as Mother Flower." The poem chosen to represent her influence, both in the magazine and on the funeral service brochure was "Outpoured" or "Spent For Jesus." Her role as "mother" was both deeply spiritual and eminently active. How did it become so?

The Flowers rejoined the Springfield church they had been members of before moving to Pennsylvania. In 1937 they began a Sunday school class together, the Homemakers Class, with special attention on the home as a divine sanctuary (the title of one of her later books). Alice's husband taught the biblical lesson and she followed with guide lines for practical application. Alice was near 50, had been a pastor's wife for many years, and had successfully negotiated parsonage life while raising six children of her own and three foster children. Additionally, the family sometimes took in professional women who were facing spiritual and emotional difficulties, nursing them back to health. Alice's tender wisdom, deep love for others, and unwavering integrity were those of a wise mother. The Homemakers Class grew to nearly 200. Following her husband's death in 1970, she continued teaching the class until she was nearly 90. During these years, she was frequently called to speak about the family in churches, camps, and civic gatherings all over the United States. Out of those lessons and lectures came three key books: *From Under the Threshold* (rev. ed. 1947),

Building Her House Well (1949), and *The Home: A Divine Sanctuary* {1955). Her loving, clear-eyed counsel for family life reflected the success of her own family and sealed her reputation as "Mother Flower."

Not long before her death, one of her grandsons recorded a conversation with Alice. Though her mind was not always clear, she could still repeat the things she held deeply and pass them on: "It was hard for me to realize that I didn't have to turn the world upside down. All I had to do was be the things that God wanted me to be." Being first, doing second. Mother Flower had captured this central truth in the third stanza of her poem "At Thy Feet":

> Just to worship-0 how sweet! Frankincense of adoration
> Rises up thy grace to meet;
> At thy feet-how swift the moments
> At thy feet-because I love thee, Pass when thus I'm lost in
> thee; Broken by thy holy passion, Thrilled with joy alone
> in thee!
>
> from *A Barley Loaf* (1938)

BIBLIOGRAPHY

Blumhofer, Edith L. *"Pentecost in My Soul": Explorations in the Meaning of Pentecostal Experience in the Early Assemblies of God*. Springfield, MO: Gospel Publishing House, 1989.

Flower, Alice Reynolds. *Grace for Grace: Some Highlights of God's Grace in the Daily Life of the Flower Family*. Springfield, MO: n.p., 1963.

McGee, Gary B. "Flower, Joseph James Roswell, and Alice Reynolds Flower," in S.M. Burgess and Ed van der Maas, ed. *The New International Dictionary of Pentecostal and Charismatic Movements*. Grand Rapids, Ml: Zondervan, 2002.

Ringer, David K. *J. Roswell Flower: A Brief Biography*. Forward by Wayne Warner. Eugene, OR: Wipf & Stock, 2016.

David K. Ringer

Lillian Hunt Trasher

illian Trasher (September 27, 1887-December 17, 1961) was a Christian Pentecostal missionary to Asyut (Assiout), Egypt, where she founded the first orphanage in that country. She was eventually called the "Nile Mother" of Egypt.

We have evidence that Lillian Trasher had a Quaker background. She was born in Jacksonville, Florida and was raised as a Roman Catholic in Brunswick, Georgia. In her late teens, she attended Bible college for one semester, and then worked at Faith Orphanage in North Carolina in 1908-

10. After she became engaged to marry the Reverend Tom Jordan, she heard a missionary to India speak, and experienced a call to Africa. Because he did not share her call, the wedding was called off. Meanwhile, she taught at a Bible College in South Carolina, where she received the infilling of the Holy Spirit. As a result, she briefly pastored a Pentecostal church, then travelled as an evangelist, and later returned to Faith Orphanage.

In 1910 she met Pastor Brelsford of Assiout at a missionary conference. She determined then to defy her family's wishes and left with her sister, Jennie, for Africa, virtually without money. After arriving in Assiout (some 230 miles south of Cairo) with no idea of what she should do, a dying Egyptian mother gave her baby to Lillian to care for. She then rented a home in Assiout, which at that time was predominantly Christian {Coptic church). A man asked her to take care of his infant daughter, whose mother was near death. Based on her previous experience in the United States, she accepted that this was a sign of God's leading. Historically, this moment marked the beginning of her life's work, the Lillian Trasher orphanage.

Lillian Trasher was ordained in 1912 by the Church of God, Cleveland, Tennessee. The orphanage family had grown to fifty children. Returning to America in 1919, she recognized that greater support was available through the newly created Assemblies of God fellowship, and she transferred her ministerial credentials to them. With added support, Lillian was able to expand her mission to include widows and the blind.

Lillian worked 50 years from 1911 to 1961, when she died. At that time, the orphanage had expanded to approximately 1,200 children. Today the institution is supported by the Assemblies of God of Egypt, with 85% of their budget met by donations of the Presbyterian churches in Egypt and other Egyptian organizations.

Lillian was buried in Assiout on the orphanage grounds. It is interesting to note that she has been venerated by the Episcopal Church in the United States. Her feast day is December 19th.

BIBLIOGRAPHY

Benge, Janet and Geoff Benge. *Lillian Trasher: The Greatest Wonder in Egypt.* Seattle, WA: YWAM Publishers, 2004.

McGee, Gary B. "Trasher, Lillian Hunt," in Gerald H. Anderson, ed. *Biographical Dictionary of Christian Missions.* Grand Rapids, Ml: William B. Eerdmans, 1998.

Shemeth, Scott. "Trasher, Lillian Hunt," in Stanley M. Burgess and Ed van der Maas, eds., *The New International Dictionary of Pentecostal and Charismatic Movements.* Grand Rapids, Ml: Zondervan, 2002.

Trasher, Lillian Hunt. *Letters from Lillian.* Springfield, MO: {AG} Division of Foreign Missions, 1983.

Stanley M. Burgess

Anna Eleanor Roosevelt

Anna Eleanor Roosevelt (October 11, 1884-November 7, 1962) was First Lady of the United States from March 4, 1933, to April 12, 1945, throughout her husband, Franklin Delano Roosevelt's four terms in office. This was by far the longest-serving First Lady of the United States. Then in President Harry Truman's administration, from 1945-1952, she was United States Delegate to the United Nations General Assembly. Truman called her the "First Lady of the World", because of her human rights achievements.

Eleanor was a member of the powerful American Roosevelt and Livingston families and was a niece of President Theodore Roosevelt. During her childhood, she lost both of her parents and one of her brothers. At the age of 15 she attended the exclusive Allenwood Academy in London. After returning to America, in 1905, she married her fifth cousin, once removed, Franklin Delano Roosevelt. They had six children. Her new mother-in-law, Sara attempted to control her, and by 1918, her husband had an affair with Lucy Mercer. All of this led her to seek her own place in public life. When Franklin was afflicted with a paralytic disease in 1921, she persuaded him to remain in politics. Because he no longer had normal use of his legs, she began giving speeches and appearing at campaign events in his place. During both his time as Governor of New York and his four terms as President, she reshaped and redefined the role of First Lady.

During these years, Eleanor was highly controversial because of her outspokenness, particularly on the civil rights of African-Americans. In addition, she advocated for expanded roles for women in the workplace-this was exceptionally important because women took men's roles when the latter were taken off to war from 1941onwards. During the war, she spoke on behalf of Asian Americans after War in the Pacific opened with

Japan's attach on Pearl Harbor. She also lobbied for families of unemployed miners. After her husband's death in 1945, she remained active, pressing the United States to join the United Nations. She became its first delegate to that body. She was first chair of the UN Commission on Human Rights and facilitated the drafting of the Universal Declaration of Human Rights. Later, she chaired the John F. Kennedy administration's commission on the Status of Women.

Eleanor was a woman of strong active Christian faith. She became a life-long member of the Episcopal Church, while Franklin was relatively inactive in religious practice. She found her home in Saint James' Parish in Hyde Park. She treasured the Bible and the teachings of Jesus. Above all, she enjoyed giving aid to the poor and disadvantaged. She loved immigrants to American shores because she taught that Jesus himself was an immigrant-an immigrant whose life was threatened. She was convinced that everyone had the right to worship their own way and had the right to changer their religious beliefs, affiliations and practices.

She was comfortable dealing with non-Christians, having excellent relations with both Muslins and Jews. Most notable was her relationship with Professor Reuven Feuerstein of Jerusalem, a world-renowned champion of the disabled and mentally/emotionally afflicted. On several occasions, she met with him to lend her support. In turn, he presented her with the Youth Aliyah Award "Mother in Israel". She is especially remembered for her concern for the plight of Jewish youth in the period immediately before and following the Second World War. She was not afraid to contradict her husband, as she did on this occasion.

Eleanor Roosevelt died in New York City on November 7, 1962, from cardiac failure complicated by tuberculosis. She is buried in the FDR National Historic Site, Hyde Park, New York. She is remembered for her heart for the poor, her love of immigrants and the oppressed. She is a prime example of truth speaking to power. In a Gallup List of Most Widely Admired People of the 20th Century (December 1999}, Eleanor Roosevelt is listed as number 9.

BIBLIOGRAPHY

Beasley, Maurine H. *Eleanor Roosevelt: Transformative First Lady.* Lawrence, KS: University Press of Kansas: 2010.

Burgess, Ruth Vassar. *Changing Brain Structure Through Cross-Cultural Learning: The Life of Reuven Feuerstein.* Lewistown: Mellon, 2008.

Glendon, Mary Ann. *A World Made New: Eleanor Roosevelt and the Universal Declaration of Human Rights.* New York: Random House, 2001.

Rowley, Hazel. *Franklin and Eleanor: An Extraordinary Marriage.* Melbourne, Australia: Melbourne University Publishing, 2011.

erpa gwu.edu *The Eleanor Roosevelt Papers Project.* Department of History, Columbian College of Arts and Sciences, Washington DC. 20007.

Stanley M. Burgess

Marie Burgess Brown

Marie Estelle Burgess Brown (1880-1971) was a pioneering Pentecostal pastor of a New York City church with significant international influence. She was the fifth of nine children, raised on a farm near Eau Claire, Wisconsin. Her life was changed during her high school years when she experienced a vision. Her health had deteriorated because of tuberculosis. Jesus appeared at the foot of her bed and asked if she would give up all her worldly pursuits and follow him. She never forgot how he stretched out his nail-pierced hand and lifted her up. Soon thereafter, she was healed of her tuberculosis through the prayer of a Congregational minister.

Studies at Moody Bible Institute in Chicago and Ripon College in Wisconsin were interrupted by demands of the family at home. Hearing of the work of Alexander Dowie at Zion City, Illinois, she led her family to move there. As a second sibling, Will, died of tuberculosis, she promised him that she would wins souls for him to present to the Lord. While at Zion, she heard of prayer meetings in a private home tarrying for the Holy Spirit to fall as in Acts chapter two. At the invitation of this prayer group, Charles Parham had come from Topeka, Kansas. Marie became convinced that these meetings were the work of God, despite the disapproval of Dowie.

She experienced a Pentecostal baptism in the Spirit with speaking in tongues on her birthday, October 18, 1906, and had another life-transforming vision that lasted through the night. She saw, in turn, scenes in China, India, and Africa, and sensed a spirit of intercession for these people. For many years, she took this to be a divine call to the mission field. Soon thereafter, Parham asked her and a Miss Jessie Brown to respond to a request for Pentecostal workers to come to New York City. She did not want to go, and put three "fleeces" out to validate whether this was God's plan. When all three fleeces were wet, she acknowledged that it must be God.

The two women arrived in New York on January 7, 1907. Their first opportunity for ministry was at a holiness mission in midtown Manhattan. When word spread that workers associated with the Latter Rain had arrived, the mission was soon filled for meetings that lasted four weeks. Because she still felt a call to evangelism, Marie was resistant to opening a Pentecostal mission, but accepted God's leading.

The formal opening service of Glad Tidings Hall on West 42nd Street, on May 5, was preached by a former Irish policeman and now Wesleyan Methodist minister named Robert Brown. It was only later that he received his own Pentecostal baptism and began to pursue a personal interest in Marie. She resisted his interest as she had resisted the call to start a mission in New York, but eventually God confirmed that Robert's interest was blessed, and they were married on October 14, 1909. The following years saw growth in ministry and both joy and heartbreak in personal life. The Browns lost their one child soon after birth.

Doctrinally, Marie went to New York as a disciple of Parham. The storefront mission displayed his identification, Apostolic Faith Mission, and proclaimed "Jesus Saves Sanctifies and Heals." By 1913, however, the church publication, *The Midnight Cry,* no longer referred to sanctification as a crisis event. One finds instead the promotion of the finished work of Christ, holding that the believer was progressively sanctified from the moment of salvation. Marie recalled being maligned by other Christians for her Pentecostal message, but accepted persecution as a sharing in the suffering of her Lord.

In October, 1921, Glad Tidings Tabernacle began meeting in a large church building on West 33rd Street and was widely recognized as a regional Pentecostal center. It affiliated with the Assemblies of God, founded in 1916, and, beginning in the early 1930's, was for many years the largest contributor to world missions in the denomination. The annual Missions Convention in the fall was one of the highlights of the church year, always represented by some of the dozens of missionaries that went out from this congregation. Marie would in time understand these missionaries as the fulfillment of the vision God gave her of the world.

Glad Tidings had three services each Sunday. Robert Brown led a morning gathering and an evangelistic meeting in the evening. Marie regularly preached at the main service in the afternoon. From early on, Glad Tidings scheduled its primary service in the afternoon to allow for those from other congregations to attend. For decades, there was a Glad Tidings broadcast on the radio in the New York area. In contrast to Robert's aggressive style, Marie's approach to preaching was more pastoral and devotional. It was said that he would cut with the sword and she would pour in the healing oil. She was drawn to biblical passages that nurtured intimate fellowship with the Lord, such as the Song of Songs. Many of her sermons were based on texts in the Old Testament, and she found deep truths in the types of Christ and the church she found there. She emphasized intimacy with Jesus, commitment to him, and the necessity of sacrifice for spiritual growth. Her favorite song was "I'd Rather Have Jesus," and her appeal could be encapsulated by the words of the invitational appeal, "Is Your All on the Altar?"

Marie Burgess Brown was my great aunt. She was Aunt Marie to me, "Ma Brown" to many. Among my memories of her: Warmth. Always a white dress on Sunday. And a handkerchief. Prayer. A love for the Lord's Supper. Words to Jews she met: "My Jesus is your Messiah!"

Influenced both by her personality and her times, she allowed her husband to be the primary spokesperson in public. After Robert died in 1948, she asked my father, R. Stanley Berg, to be her assistant, and even then she had him conduct church business meetings. But everyone knew that she was the spiritual head of the congregation.

BIBLIOGRAPHY

Blumhofer, Edith L. "Brown, Robert and Marie," in Stanley M. Burgess and Ed van der Maas, eds. *The New International Dictionary of Pentecostal and Charismatic Movements*. Grand Rapids, MI: Zondervan, 2002.
Christ's Ambassadors Herald (June- November 1940)
Glad Tidings Tabernacle Golden Jubilee (May 1957)

Robert Berg

Mahalia Jackson

M ahalia Jackson (October 26, 1911-January 27, 1972) was a famous American gospel singer. Music historians and her many fans declare that the great contralto was "The Queen of Gospel." She was born in 1911 in New Orleans, Louisiana, the third of six children. Her father, John A. Jackson Sr., was a dockworker and a barber and later became a Baptist preacher. Her mother, Charity, died when she was four or five years old, and she was sent by her father, along with her ten-year-old brother, William, to live with her aunt Duke. She was forced to work at menial tasks after school.

The center of Mahalia's life was her family and the Mount Moriah Baptist Church, where she sang on Wednesdays and Fridays and four times on Sundays. At the age of twelve, she was baptized in the Mississippi River. In 1931, when she reached the age of 20, she moved to Chicago, Illinois. Before long, she began touring the Chicago area, singing with the Johnson Gospel Singers. She met the composer, Thomas A. Dorsey (known as the "Father of Gospel Music"), and began touring with him. Her signature song was his "Take My Hand, Precious Lord."

In 1936, Mahalia married Isaac Lanes Grey Hockenhull, a graduate of Fisk University, and ten years her elder. Unfortunately, this marriage did not last, for Isaac insisted that his wife sing secular music, and she resisted. She pledged to sing sacred music throughout her life. In 1941 the couple divorced. She later married a widower, but this marriage also was unsuccessful. Mahalia's career as a gospel singer led to recording contracts with Apollo and Colombia Records. She sang at Carnegie Hall in 1950, and by 1954 she had her own gospel program on CBS television. In 1956 she made her debut on The Ed Sullivan Show, and by 1958 she performed with Duke Ellington and his band. She was selected to sing at President John Fitzgerald Kennedy's inauguration in 1960.

Her growing fame and her struggles with racism led her to become a leader in the civil rights movement. She was invited by Martin Luther King Jr. to sing in front of 250,000 protesters in the second march on Washington in 1963. Just five years later, she sang at Martin Luther King's funeral. Unfortunately, Mahalia became known for her stubbornness, her temper and her stinginess. Notwithstanding these shortcomings, she remained faithful to her commission-to "make a joyful noise unto the Lord." She died on January 27, 1972, in Evergreen Park, Illinois.

BIBLIOGRAPHY

Burford, Mark. *Mahalia Jackson and the Black Gospel Field*. New York: Oxford University Press, 2019
Schwerin, Jules. *Got to Tel/It: Mahalia Jackson, Queen of Gospel*. New York: Oxford University Press, 1992.

Stanley M. Burgess

Mother Teresa: 'Saint' of the Gutters

M other Teresa is a figure who hardly needs any introduction to the world, but the lasting impact of her life is perhaps best measured in the light of its transforming effect on individuals. When the cynical English journalist Malcolm Muggeridge encountered Mother Teresa, he was struck by the mystical aura of her presence, and saw her life as "a light which could never be extinguished", eventually leading him to embrace her Roman Catholic faith. His television interview of Mother Teresa and the follow-up publication of his highly influential account of her life, *Something Beautiful for God,* catapulted Mother Teresa to international prominence and brought her cause much needed international support.

By the end of her life Mother Teresa's achievements had received unparalleled recognition across the globe. She had topped Gallup's list of most widely admired people of the twentieth century, addressed the United Nations in 1985 on its fortieth anniversary and received honorary degrees from Harvard University and Cambridge University. She received over 120 prestigious awards and honors including: the inaugural *Pope John XXIII Peace Prize* [1971], the *Templeton Prize* [1973] the *Nobel Peace Prize* [1979], honorary *Companion (The Order of Australia* [1982], two of the highest civilian awards in the U.S.A.: the *Presidential Medal of Freedom* [1985] the *Congressional Gold Medal* [1997], the *Bharat Ratna,* the highest civilian award in the country of her adoption, India [1980].

What made Mother Teresa's accomplishments especially remarkable was that her early life and experience seem quite unremarkable. She was born Agnes Gonxha Bojaxhiu on August 26, 1910 in Skopje in Macedonia, the third and youngest child of her parents Nikola Bojaxhiu & Drana. Her father Nikola was a successful businessman who took special delight in his children. But it was the faith and selfless charity of Drana, Agnes' hardworking, devout Catholic mother which decisively shaped the course of her life and ministry. Her colleagues in later years described her as— to all appearances—an ordinary nun, with average intelligence, adequate education at best, but devoted to her religious duties. It was this very ordinariness that made Mother Teresa's journey to iconic global prominence so extraordinary. There were three key features that marked her life's work and contributed to her phenomenal rise and lasting impact:

Her Compelling Call & Mission

Agnes' journey began at the age of twelve, when after returning home from a retreat, she told her mother that she had made up her mind to become a nun. She was clear about her decision, believing firmly that God had made the choice for her. While in her teens, she joined prayer groups that were praying for India, and eventually applied to the order of the Loreto Sisters who worked with the Jesuits in Bengal. Agnes left for India in August 1928, where she first did her novitiate at Darjeeling in North Bengal, taking her vows in 1937. Having chosen the name 'Teresa' she was sent to serve as a teacher with the Daughters of St. Ann in Calcutta [now Kolkata]. Teresa experienced what she described as a "call within a call" on September 10. 1946, while traveling to Darjeeling on it dusty, noisy train. Again, the message to her was quite clear and she described it as an order from above which she could not disobey. She was to leave the convent and start a new order of nuns who would take a special vow of charity to work and live among the poorest of the poor, the destitute. unwanted and marginalized in society. In 1950 the Pope gave his permission to set up this new order with the name *Missionaries of Charity,* and as mother superior, Sister Teresa became "Mother" Teresa.

Despite her failing health following a heart attack in 1989, she insisted on keeping up her frantic pace. When her doctors who advised her to slow down and rest, she protested, insisting that much remained to be done and that she had all eternity to rest. Mother Teresa identified deeply with the needs of the poor, but the driving impulse of her ministry was her sense of divine calling- -she was convinced that God had called her to serve the poor.

Her Courageous Compassion

Teresa arrived in Kolkata when the Indian nationalist struggle against the British occupation of India was at its peak. Calcutta was flooded with thousands of migrants who had fled to the city in their desperation to survive. With food in short supply and housing for the poor already overstretched, thousands of people died in the streets daily. Calcutta's struggle to cope with hunger and poverty on the streets only intensified with the refugee crisis in the wake of the partition of India and India's independence in 1947. Teresa displayed exceptional courage needed to serve the poor in these circumstances even while she still served as a teacher at the convent.

It was this same courageous compassion that propelled her life-long crusade against poverty, providing food, shelter and care for the poor. It also motivated her to establish clinics, mobile dispensaries, nurseries, orphanages and homes for abandoned babies, the destitute and dying, and leprosy and AIDS patients. In 1952, two years after the launch of the *Missionaries of Charity* she started *Nirmal Hirday,* a home for the destitute and dying in an abandoned Kali temple in Calcutta, and the following year she opened *Nirmala Shishu Bhavan,* a home for orphaned children and those with other needs. In 1957 she established *Shanti Nagar,* a colony where families leprosy patients were cared for and could work their own fields, learn new trades and build their own houses.

'Motherhouse', a modest three-story building in the heart of Kolkata has served as the headquarters of the *Missionaries of Charity* since 1953, but over the years the work has expanded to 20 centers across the city. Recognizing the need for men to help serve the needs of boys and men in their homes and in extremely dangerous locations, Mother Teresa launched the *Missionary Brothers of Charity* in 1963. In 1965 she received the Pope's permission to expand her compassionate mission outside of India, and today *Missionaries of Charity* homes may be found in 139 countries with close to 5,200 sisters and brothers serving in over 750 homes across the globe.

Her Christ-centered Devotion

It is impossible to explain Mother Teresa's passionate commitment to the plight of the suffering without understanding its source - her unflinching devotion to Christ. Her most celebrated biographer captured it best when he observed: "Her face shines with the love of Christ on which her whole life is centred." (Muggeridge, *Something Beautiful:* 1). She never hesitated to point to Christ as the source and inspiration for her love for the poor. She saw Jesus in the hungry, diseased, homeless, unwanted, dying, unloved, mentally disturbed and spiritually impoverished, and quoted Jesus' words in Matthew 25:40 in challenging others to do the same: "Truly I tell you, just as you did it to one of the least of these who are members of my family, you did it to me."

During the last 20 years of her life Mother Teresa and her work were dogged by unfortunate controversy, in part because her love for the poor was accompanied by a stern indictment of the rich and powerful. Criticism centered around reactions to her vocal opposition to abortion, questions about effective stewardship of finances, and doubts and distrust about the standard of services offered in *Missionaries of Charity* homes. In truth, her growth in fame and popularity had exposed Mother Teresa to excessive and at times unfair public scrutiny. Her life was a paradoxical mixture of simple piety, single-minded vision and steely determination, which in her humanness could be headstrong, demanding and difficult. But she never denied her humanity, referring to herself as "a pencil in God's hand" - merely God's human instrument. A book of her letters published posthumously, gave the world a glimpse into her personal spiritual struggles, her "dark night of the soul", both a reflection of her humanity and a testament to her spiritual strength in how she was able to pursue faithfully her Christ-centered purpose and mission even as she fought to overcome her own crisis of faith.

Following a fatal heart attack Mother Teresa breathed her last on September 5, 1997. The Indian government gave her a state funeral at which nearly half-million mourners came from far and wide to bid her final farewell. Mother Teresa was "beatified" by Pope John Paul II in October 2003 and canonized a saint in September 2016. Her life and legacy will continue to inspire selfless service to the poor for generations to come as they ponder over the staggering accomplishments of the little nun whose life cast such a big bright beacon of light in the darkness of our world.

BIBLIOGRAPHY

Allegri, Renzo. *Teresa of the Poor: The Story of Her Life*. Ann Arbor, Michigan: Charis Books, 1996.

Cannon, Mae Elise. *Just Spirituality: How Faith Practices Fuel Social Action*. Downer's Grove, Ill: InterVarsity Press, 2013.

Chawla, Navin. *Mother Teresa: The Authorized Biography*, London: Collins, 1998.

Greene, Meg. *Mother Teresa: A Biography*. London: Greenwood, 2004.

Kolodiejchuk, Brian. *Mother Teresa. Come be My Light*. Garden City, N.Y: Doubleday, 2007.

Kudo, lliromi J. *Mother Teresa: A Sctintfrom Skopje*. Anand, Gujarat: Gujarat Sahitya Prakash, 2006.

Muggeridge, Malcolm. *Something Beautiful*. New York: Ballantine Books, 1971.

Scott, David *A Revolution of Love: The Meaning of Mother Teresa*. Chicago: Loyola Press, 2005.

Spink, Kathryn. *Mother Teresa: A Complete Authorized Biographv*. New York: HarperCollins, 1997.

Teresa, Mother, et al. *Mother Teresa: In My Own Words·*. Bexley, OH: Gramercy Books, 1997.

Ivan Satyavrata and Elizabeth (Sheila) Shinde Satyavrata

Lenora Isabel Scott Vassar

Nebraska prairies promised a bright future for the recently arrived Scotch- Irish immigrants in the late nineteenth century. Among the folk in the westward covered wagons was Ira Abner Scott and his young bride Amanda Almeda McClain. As the youngest McClain child, Amanda was known for her music and love of books. With courage, perseverance and teamwork the Scotts welcomed their first child, Lenora Isabelle Scott, on February 9, 1889 to the extended family farm near Holland, Nebraska.

Twelve children were born to Ira and Amanda Scott. Being the eldest meant Lenora was expected to participate in women's work in the house as well as family work in the field. At the age of three years the child was crying, not wanting to shuck corn. Grandfather McClain said in a stern voice, "You are nobodies, honey. Grab a sack and get out in the field, girl."

Soon it was rumored additional free land was available in the Oklahoma Territory. So, the Ira Scott family, after several attempts elsewhere, settled in Tryon, Oklahoma Territory. It was here Lenora played the pump organ, taught card Sunday School and was secretary for the First Christian Church (Disciples of Christ). She joined this church when she was 12 years 3 months. Then in Lincoln County Lenora taught at multiple grade levels in a one room schoolhouse.

By the age of seventeen Lenora was accomplished in canning, sewing, quilting and crocheting. Match makers were whispering that Lenora Scott would be a good match for John Alexander Vassar, whose family had come to the Oklahoma Territory from Missouri. After arrangements were made, the newly wed couple started a marriage full of anticipation. Realizing significant opportunities existed in the future for settlers, both John and Lenora completed correspondence courses. John became a certified veterinarian and Lenora was certified in tailoring. By December, 1913 long range planning propelled the couple to load belongings and four children in a covered wagon and travel northward to Osage County.

Since 1907when Indian Territory and Oklahoma Territory merged to form the state of Oklahoma, civil unrest rumbled among the Osage tribe, mixed breeds, oil speculators, the feds and those who saw economic possibilities. In addition, oil revenues during the twentieth century affected the stability of an ancient tribe of people. Their culture had been mutilated and marginalized by outsiders. Pawhuska, Oklahoma struggled with critical changes at the cost of minimalizing cultural continuity.

Lenora and John with their four children (Nellie May, Theodore Roosevelt, Benjamin Franklin, and Wallace Walker) built a home near Bird Creek. Here their trades were valued. So were those of their neighbor, including a bootlegger, Stella, who had been married thirteen times, and the Hahn family who invited Lenora and family to a Holy Ghost tent revival. Her Disciples of Christ and newly acquired Pentecostal seeds took root, much to John's dismay.

An evangelistic plan was put into place for the neighborhood teenage boys. Ted, Ben and Wallace enjoyed playing softball and basketball on Thursday evenings. The Vassar's front yard filled up with youngsters. Each week Lenora cooked an evening meal for the boys. While they ate, she taught them that week's Sunday School lesson. When asked "why" she did this she replied, "They needed to participate in the lesson if they went to church on Sunday." Numerous individuals replicated her insights and kindnesses later in life.

Many examples of mercy are found in Lenore's life. She paid college fees for Ted and Ben, purchased a house for Wallace and assisted getting a farm for Nellie. She gave tuition funds for everyone who wanted to be trained as a minister. Even as an octogenarian and bedfast with arthritis, Lenora insisted the home care workers sit by her bed and take a Bible lesson. Her many years of teaching Bible meant a lifetime of spiritual services.

Lenora Isabel emerges as a cultural icon. She valued her, no, our past, in such a way that she lovingly and purposefully transmitted it to each of her "little ones." We lived through three dimensions - her past, our conjoining present and our possible futures with her memories guiding our thoughts and ways. This pioneer Pentecostal passed away in 1979, and she was buried in Pawhuska, OK.

> She walked in beauty as the night. She walked with light shining brightly Bringing comfort with her soul light Leonora Isabelle provided the loving bond that braided cultural strands while weaving steady and vibrant bands that would bring her loved ones into a way of knowing, believing, Behaving and transmitting her culture to future generations.
>
> RVB

BIBLIOGRAPHY

Burgess/Vassar family archives. Strafford, MO. Ruth Vassar Burgess is a granddaughter of Lenora Isabel Scott Vassar.

Burgess, Ruth Vassar. *Spirited Sisters*. Bloomington, IN: Xlibris, 2014.

Burgess, Stanley M., and Ed van der Maas, eds. *The New International Dictionary of Pentecostal and Charismatic Movements*. Grand Rapids, Ml: Zondervan, 2002.

Vessar, Lyndal G. *The Descendants of John Vasser of Virginia {1635-1984}" A Family History*. Stillwater, OK: First Word Desktop Publishing Co., 1988.

Wilson, Terry P. *The Osage*. New York/Philadelphia, Chelsea House Publishers, 1988.

Ruth Lenora Vassar Burgess

Aimee Kennedy Semple Mcpherson

The history of Spirit-filled women has its own superstars, and Aimee Kennedy Semple McPherson (1890-1944) is arguable the brightest on the marquee. Sister Aimee, as she preferred to be called, was a dynamic and complex leader in early Pentecostal and charismatic Christianity. Born in Ontario, Canada, Aimee Kennedy was raised in a Methodist and Salvation Army home until a visiting evangelist, Robert Semple, caught her eye. Semple's appeal for Aimee was likely complex. He was, according to reports, a handsome and well-spoken man, and he preached a fascinating new way of being Christian: Pentecostalism, with its miracles of divine healing and blessing of tongues. Aimee was attracted by the man and the message, and also was ready to be away from her hovering mother Minnie. She and Semple married, and in short order Aimee became pregnant and the couple left for a missionary tour of China. Sadly, they both contracted malaria, and Semple died in 1910, leaving Aimee and newborn daughter Roberta to make their way back to the United States alone. Only in her twenties, we already see in Aimee Semple the bravery and determination, as well as the simple grit, that would act as the foundation of her future successes.

Aimee, with the help of her re-instated mother Minnie, continued in "the work," evangelism and reform, upon return to the United States. In 1914 Aimee married Harold McPherson, and it seemed she had accepted a life deemed more appropriate by the surrounding culture. Harold McPherson took up a steady job as an accountant in Providence, Rhode Island, and Aimee stayed home raising Roberta and her newborn son, Rolf. But Aimee felt a continuing call to ministry. This set up a quandary familiar to many women who sensed a vocational mandate from God. Women in religious leadership were not common or comfortable for much of American Christianity in the early twentieth century. Women served alongside their husbands, as Aimee had done in China, satisfying the cultural preference for male headship in the church. In Pentecostal worship, however, women testified to their experiences of the Holy Spirit, including their own acts of healing and witnessing. This testifying easily slipped into de facto preaching, as women exhorted and taught scripture at so-called "promiscuous" meetings that included both men and women. Men even allowed women to lay on hands and pray for them, with the accompanying submission to the women's authority. This served as a testimony to the Pentecostal belief concerning the directing hand of the Spirit over worship, even if that hand directed a man to submit to a woman. Aimee was a seasoned participant in these types of worship environments, and her desire to continue to be so began to cause dissatisfaction in her marriage to Harold. Aimee recalled this time in her life as reflective of the Bible stories of God calling the reluctant prophet to task. Caught up by God's directive, Aimee had *no choice* but to preach and teach. This narrative of resistance and relinquishing, while sincere, stands in intriguing tension with the intrepid actions of the young wife and mother. Her confidence was rooted in her understanding of God's sovereignty over her life, marriage or no marriage. In her famous "From Milkpail to Pulpit" sermon, Aimee, recounted a conversation she had with God. The audiotapes of Aimee giving this often-repeated testimony capture her throaty voice with a hint of fun in it as she asks, "Lord I never heard of a woman preacher. They're all men. I don't know why. Why wasn't I a man? I'd like to be a young man so I'd go out and preach." In other words, this job of preaching would be easier, Aimee argued, if she'd just been a man. But Aimee continued, "Lord said, 'Hold your peace, now.'" It was a humorous and rhetorically brilliant move by Aimee, used effectively to cover her ministry with the headship of God, and to tell her detractors to quit bothering her and take it up with the management. Aimee was determined to preach and teach, and even succeeded in helping her husband realize the authenticity of her call. Still, after several years of itinerant ministry together in a "gospel car," travelling the country with the message of Pentecostal glory, Harold and Aimee divorced amicably. With the divorce understood by her followers as the act of a yielded woman to the demands of God, Sister Aimee was free to move into the life she was resolved to pursue.

From 1919-1922, Aimee was a credentialed minister with the young Pentecostal denomination, the Assemblies of God. She continued her itinerant ministry in the American west and back home in Canada. Pictures and recordings of McPherson often show her in a white pulpit dress, loosely (and glamorously) modeled after a Salvation Army uniform. McPherson spoke with a stylized inflection similar to the fashion of movie stars of her time, a way of speaking called the Mid-Atlantic accent because of its mythical positioning somewhere between an American and British accent. With her panache and powerful speaking, she gathered audiences in the hundreds, then thousands, as her ministry grew in popularity. In time, she came into conflict with the Assemblies over doctrinal and political issues, and so she left. What would she do now? She simply established her own church: The International Church of the Foursquare Gospel, a holiness-Pentecostal denomination headquartered in Los Angeles. From here Aimee's own brand of Christianity was promoted, the Foursquare Gospel: Jesus the Savior, Jesus the Baptizer with the Holy Spirit, Jesus the Healer, and Jesus the Soon-Coming King.

The inclusion of Jesus as Healer in her Foursquare Gospel revealed a phenomenon that was on the rise in her meetings at the time. Divine healing, one of the marks of Pentecostal practice, accompanied McPherson's preaching and teaching. She soon became known as a healing evangelist, and her understanding of divine healing made her appeal wide, even as it brought her into conflict with some of the Pentecostal gatekeepers. McPherson taught the controversial doctrine that healing was in the atonement of the crucifixion of Jesus Christ. The salvation message included healing, since appropriating Christ's atoning work included "the whole man." When McPherson's followers sang the hymn *Rock of Ages,* it was the atonement of Jesus Christ that was the "double cure" claimed in the words of the song: Rock of ages, cleft for me, let me hide myself in Thee. May the water and the blood, from Thy wounded side which flowed, be of sin the double cure, save from wrath and make me pure. The atonement, the "water and the blood" of the hymn, included ransom for both sin and sickness, a reinterpretation of the old hymn's message of the double cure of salvation and sanctification. For the Angelus Temple believers, Jesus died not only to save souls, but to cure bodies. His atonement was for spirit and flesh. Simple appropriation of that atoning grace was all one needed to be healed. McPherson became a celebrity spokesperson for this understanding of divine healing and was instrumental in making the exotic practice more appealing to the general public.

As Sister Aimee continued to gather a large following in LA, she built in 1923 the 5300 seat Angelus Temple. From the Temple headquarters she published a monthly periodical entitled "The Bridal Call" and opened her Lighthouse for International Foursquare Evangelism (L.I.F.E.) Bible College. In her typical early-adopter pattern, she developed the first religious radio station in the United States, KFSG, from the Temple. Kall Four Square Gospel began broadcasting Pentecostal Christianity across the airwaves in February 1924. McPherson aired her rousing sermons on divine healing and issued prophetic teaching on the nearness of the end-times. Radio unlocked the American home to Foursquare teaching in a new way, and the media savvy Sister Aimee made quick use of the new access point. Aimee's big, dramatic style was perfectly suited for broadcasting. And Aimee offered a bonus: her audiences could be "born again" by listening and responding to her broadcast altar calls, but by stopping the dial on KFSG and choosing to listen to Sister Aimee, they could also be divinely healed through the power of the Holy Ghost on the radio. Aimee's worship services were soon echoing throughout homes all across the western United States. The preaching and teaching of Sister Aimee Semple McPherson now radiated from one of the first large-scale radio stations in the country.

Sister Aimee Semple McPherson was one of the most successful women leaders of the early twentieth century. She stood at the head of a thriving, innovative church organization, whose Foursquare Church in 2020 includes more than 68,500 churches in 150 countries around the world, and more than 1,700 churches in the U.S. In her ministry she pushed at boundaries for religious authority for women and against racial prejudices. She was difficult and fragile and fabulous. Although she had great successes, Aimee's story continued to have its share of sadness. She married again, only to quickly divorce. It is likely she struggled with addiction. For many of her later years she was best known for a scandalous, media-soaked disappearance she defended in court as a kidnapping. She was estranged from her daughter and in an unending power struggle with her mother. Her life ended much too soon at the age of 53. At the time of her death, the public saw her mostly as disgraced and dishonest, and her Temple continued to proclaim her as their beloved and powerful leader. As was typical of the complicated Sister Aimee, they were both right.

BIBLIOGRAPHY

Blumhofer, Edith Lydia. *Aimee Semple McPherson: Everybody's Sister.* Grand Rapids, MI: 1993.

Declaration of Faith. The International Church of the Foursquare Gospel. 1920.

McPherson, Aimee Semple. *This is That: Personal Experiences, Sermons and Writings of Aimee Semple McPherson Evangelist.* Los Angeles, CA: The Bridal Call Publishing House, 1919, 1923.

_____. *In the Service of the King: The Story of My Life.* New York, NY: Boni and Liveright, 1927.

Obituary, *Variety.* October 4, 1944.

Amy Artman

Margaret Gaines

In 1964 Margaret Gaines (1931-2017), a graduate of Lee College and eleventh generation missionary on her mother's side, arrived in Israel after serving 10 years in Tunisia and 2 years in France as a Church of God (COG) missionary.

Gaines immediately faced cultural tensions, which she attributed to differing norms of Arab and Western cultures. In her autobiography Gaines describes an immediate conflict with her supervisor, George Kuttab. The conflict started when Kuttab reacted angrily because Gaines had gone to the post office without asking for his permission. Gaines had violated the custom that wives and all women in an Arab household must explicitly obey the patriarch. She made matters worse by standing up to Kuttab: "I told him his customs and traditions would not be binding on me. I was not a member of his household and neither the church nor the government required that type of subjugation" (Gaines 2000, 141). Although Gaines regretted her cultural blunder, the confrontation left scars on her relationship with Kuttab. A second event led to a further deterioration of that relationship. Gaines questioned the manner of disciplining children in the day school after observing that the teachers made liberal use of corporal punishment which she interpreted as a venting of frustration on the students. Her attempt to correct what she perceived as "unmerciful beatings" backfired and led to the closing of the school. As Gaines recalls, the Arab leaders of the church "slyly referred to me in their sermons by telling stories of how 'a queen who is allowed to rule for one day will destroy a kingdom.'"(Gaines 2000, 143) Gaines was off to a shaky start, yet she quickly proved herself to be a tireless worker. Early in her ministry Gaines started two churches. The first was in the village of Aboud, 33 miles northwest of Jerusalem, which was the birthplace of the Old Testament prophet Obadiah (Gaines 1969, 7). Aboud had been an important Christian site with a population of 40,000 in the fifth century. Since then its population decreased to 3,000, of which half were Christian and half were Muslim. The second church planted by Gaines was in Amman, Jordan, where she rented an apartment and spent Friday to Sunday (Gaines 2000, 168-170). Along with the COG overseer of the Middle East, Gaines organized the Middle East Theological Institute, which under her supervision offered theological education by extension with a curriculum of worship, study, work, and recreation (Gaines 1969, 7).

Political events placed a damper on the COG mission and exposed Gaines to many ordeals. In 1964 the Palestinian Liberation Organization was founded by the Arab League with the purpose of waging an armed struggle for the liberation of Palestine. In 1967 King Hussein of Jordan went to Egypt and pledged his loyalty to Egypt and the Arab nations in the event of an attack of Israel. Provocation on both sides had led to a war that neither side wanted. Surprisingly, in a mere six days Israel soundly defeated the armies of Egypt, Jordan, and Syria. In the process the Israelis occupied the West Bank, East Jerusalem, Gaza, the Sinai Peninsula, and the Golan Heights.

When East Jerusalem came under the jurisdiction of Israel, Gaines was forced to go through the tedious process of waiting in lines to secure a new identity card, register the church property and her car in Israel, and obtain an Israeli driver's license. An Israeli military commander accused Gaines of being a spy and interrogated her for two hours. She was ordered to appear before a higher official in Ramallah, who also interrogated and released her. At the request of the COG Missions Board, on July 18, 1968 Gaines left for a furlough in America (Gaines 2000,165).

While Gaines was on furlough, she managed to scrape together enough money to launch a building project in Aboud, which was completed during the summer of 1969. The building consisted of a stone edifice and an enclosed garden. Including furniture and an electric generator, the cost was $10,000, all of which was paid for before the dedication on September 13, 1969, which was remarkable given that the only means of livelihood for most of the congregation was their olive trees and small gardens.

The next years saw the expansion of the mission work in Aboud beyond what Gaines could have imagined. In February, 1970 plamling for an elementary school project kicked into high gear. An application was submitted to the director of education of the Ramallah District for a license to operate a school. Some said approval would take a long time, but the application was approved in six weeks. Gaines found a carpenter who could build the desks, benches, and chalkboards at a reasonable price. She then rented the lower level of a house and readied the facility for the 1970-71 school term. In the meantime, she designed a curriculum and prepared materials. Gaines assumed the role of head mistress, aided by a strategic book she procured in a bookstore in Jerusalem, entitled *What To Look For When Inspecting Schools.* This book covered the wide array of issues in administrating a school, such as sanitary conditions, scheduling, attendance records, faculty meetings, supervision of teachers, lesson plans, and testing. During the summer she interviewed candidates and hired a faculty of four teachers. The Aboud Elementary School began according to schedule (Gaines 2000, 172-75).

Not long afterward, as Israel came under attack in 1973, Gaines was undergoing an electrocardiogram at the Hadassah Hospital in Jerusalem. Doctors informed her that she was likely to have a heart attack. A year later, in April 1974, due to the stress of an unrelenting work load, Gaines suffered the predicted heart attack as she was driving from Ramallah to Aboud. Nonetheless, Gaines was back at her post for the 1974-75 school year, in spite of her diminished physical strength.

For the next four years Gaines was absorbed in her duties as the school administrator, developing curriculum, performing class inspections, and supervising teachers. She was pleased to report that the director of education told her that her school ranked the highest in the West Bank. However, the strain of a heavy workload left Gains totally exhausted and in dire need of rest. In twenty-seven years of active mission service, she had taken a total of only seventeen months of furlough, most of which were spent in deputation. After the World Missions Board granted her a year's leave of absence, Gains left Israel in time to arrive home for Christmas 1978.

The installation of electricity in 1983 boosted the quality of life in Aboud. From this time on the villagers were able to enjoy of the conveniences of refrigerators, washing machines, televisions, and other household appliances. By this time most of the people were sleeping on beds and relaxing on sofas and armchairs. Work in Israel even at the minimum wage allowed families to enjoy a sense of prosperity and relief from hardship. The population grew as young married couples settled in Aboud. Small two-room houses sprung up and the streets were paved.

In February 1983 Gaines devoted herself full-time to leadership development, which was essential to the sustainability of the Palestinian church. Gaines organized a weekly Ladies Ministry with the intention of meeting the spiritual needs of women and offering a ministry to children. The ladies held bazaars in which they sold their embroidery, foods, and novelties. Gaines also worked with the women of Aboud to develop a number of children's ministries, such as the Blue Belles, the Joy Belles, the Young Ladies Ministries, and the Christian Service Brigade. Gaines raised up a number of promising women leaders through the Girls Club Counselor Enrichment Training Course. These leaders included Raika El Khoury, her nieces Mary and Hannie El Khoury, and Selwa Subhi, who later married Nihad Salman (Gaines 2000, 207).

With political tensions escalating in the Palestinian territories, the First Intifada erupted in 1987. This uprising began with boys throwing rocks at Israeli tanks and then escalated into a massive strike. The Intifada was the cause of polarization in the West Bank. When the Gulf War erupted on January 16, 1991, Gaines was one of the few missionaries who remained in the West Bank under a curfew imposed because of the threat of scud attacks. For forty-two days no one was allowed to go outside. Schools, churches, and shops were closed. The horror of scuds was not the only problem faced by the people of Aboud. They faced food shortages. Living under impoverished conditions, they did not possess the wherewithal to procure supplies of food. For years they had not been allowed to work in Israel and few jobs were available in the West Bank, resulting in the lack of money to buy food. Gaines played a crucial role in securing food for the people of Aboud. She later observed that violence was practically unknown in Aboud due to the charitable work of the mission (Gaines 2011, 52).

Beset with a worsening heart condition in 1991-1992, Gaines was relying more and more on the local leadership she had equipped to carry on the ministry of the church and school in Aboud. During her last trip to Aboud in 1999 Gaines inspected the fruit of her ministry in the church, the parsonage, the original school building, and the new ministry building.

She felt that anyone with common sense or uncommon sense would know that a 20-year-old Alabama girl who left America with only two years of college, little experience and no money could never have achieved such results.

In March 1999 Gaines retired and left the field. The COG sent out a missionary couple to Aboud in 1999, but they returned home in 2001 due to a medical emergency ("Our Missionaries in the Holy Land" 2002). Despite the short tenure of her successors, Gaines could take satisfaction in the fruit of her ministry. School enrollment had increased from 32 to 121 between 1993 and 1999. The women to whom she had passed the leadership baton were performing brilliantly. Led by the head administrator, Suhaila El Khoury, the faculty was held in high regard by the Department of Education. As Gaines recalls, "The Aboud Elementary School is rated as superior in all the Occupied West Bank" (Gaines 2000, 213).

The most significant achievement of Gaines was the achievement of "a contextualized ministry." During a 1976 interview, a COG official surmised, "Sister Gaines, if I understand correctly, you are a missionary to Israel." Gaines replied, "To be more exact, I think we will have to say I am a missionary in Israel. The terms in the Middle East are very indigenous. We hear Palestine. We hear Israel. We hear the Holy Land, and for the people stateside, this can be rather confusing. My address is Israel, but I am a missionary in a village on the occupied West bank of the Jordan."

Gaines expressed her support for the Palestinian cause in her *Small Enough to Stop the Violence? Muslims, Christians and Jews* (Gaines 2011, 15-23) As a result of her endorsement of Arab claims to Palestine, unlike other Pentecostal missionaries to Israel Gaines, was successful in developing indigenous leaders (Newberg 2012, 147). However, as Kimberly Alexander rightfully notes, Gaines was an enigma to the COG. She was celebrated by the denomination, yet her challenge to the accepted pro-Israel stance of the denomination was an uncomfortable fit. Her ability to think outside the denominational box and advocate for justice from a contextualized perspective explains why the indomitable Margaret Gaines is highly regarded among leading Palestinian Christians in the West Bank (Alexander 2019, 58).

BIBLIOGRAPHY

Alexander, Kimberly Ervin. "Nevertheless, She Persisted: Margaret Gaines, Patriarchal Cultures and a Passport of Love." *The Holy Spirit and Social Justice: Interdisciplinary Global Perspectives, History, Race and Culture.* Eds. Antipas L. Harris and Michael D. Palmer. Lanham, MD: Seymour Press, 2019, pp. 58-91.

Biographical Sketch, Margaret Gaines Collection, Dixon Research Center, Cleveland, TN. Collection Number: M0039; Accession Number: 2013-42.

Gaines, Margaret, "Birth of a Church," *Church of God Evangel* (December 1, 1969): 7.

Gaines, Margaret. *Of Like Passions: Missionary to the Arabs.* Cleveland, TN: Pathway, 2000.

Gaines, Margaret. *Small Enough to Stop the Violence: Muslims, Christians and Jews.* Cleveland, TN: Cherohala Press, 2011.

Newberg, Eric N. *Pentecostal Mission in Palestine: The Legacy of Pentecostal Zionism.* Eugene, OR: Pickwick, 2012.

"Our Missionaries in the Holy Land," *Mission Line* 18, no. 3 (Summer 2002): n.p.

Eric Newberg

Corrie Ten Boom

ornelia Arnalda Johanna "Corrie" ten Boom (April 15, 1892-April 15, 1983) was born in Amsterdam, Netherlands, to a working- class family. She was named after her mother, Cornelia. Her father, Casper ten Boom, was a jeweler and watchmaker. Corrie trained to be a watchmaker herself and was the first woman to be licensed as a watchmaker in the Netherlands. In addition to serving their society as a member of the Dutch Reformed Church by offering shelter, food and money to those who were in need, Corrie established a youth club for teenage girls, with religious instruction and training in sewing, handicrafts and the performing arts.

The German army invaded the Netherlands in May 1940. They forced the youth club to close. In May 1942, a Jewish lady came to the ten Booms' house with a suitcase in hand, informing them that her husband had already been arrested by the Nazis, and her son had gone into hiding to avoid the Occupation authorities. The ten Booms immediately accepted her into their home, although they lived close to the police station. They reasoned that the Jews were God's chosen people and that God's people were always welcome. The ten Booms then became active in the Dutch underground, hiding refugees and honoring the Jewish calendar, including Sabbath.

Thus was born "The Hiding Place." Corrie and her elder sister Betsie opened their home to Jewish and Gentile refugees who were members of the resistance movement. They were henceforth sought after by the Gestapo and its Dutch equivalent. The secret room was in Corrie's bedroom, behind a false wall and holding six people. This area was enlarged later by the Dutch Resistance with an alert buzzer to warn refugees to get into the hidden room.

On February 28, 1944, a Dutch informant, Jan Vogel, informed the Nazis about the ten Boom's work. At around 12:30 p.m., the Nazis arrested the entire ten Boom family. Corrie and Betsie were sent to Scheveningen

Prison, the rest of the ten Boons were released. Father Casper died ten days later. Six people remained undiscovered in the "Hiding Place".

Corrie argued that she was helping the mentally disabled, while the Nazi lieutenant scoffed, because the Nazis had ben exterminating mentally disable people for years. She suggested that a disabled person might be greater in the eyes of God than a watchmaker, or a lieutenant! At that time, Corrie and Betsie were sent to two concentration camps, finally arriving at the death camp of Ravensbruck in Germany.

Betsie's health continued to decline. She died in the camp on December 20. 1944 at the age of 50. Before passing, she told her sister that there was no pit so deep that God is not deeper still. Fifteen days later, Corrie was released from Revensbruck, probably by mistake, because the remainder of the women there were executed a week later in the gas chambers. Corrie returned home to the Netherlands, opening her doors to the mentally disabled who were still in hiding.

After the war ended in 1945, Corrie established a rehabilitation center which served concentration-camp survivors and also jobless Dutch who had collaborated with the Germans. She returned to Germany in 1946 to forgive Germans who had been employed at Ravensbruck and had been particularly brutal to the sister there. She then travelled the world, speaking in over sixty countries. During the next few years she also wrote extensively.

In 1971 Corrie wrote her bestselling book, *The Hiding Place,* which later was made into a 1975 Hollywood film, *The Hiding Place.* She wrote many other books before her death on April 25, 1983, at the age of 91(from her third stroke).

BIBLIOGRAPHY

Atwood, Kathryn J. *Women Heroes of World War II.* Chicago, IL: Chicago Review Press, 2019.

Corrie ten Boom Papers. Billy Graham Center Archives, Wheaton College, Wheaton, IL.

ten Boom, Corrie. *The Hiding Place.* Peabody, MA: Hendrickson, 2009.

Stanley M. Burgess

Kathrn Johanna Kuhlman

Born in the heartland of the USA and known worldwide at her death, healing evangelist Kathryn Johanna Kuhlman (1907-1976) was the most well-known female leader in mid-twentieth century charismatic Christianity. Her life as an evangelist began early. At age 14, Kuhlman left her home in Concordia, Missouri with her sister and brother-in-law Myrtle and Everett Parrott to travel the west as a part of the Parrott's preaching tour. Kuhlman and her sister and brother-in-law travelled together on the "sawdust trail" across the western states to California, then on to Idaho. After five less-than-successful years working with Mytile and Kathryn, Everett apparently tired of the arrangement. After a series of arguments with Myrtle in Boise, Idaho, Everett abandoned Myrtle as well as 21-year old Kathryn and Helen Gulliford, the revival pianist, as he traveled on to South Dakota. The women were unable to make enough to continue by themselves. Outside the Boise Women's Club where Myrtle Parrott continued to preach after Everett's departure, a local Nazarene pastor encouraged the three women to persevere. Myrtle was unwilling to continue due to the dire financial situation and had already decided to return to Everett. But the man said to Myrtle, "Let the girls stay." Kuhlman was ready. She was an eager, enthusiastic, ambitious young woman determined to take the revival circuit by storm. Kuhlman began to travel with Helen throughout Idaho to preach. One participant in her Idaho services remembered the evangelists regularly filled the Baptist churches during their two to six weeks revival meetings.

Soon Kuhlman realized a call to take up her own ministry, and in 1933 she became the leader of the Denver Revival Tabernacle in Colorado. Judging by photographs from Kuhlman's own albums of the time, she spent several happy years in Colorado with close friends and ministry companions. Kuhlman was young, out on her own, preaching and teaching to a packed house. At the age of 28 she was finally coming into her own as a leader of the thriving congregation at the Tabernacle.

The death of her beloved father began the disruption of Kuhlman's life in Denver. Kathryn Kuhlman adored her father Joe, who she always called Papa. Joe Kuhlman was killed instantly when hit by a car driven by a college student home for the holidays in Concordia. After her father's funeral, Kuhlman returned to her ministry in Denver, determined to persevere. Soon she made the acquaintance of Burroughs Waltrip, an evangelist who came to Denver on a preaching junket in 1935. This was followed by a disastrous romance between Kuhlman and Waltrip, who abandoned his wife and two children to marry Kuhlman in 1938. Facing rejection by her former parishioners, Kuhlman quickly regretted the marriage. She spoke of her re-consecration to ministry during this time, stating that Kathryn Kuhlman "died" as the Holy Spirit claimed her life once again. She relocated to Pennsylvania in 1946, divorced Waltrip by 1947, and began a new phase of ministry marked by miracles of healing.

Kuhlman identified what she called "the beginning of miracles" in her ministry with the testimony of an anonymous woman who claimed to be divinely healed in one of her services in Pennsylvania in 1947. Even after the attestation to this miracle, Kuhlman continued to preach a standard evangelical message of born-again Christianity. Increasingly, though, she was known as a faith healer, a term she rejected for its association with Pentecostal healers such as William Branham and A.A. Allen. Kuhlman practiced healing through Words of Knowledge, a style similar to her predecessor Aimee Semple McPherson (although Kuhlman never acknowledged McPherson's influence). Kuhlman did not "lay on hands" to heal, or claim a "point of contact" for healing such as her contemporary, Oral Roberts. Kuhlman would preach until she perceived the healing power of the Holy Spirit, then call out the healings taking place in the room or auditorium around her. According to Kuhlman, she was simply identifying what God was already doing in the bodies and lives of her audiences. Kuhlman produced a short-lived television show in the 1950's called "Your Faith and Mine," where she drew miracle stories from her congregations in Pennsylvania and Ohio. She collected these testimonies in a best-selling book entitled "I Believe In Miracles," published in 1962, the first of several popular titles about Kuhlman's healing and salvation ministry. Her books were translated into as many as 13 different languages and were known world-wide. Kuhlman led weekly services in Pittsburgh, now the center of her ministry and the site of her Kathryn Kuhlman Foundation offices. She recorded weekly episodes of a popular radio show called *Heart to Heart with Kathryn Kuhlman*. In 1965 she added monthly Miracle Services at the seven thousand seat Los Angeles Shrine Auditorium and the following year launched her syndicated television talk show, *I Believe in Miracles*.

Between 1966 and 1975, during the height of the charismatic renewal movement, Kuhlman recorded over 500 episodes of *I Believe in Miracles*. Her show was broadcast in syndication throughout the United States and Canada. Never before had a religious leader hosted a television talk show like *Miracles*. Kuhlman's talk show caught the wave of cultural excitement surrounding the new medium of television, not to mention the novelty of the talk show format in itself, catering to formerly overlooked audiences in daytime and late night. In the new format of the talk show, the experience of the audience changed from worship participant to detached onlooker. In the mid twentieth century, popular culture, the press, and mainstream Christianity still regarded charismatics as unusual. As audiences tuned in to Kuhlman's show, they entered into a world where charismatic Christianity was unexceptional. In each episode they were exposed to testimonies of charismatic experiences of "normal" Americans. The non- threatening space of television combined with the everyday appearance and behavior of the guests made *I Believe in Miracles* a significant contributor to the eventual acceptance of charismatic Christianity in mid twentieth century America and beyond.

The last years of Kuhlman's life were hectic and remarkable. Her popularity within the Catholic Charismatic Renewal movement was reinforced by her audience with Pope Paul VI in 1972. By 1974 Kuhlman was invited to *The Tonight Show* with Johnny Carson and in 1975 the *Dinah!* show starring Dinah Shore. As Kuhlman appeared on national television, her Foundation was operating a radio program, a television show, coordinating multiple worship services and Bible studies in Pittsburgh, Ohio, and LA. Despite her enthusiasm for all media, especially television, Kuhlman did not record a Miracle Service in its entirety until very late in her career, preferring to share the testimonies of those who experienced the miraculous through her books and talk show. In 1975, she finally allowed a miracle service to be filmed in its entirety. Filmed May 3, 1975, the syndicated special *Dry Land, Living Water* was a rare glimpse into the workings of Kuhlman's trademark meetings. The film captured on camera the striking style of Kuhlman as preacher, the manifestation of Words of Knowledge, and the phenomenon of audience members being "slain in the Spirit," or apparently passing out under the influence of the Holy Spirit. Where Kuhlman the talk show host shared cultural space with genteel colleagues such as Dinah Shore and Barbara Walters, Kuhlman the miracle lady did not share such refined associates. The Kuhlman of the miracle service platform was a figure who was heir to the theatrical Sister Aimee Semple McPherson, "holy roller services," and old-fashioned tent revivalists. The meeting was characterized by wigs flying off as women collapsed, children rising from wheelchairs, and lines of eager audience members waiting to take the microphone to testify to divine healing. And then there was Kuhlman, the extraordinary deliverance evangelist in full form, finally captured on film.

Kuhlman's grueling schedule exacerbated an already serious heart condition, and she became weak as she approached the age of 70. She fell ill due to an enlarged heart and died after surgery February 20, 1976. Kuhlman was buried in Forest Lawn Memorial Park in Glendale, California, her tombstone carved with her trademark words, "I Believe in Miracles Because I Believe in God."

BIBLIOGRAPHY

Artman, Amy. *The Miracle Lady: Kathryn Kuhlman and the Transformation of Charismatic Christianity*. Grand Rapids, Michigan: William B. Eerdmans Publishing Company, 2019.

Buckingham, Jamie. *Daughter of Destiny*. Florida: Bridge-Logos, 1999.

De Alminana, Margaret and Lois E. Olena, eds. *Women in Pentecostal and Charismatic Ministry: Informing a Dialogue on Gender, Church, and Ministry*. Boston: Brill, 2016.

Dry Land... Living Water. Pittsburgh, PA: Kathryn Kuhlman Foundation, 1975.Videocassette (VHS), 85 min.

Kathryn Kuhlman Foundation Collection, Collection 212.Billy Graham Center Archives, Wheaton College, Wheaton, Illinois.

Warner, Wayne E. *Kathryn Kuhlman: The Woman Behind the Miracles.* Ann Arbor: Servant Publications, 1993.

Amy Artman

Billie Clare Davis

D r. Billie Clare Davis (April 18, 1923-August 3, 2019} was born in Grants Pass, Oregon, the eldest of John and Daisy Crawford's nine children. She began her life in this extremely poor migrant family that picked crops from the West Coast to the Midwest. Inevitably, they moved frequently, with Billie attending numerous schools. She is reported to have found stability in her school life, the church, and in public libraries. Despite her migrant circumstances, she found educational opportunities wherever and whenever they were made available to her.

Eventually, Billie graduated from high school and attended Drury University in Springfield, Missouri, where she graduated. Later she attended the University of Miami in Coral Gables, Florida, where she earned her Ed.D. in 1976. By that time, she had been made famous as the result of her story, *I was a Hobo Kid,* appearing in the *Saturday Evening Post* in December 1952. Shortly thereafter, a film was produced in 1956 by Agrafilms for the National Education Association, directed by Irving Rusinow, entitled *A Desk for Billie.*

Meanwhile, Billie became an ordained minister in the Assemblies of God, and married the Rev. George H. Davis. Together, they became missionaries to several countries in Central and South America, as well as in the West Indies. From 1981to 1992 Billie taught at Evangel University in Springfield, Missouri, eventually serving as head of the Behavioral Sciences Department. She founded the university's Social Work Department major in 2018. The program was named for her. Upon her retirement, she was honored as professor emeritus.

Billie was the author of five books and hundreds of articles. She served on the Springfield, Missouri Mayor's Commission on Human Rights, beginning in 2008 and serving two terms. She passed away at her home in Springfield on August 3, 2019.

Dr. Davis is remembered for her rise out of obscurity to relative prominence because of taking advantage of opportunities and her spiritual devotion. She is a strong example of individual potential in a world seeking high character and determination.

BIBLIOGRAPHY

The Flower Pentecostal Archives and Missions Archives, Springfield, Missouri.

"I was a Hobo Kid," *Saturday Evening Post,* December 1952. (The article was later reprinted in the *Reader's Digest* and several anthologies.)

"*Longtime educator Billie Davis honored by Evangel,*" Springfield (Missouri) News-Leader, January 4, 2015.

Obituary, Springfield (Missouri) News-Leader, August 6, 2019.

Stanley M. Burgess

Betty Peterson

At age 100, Betty died peacefully on Saturday, February 24, 2018 in Halifax, Nova Scotia. She was born in Reading, PA. on November 27, 1917 and was brought up in the aftermath of the First World War in Syracuse, NY, during the rigors of the Stock Market Crash and the Great Depression. Having always loved music, she performed widely in high school and university groups on radio and stage. She graduated in 1939 from the College of Fine Arts at Syracuse University, majoring in music, classical and folk (both in and out of the classroom, kindergarten through high school), and won honors conducting many school, college, and church choirs. Betty often stated that the formative strands of her life were clearly marked. Her work for social justice was influenced by experiences during the Great Depression. Her interest in the environment and the natural world were nurtured through nature study in Girl Scouting and Albert Schweitzer's "Reverence for Life". While at Syracuse University she met Gunnar Arthur Peterson of Pittsfield, MA. Her love of the outdoors was augmented by Gunnar's interest in skiing, climbing, and canoeing. In 1939 they were married, but during the Second World War she and her husband were separated for periods when he served in different locations as a conscientious objector.

During Gunnar's service, Betty gave birth to their first child, Larry Lars, while living at her mother's house in Syracuse. Betty and Larry joined Gunnar for the last part of his service at The State School for the Developmentally Disabled in Pownal, Maine, where they lived in a small cabin. A major life change occurred with the bombing of Hiroshima and Nagasaki at war's end and the full disclosure of the death camps in Europe. They both determined to devote their lives to peace and social justice. In 1946, their daughter, Lisl Ann, was born. For several years they lived in Connecticut and New York state, becoming Quakers in 1949 and volunteered with the American Friends Service Committee periodically.

Unfortunately, also in 1949, their son, Larry, died of complications due to measles and they threw themselves all the more into peace and social activism. Betty participated in early sit-ins and civil rights protests with Bayard Rustin, Jim Farmer, and other well-known leaders of that era. In 1950 the family moved to a suburb of Chicago, IL. where, in 1952, their son Eric was born. In the 1950s and 1960s while raising a family, she served as a trainer and camp director in professional Girl Scouting, participated in sit-ins and civil disobedience, and was a founder of the South Suburban Human Rights Organization. For many years she was a community educator and organizer for voting equality with the League of Women Voters, and for open housing for all.

Under the War on Poverty Betty taught English as a Second Language at Thornton Community College, Harvey, IL, and later became the director of learning centers in several Chicago south suburbs for Spanish-speaking migrants, Vietnam war brides and African Americans moving from the South during the 60s. Betty was also active in protesting the Vietnam War in 1969.

The Petersons acquired a summer home/farm in Janvrins Harbour, Cape Breton. In 1975 after the fallout from the Vietnam War and Watergate, disillusioned with American Politics, they moved, partly in political protest, to Canada, and to their farm in "Small is Beautiful" Nova Scotia. Gunnar died suddenly in 1976 and Betty at loose ends, decided to stay in Canada and spent a few years traveling and continuing her work from Cape Breton. Doors then opened in 1980 when she moved to Halifax during the winter months and became active in the women's movement and an organizer of many peace activities with the Voice of Women. Through the years with the Canadian Friends Service Committee she became very involved with Native American peoples in Canada, particularly the Innu of Labrador, with whom she camped many times in protest of the NATO low-flying training flights and on whose behalf she spoke at public gatherings throughout the Maritimes. She also camped and protested with the Lubicon in Alberta in their struggle against the oil drilling on their land and continued to rally support for them. She was named Grandmother of the Lubicon and was affectionately referred to as "Rambo Granny". The Innu called her Kukuminash (Old Lady with a Hug); both names she considered an honor. Betty was increasingly appreciative of Native spirituality, particularly in her work with the Native Brotherhood in Prisons.

She became a familiar figure in Halifax and Nova Scotia for the next 35 years; emphasizing non-violent protest in a time of wide-spread wars and revolution. She was involved in organizing rallies, vigils, marches and educational programs to further peace and social concerns. She valued highly the community of activists with whom she worked, and was a member of Halifax Friends Meeting; Voice of Women; Aboriginal Rights Coalition; Project Ploughshares; Canadians, Arabs and Jews for a Just Peace; Fellowship of Reconciliation; War Resisters' League; the Raging Grannies; Kairos; and many justice and inter-faith organizations. Betty's experience of collecting names for the Women's International Peace Petition and taking them to the United Nations Second Session on Disarmament in New York City in 1982 on the March of a Million International Peace Activists, was a life-changer.

As a Quaker, Betty served more widely for many years on the Canadian Friends Service Committee, working for Social Justice and Human Rights in Canada, as well as internationally. She joined Witness for Peace in Central America and travelled on several educational trips to China, Japan and Russia during the Cold War promoting peace and understanding.

She continued her lifelong advocacy for environmental protection and the conservation of land and animals. She was devoted to her Cape Breton farm and to her neighbors there. In her eighties and nineties. Betty spent major time doing archival work for various groups as well as for herself. Her personal papers and organizational records have gone to the Nova Scotia Archives; she also compiled the history of the Quaker Movement in Canada and donated them to the Quaker Society of Canada Archives.

Betty is survived by her daughter, Lisl Peterson Fuson of Farmington, Me.; son, Eric Knute Peterson of Ozark, Mo.; grandsons, Joshua Peter Jacob Fuson (Sarah Tyson) of Denver, CO; and Gabriel Chester Fuson of San Francisco, CA; and great-grand-daughter, Iris Phoebe Tyson. She was predeceased by son, Larry Lars Peterson in Cato, NY in 1949, and by her husband, Gunnar Arthur Peterson in Antigonish, NS in 1976; and brother, William Farber in Woodstock, CN. in 1995. Betty's ashes were scattered over her beloved "Sea farm" in Cape Breton, and next to her husband in Pittsfield, MA.

Betty tried to follow the leadings of the Spirit and to move through life as a Friend. She sometimes referred to her great-grandmother's epitaph in a quiet Pennsylvania graveyard: "She believed in God and did what she could".

BIBLIOGRAPHY

Beckwith, Dave. Interview of Betty Peterson. November 11, 2000. Halifax, Nova Scotia.

Greenberg, Sandy. Canadian Voice of Women for Peace. February 27, 2018.

Obituary, Betty Peterson, in *The Globe and Mail.* Halifax, Nova Scotia, March 16, 2018.

Peterson, Betty. *History of the Quaker Movement in Canada.* Unpublished volume presented to the Quaker Society of Canada Archives.

Eric Knute Peterson

Elisabeth Caspari and
Marie Montessori

Among the most innovative educators in the twentieth century were Elisabeth Caspari and the more famous Marie Montessori. Caspari (1899-2002) was born and raised in Switzerland, in a small mountain village, Chateau d'Oex, near Lake Lausanne. Because Elisabeth was briefly an invalid during childhood, her father introduced her to the piano. She was educated in Lausanne, ultimately receiving a Doctorate in Music Pedagogy in 1927. She married her husband, Charles Caspari in Chateau d'Oex, and taught for fifteen years at the Ecole Normale de Musique de Lausanne, Switzerland.

During a trip to Tibet, studying comparative world religions, she met Dr. Marie Montessori, who changed the direction of her life. Suddenly, it was 1939, and World War II had begun, stranding both the Casparis and Montessori in India until they finally were released to return home as the war ended in 1945.

Marie Montessori (1870-1952) is world-famous for her transformational work among children, beginning with children in the slums of Rome, Italy, and culminating in her famous Montessori educational program for children that continues to be practiced throughout the world to the present.

In 1941Montessori, joined by the Casparis moved to Madras State in India, to the lovely hill station of Kodaikanal, where Madame Caspari and Marie Montessori taught children of missionaries stationed in India.

Madame Caspari continued the work of Montessori until she passed at the age of 101. She became known as the "Montessori Gypsi". The work of these two memorable Christian women continues into the future, with numerous followers, their trainer of trainer programs, and the Montessori societies stationed throughout the world.

BIBLIOGRAPHY

Burgess, Ruth Vassar. Burgess family archives (the author was a third-grade student of Madame Caspari at the International School in Kodaikanal, South India during Caspari's internship there between 1941-45).

Maunz, Mary Ellen. "Dr. Elisabeth Caspari," *Age of Montessori: Certifying Teachers and Educating Parents.* Age of Montessori.org.

Montessori, Maria and Gerald Lee Gutek. *The Montessori Method: The Origins of an Educational Innovation Including an Abridged and Annotated Edition of Maria Montessori's The Montessori Method.* New York, London: Rowman and Littlefield, 2004.

Ruth Vassar Burgess

Mary Ann Louise Hoover

Mary Ann Louise Hoover, together with her husband, Willis Collins Hoover (1856-1936}, were founders of the Pentecostal movement in Chile. She married Hoover, who had been credentialled in medicine in 1884 (M.D.). Willis and his wife were part of the Wesleyan/Holiness tradition. Willis experienced a call to serve as a missionary to South America. Mary Ann Louise was a graduate of the Chicago Training School for home and foreign missions. Both of the Hoovers were part of the Holiness Movement and began their missionary careers in the Methodist Episcopal Church. As such, they were close friends to Phoebe and Walter Palmer, well known members of the Wesleyan Holiness Movement in the nineteenth century.

The Hoovers did not go to Chile with the Methodist Episcopal Missionary Society. Instead, they chose to go with the support of the William Taylor Building and Transit Fund. The great missionary Taylor enabled self-supporting Wesleyan Holiness missionaries to enter missionary service. Taylor had initiated Methodist-related missions in Chile in 1878 in an effort to prove to the Methodist Missionary Society that self-supporting, self-governing, and self-perpetuating churches would result from the work of self-supporting missionaries.

The Hoovers began their missions work in 1889 as the rector of the *Collegia Ingles* in Iquique, Chile. Willis learned Spanish easily and then he also became pastor of the first Spanish-speaking Methodist church in the area. Unfortunately, the United States Methodist governing system then dealing with the Hoovers disenfranchised women missionaries working throughout Chile.

Willis Hoover' work led to large congregations in Northern Chile, and many of the lay leaders in his church became pastors of new groups.

Willis was named pastor at Valparaiso. Meanwhile, new missionaries were being sent out to Chile with greater funding than the self-supporting Hoover branch of Methodism. Strife broke out between older and newer missionaries.

This strife led Mary Ann Louise and her husband to search for spiritual revival in other places. In 1907, Minnie Abrams, a Wesleyan Holiness missionary in India who had resigned from the Methodist Episcopal Missionary Society, sent the Heavers a copy of her book, *The Baptism of the Holy Ghost and Fire*. Minnie had been a close friend of Mary Ann Louise and a classmate of hers in Chicago. Mary Ann Louis Hoover then began to correspond with Pentecostal leaders and their wives around the world. In 1909 Mary Ann Louis and Willis Hoover experienced the Pentecostal baptism of the Holy Spirit.

By 1910 the Hoovers had led a movement to transform their congregations into Pentecostal churches. On May 1 Willis resigned his pastorate in Valparaiso. The resistance to the new movement led to his being arrested, and with them being pressured to leave Chile. He was freed from prison by the local magistrate, and he proceeded to establish the Methodist Pentecostal Church of Chile and later the Iglesia Evangelica Pentecostal. By 1975 these two denominations ranked as first and second largest Protestant denominations in the country, with a combined communicant membership of 350,000. By 1998, Pentecostal denominations of all kinds made up approximately one fifth of the total population of Chile.

Willis died in 1936.

BIBLIOGRAPHY

Abrams, Minnie. *The Baptism of the Holy Ghost and Fire*. 2nd ed. Khedgaun: Mukti Mission Press, 1906.

Anderson, Gerald H. *Biographical Dictionary of Christian Missions*. New York: Macmillan, 1998.

Bundy, David D. "Chile", and "Hoover, Willis Collins", in Stanley M. Burgess and Ed van der Maas, eds. *The New International Dictionary of Pentecostal and Charismatic Movements*. Grand Rapids, Ml: Zondervan, 2002.

Hoover, Mario G. *Willis Collins Hoover: History of the Pentecostal Revival in Chile.* Santiago: lmprenta Eben-Ezer, 2000.

Hoover, Mary Louise. "Pentecost in Chile, South America," *The Upper Room* 1(6 Jan. 1910).

Hoover, Willis Collins. *Historia del Avivamiento Pentecostal en Chile.* Valparaiso, Chile, lmprenta Excelsior, 1948.

Stanley M. Burgess

Soong Mel-Ling Madame Chiang Kai-Shek

adame Chaing Kai-Shek (March 5, 1898-0ctober 23, 2003) was the First Lady of the Republic of China (1928-April 5, 1975), the wife of Generalissimo and President Chiang Kai-Shek. She also was the sister-in-law of Sun Yat-sen, the founder and leader of the Republic of China. A strong Christian, she was chairwoman of Fu Jen Catholic University.

She was born in Shanghai in 1898—although Eastern culture insisted that her conception in 1897 was the acceptable date of origin. She was the fourth of six children of Charlie Soong, a wealthy business tycoon and former Methodist missionary from Hainan, and his wife Ni Kwei-tseng. At the age of 15 she moved to Macon, George, to attend Wesleyan College. Two years later she transferred to Wellesley College, to be close to her brother, who was studying at Harvard. She excelled in her studies, graduating as a "Durant Scholar" in. 1917. She spoke excellent English, with a strong Georgian accent.

In 1920 Mei-ling met Chiang Kai-shek. He was eleven years her elder, already married, and a Buddhist. Her mother opposed the marriage unto Chiang showed proof of his divorce and promised to convert to Christianity. They married in 1927. Madame Chiang became her husband's English translator and advisor. She promoted the Chinese cause during World War II, and attempted to build up her husband internationally to be on a par with Roosevelt, Churchill and Stalin.

Madame Chiang also began ambitious social welfare projects for "warphans", orphans of Chinese soldiers, including schools, playgrounds, swimming pools, and dormitories. She personally picked all of the teachers. These efforts became even more important when China entered the war with Japan in 1937.

She also made numerous trips to the United States to rally money and support for the Republic of China. On February 18, 1943, she became the first Chinese national to address both houses of the US Congress. When her husband was defeated in the Chinese Civil War in 1949, she and her husband moved to Taiwan. In 1975, Chiang died. Madame Chaing suffered from breast cancer, and had ovarian surgery in 1991. She died in New York City, on October 23, 2003, at the age of 105, and was buried with her husband, first in Hartsdale, New York, and finally, in Cihu, Taiwan. Clare Booth Luce compared her to Joan of Arc and Florence Nightingale, and Ernest Hemingway called her the "empress" of China. Without question, Madame Chiang must be considered one of the most significant Christian women of the twentieth century.

BIBLIOGRAPHY

Chu, Samuel C., & Thomas L. Kennedy., eds. *Madame Chiang Kai-shek and her China*. Norwalk, CN, 2005.

Pakula, Hannah. *The Last Empress: Madame Chiang Kai-shek and the Birth of Modern China*. New York: Simon & Schuster, 2009.

Tyson Li, Laura. *Madame Chiang Kai-Shek: China's Eternal First Lady*. New York: Grove Press, 2006.

Stanley M. Burgess

Jashil Choi

C hoi was born in 1915 in Haeju City in Hwang-hae Province of North Korea during the Japanese occupation. While she was still young, her father died and she had to take up the heavy responsibility of assisting her mother, who made a tiny income from her sewing job. At the age of twelve, she and her mother had a chance to attend a tent revival meeting led by Sung-Bong Lee, a well-known Holiness preacher in early Korean Christian history. During this meeting, they accepted Christ as their personal Savior. Their great desire was to be able to overcome poverty and become rich. To achieve this goal, Choi entered a nursing school to become a nurse and to work as a midwife as well. During those days, nurses earned good money while enjoying a decent life and respect. Choi's diligence and hard work led her closer to her goal, and she later married an affluent and educated man.

After moving to Seoul, South Korea from the North, she opened a new business and it became successful. However, the more money she made, the more empty her heart became. However, she refused to go to church. Then a tragedy befell her: her mother and the oldest daughter died within about a ten-day interval of each other. That incident shook Choi so badly that she developed complex illnesses. She interpreted this as a penalization from God for her ambition and worldly desires, and her life away from him. Coincidentally, her business failed miserably. In 1956, she attempted to kill herself as she was losing all hope to live.

During this desperate period, she turned to the Lord. She headed to a prayer mountain, where a famous revival speaker Sung-Bong Lee was conducting a revival meeting, and there she came back to the Lord. Lee's message strongly ministered to her heart and helped her open up to the Holy Spirit. During the prayer time, she experienced fire running throughout her body from above, and her tongue became twisted, and she spoke in a strange language, as the Holy Spirit baptized her. She had a true encounter with the Lord and made a full commitment to him. She entered the Full Gospel Bible College to prepare for her future ministry. (See more sources about her early spiritual journey, Choi, 1-125)

The Yoido Full Gospel Church was founded in the outskirt of Seoul on 15 May 1958 by David Yonggi Cho and Jashil Chio, who was Cho's mother-in-law. It was a tent church with a few members. But she served the church as the associate pastor. After moving to the new location, Yoido Island, the church grew rapidly became the largest church in the world by reaching 800,000 membership in 2007. David Yonggi Cho retired in 2008 and Yonghoon Lee became his succesor.

The spirituality of Choi's life can be attributed to two keys components: prayer and fasting. Choi's prayer life was shaped during her Bible College years. In a sense, her life of being a student in her older age could have been exciting, but it was not. She had many responsibilities, including the burden of leaving her children to someone else's care and supporting them. Such difficult situations drew her closer to God and her spirituality in prayer was developed. Choi not only prayed at designated hours she set up, but she also prayed constantly. Her spirituality was not confined just to her private life but was often demonstrated in her life of ministry, and such a display of concern for others as part of her spiritual exercise.

She met Yonggi Cho at Bible College and found him terribly ill with tuberculosis. While no one else paid any attention to or cared for him, she showed her affection towards him with an intense prayer for his healing. (Choi, 147-52) Perhaps this incident encouraged them to cultivate a close relationship with each other.

Choi fasted as often as her spirit was led. She firmly believed that fasting could draw one closer to the Divine presence and enable more powerful prayer. Her desire for a sound spiritual life led her to the establishment of a prayer mountain dedicated to fasting. Long and intensive prayer with frequent fasting naturally characterized this process. The more time she spent in prayer and fasting, the stronger her faith became for the very first prayer mountain, with a distinct emphasis on fasting.

She began to search for a good location for the prayer facility. While she was praying and fasting, one night she clearly heard the voice of God directing her to a parcel of land for the prayer mountain. The place had been a cemetery for many years and she may have felt a strong reluctance about using it. However, when she made an immediate visit to the place called Osan-ni village, she knelt on her knees on the barren ground, surrounded by graves, and prayed. (Ma, 235-54)

Choi had a marvelous heart for serving lost souls. She always availed herself to be used for the work of God's kingdom. During her training in the Bible College, she took every opportunity to bring the unsaved to Christ. Her unique evangelism strategy was to approach children, as Choi had a natural ability to draw children to her. Even in evangelism, prayer was the bedrock of her ministry. She spent more time in prayer and fasting than in actual evangelism.

She gradually expanded her evangelistic activities to adults. Each Sunday, Choi had about 70 attendees in fellowship, plus a good number of children. As there was no suitable meeting place, their gathering often took place under a pine tree. Thus, rainy days posed extreme challenges. Once, during her regular prayer time in a quiet place, she heard the voice of God instructing her to start a tent church. "Hearing God's voice" was a regular part of her prayer life.

The church became particularly known for its healing ministry. When the church held a tent revival meeting, together with missionary Sam Todd, about 200 people received healing. (Choi, 355-56) As the church constantly grew in number, Cho and the church began to search for another location for a new church building. When Yoido Island was suggested, odds were against Cho. First, Yoido was too far from the city center, and the future of the deserted military airfield was uncertain. This challenge took Choi frequently to a prayer mountain near Seoul. Every night she went to the cemetery in Osan-ri and spent her time in prayer. Through the ministry of the prayer mountain, she wanted to bring the people of God to prayer life. (Choi, 415-32)

The Lord showed a clear sign of his will: People from different places flocked into Osan-ri, even though it was not yet purchased and was still barren. Those people who came prayed with fasting and this became a rule of this prayer mountain. Soon the place began to attract people from Japan and other parts of the world, and they too discovered a new spiritual dimension through prayer with fasting. The Osan-ri Prayer Mountain was established in 1973 and became the first international facility for prayer and fasting. An increasing number of sick came to experience divine healing. Soon many experienced healing from incurable sicknesses through intensive and fervent prayer accompanied by fasting. Some fasted for forty days. Such news soon spread throughout the nation and more people who were in a desperate situation came to pray. The name of the prayer mountain changed to Osanri Choi Jashil Memorial Fasting Prayer Mountain. Jashil Choi passed away on Nov. 6, 1989.

BIBLIOGRAPHY

Choi, Jashil. *I was Mrs. Hallelujah.* Seoul: Seoul Books, 1978.
Ma, Julie. "Korean Pentecostal Spirituality: A Case of Jashil Choi," *Asian Journal of Pentecostal Studies* 5:2 (2002): 235-54.

Julie Ma

Maya Angelou

Maya Angelou was born Marguerite Annie Johnson (April4, 1928) and died on May 28, 2014. She was the second child of Bailey Johnson, a doorman and navy dietitian, and Vivian (Baxter) Johnson, a nurse and card dealer. Angelou's older brother, Bailer Jr., nickname her "Maya" or "My" or "My Sister." When Angelou was three, the parents' "calamitous marriage" ended, and her father sent them to Stamps, Arkansas, alone by train, to their paternal grandmother's house. It so happened that this grandmother was prospering financially during the Great Depression and World War II because she owned a general store, where basic commodities were sold and she made wise investments. Four years later the father came to Stamps without warning and returned them to their mother's care in St. Louis.

Sadly, while living with her mother, Maya was abused and raped by her mother's boyfriend. The abuser was eventually murdered by family members. Maya became mute for almost five years, thinking that she had killed the rapist by revealing his identity. She was returned to her grandmother's care in St. Louis where she learned to speak again and was introduced to such authors as Charles Dickens, William Shakespeare, Edgar Allan Poe and others. She also learned about black female artists like Frances Harper, Anne Spencer and Jessie Fauset.

When Maya was fourteen, she and her brother moved in with their mother again, now in Oakland, California. During World War II she attended the California Labor School. At the age of 16, she became the first black female cable car conductor in San Francisco. Three weeks after completing school, she gave birth to her son, Clyde (who later changed his name to Guy Johnson).

In 1951Maya married Tosh Angelos, a Greek electrician and former sailor, and aspiring musician. This despite the opposition of her mother to the interracial marriage. Maya took modern dance classes at this time, and later joined a dance team, performing throughout San Francisco, although never becoming successful. Her marriage ended in 1954, at which time she began to dance professionally at a variety of nightclubs in San Francisco, including the Purple Onion, where she changed her name to "Maya Angelou". In 1954-1955, she toured Europe with a production of the opera *Porgy and Bess.* She became a multi-linguist, gaining proficiency in several languages. She then moved to New York City to concentrate on her writing career.

In 1961, Maya moved with her new friend, Vusumzi Make, and her son, Guy, to Cairo, where she worked as an associate editor for the weekly English-language newspaper, *The Arab Observer.* In 1962, she moved to Accra, Ghana so Guy could attend college, but he suffered a severe injury in an auto accident. As he recovered, Maya became an administrator at the University of Ghana, and was active in the African-American expatriate movement.

In Accra, Maya became close friends with Malcolm X during his visit in the early 1960s. Maya then returned to the States in 1965 to help him build a new civil rights organization. But Malcolm was assassinated shortly afterward, and Maya was devastated and adrift. She moved briefly to Hawaii, where her brother resided, and where she resumed her singing career. Then she returned to Los Angeles to focus on her writing.

In 1968 Martin Luther King, Mr. asked Angelou to organize a march. She agreed, but sadly King was assassinated on her 40th birthday (April 4th). Again, depressed by this loss, she was encouraged to write a series of documentaries on National Educational Television (precursor to PBS}. Then encouraged by friends and Random House Publishers, she wrote her first autobiography, *I Know Why the Caged Bird Sings* (1969}. In years to come, she would write six additional life stories. Maya was now internationally recognized and acclaimed.

In 1972, her play *Georgia, Georgia* was produced by a Swedish film company-the first screenplay written by a black woman. In her late career she wrote articles, short stories, TV scripts, documentaries, autobiographies, and poetry. In 1977 she appeared in a support role in the TV miniseries *Roots.* She received many awards, including over fifty honorary degrees from colleges and universities world-wide, and became a close friend and mentor to Oprah Winfrey.

In 1981 she returned to the southern United States, accepting the lifetime Reynolds Professorship of American Studies at Wake Forest University in Winston-Salem, North Carolina, where she was one of the very few full-time African-American professors (she had never earned a college degree). Instead, she had learned that if God loved her, what is it that she could not do?

In her last years, Maya campaigned for the Democratic party—in 2008 for Hilary Clinton, and then for Barack Obama, who then became the first black President of the United States. Maya died on May 28, 2014. At her funeral, her son, Oprah Winfrey, Michelle Obama, and Bill Clinton spoke.

BIBLIOGRAPHY

Angelo, Maya. *I Know Why the Caged Bird Sings.* New York: Random House, 1969.

Toppman, Lawrence. "Maya Angelo: The Serene Spirit of a Survivor," in *Conversations with Maya Angelo,* Jeffrey M. Elliot, ed. Jackson, Mississippi: University Press, 1989.

Stanley M. Burgess

Helen Adams Keller

H elen Adams Keller (June 27, 1880-June 1, 1968) was the first deaf-blind person to earn a Bachelor of Arts degree (Radcliffe College at Harvard University). She became a significant American author, political activist, and lecturer, and one of the 20th century's leading humanitarians. She was born in Tuscumbia, Alabama. Her father, Arthur Henley Keller, was a newspaper editor as well as a captain in the Confederate Army. Her mother, Catherine Everett (Adams) Keller, was the daughter of a Confederate general. Interestingly, one of Helen's Swiss ancestors was the first Swiss teacher for the deaf in Zurich.

At the age of 19 months, Helen Keller contracted an illness, "brain fever", unidentifiable at the time, but probably either scarlet fever or meningitis, that left her both deaf and blind. At that time, she was able to communicate with the six-year-old daughter of the family cook, who understood her signs. By the age of seven, Helen had developed more than 60 home signs to communicate with her family. In 1886, Helen's mother arranged for her to be examined by a leading ear, nose, and throat specialist in Baltimore. He referred them to Alexander Graham Bell, who was treating deaf children at that time. Bell arranged for her to work with Anne Sullivan, also visually impaired, who became both her governess and later her companion. This became a fifty-year-long relationship (until Sullivan's death in 1936).

In May 1888 Helen began to attend the Perkins Institute for the Blind. By 1890 she had moved to the Cambridge School for Young Ladies, before she was admitted two years later to Radcliffe College of Harvard University. There she met Mark Twain. Her education was paid for by friends of Mark Twain, Standard Oil magnate, Henry Huttleston Rogers and his wife Abbie. In 1904, at the age of 24, she graduated Phi Beta Kappa from Radcliffe.

In 1905, Anne Sullivan married John Macy, an instructor at Harvard, a social critic and a prominent socialist. In the same year, with the help of Anne and Macy, Helen wrote her first book, *The Story of My Life*. Helen went on to become a world-famous speaker and author. She is remembered as an advocate for people with disabilities, especially impacting the deaf community. Helen had many other roles, including being a suffragette, pacifist, radical socialist, birth control supporter, and an opponent of Woodrow Wilson.

Having a strong Leftist position, she opposed all wars and supported the working class and women's right to vote. She opposed all military intervention, and joined the Socialist party, including candidate Eugene V. Debs in his campaign for the presidency. She wrote a total of 12 published books and numerous articles.

Strongly Christian, Helen wrote her spiritual autobiography, *My Religion,* which was later revised after her death under the title, *Light in My Darkness* (1994). She followed the teachings of Emanuel Swedenborg, who claimed that the Second Coming of Christ had already occurred. She suffered a series of strokes in 1961and died in her sleep on June 1, 1968. She was buried at the Washington National Cathedral in Washington, D.C In 1999, Keller was listed in Gallup's Most widely Admired People of the 20th Century.

BIBLIOGRAPHY

Lash, Joseph P. *Helen and Teacher: The Story of Helen Keffer and Anne Sullivan Macy.* New York: Delacorte Press, 1980.

Herrmann, Dorothy. *Helen Keller: A Life.* New York: Knopf, 1998.

Keller, Helen with Anne Sullivan and John A. Macy. *The Story of My Life.* New York: Doubleday, Page and *Co.,* 1903.

Stanley M. Burgess

Coretta Scott King

Coretta Scott King (April 27, 1927-January 30, 2006) was the wife of Dr. Martin Luther King Jr. (Ph.D., Boston University; born in 1929, married in 1953, died in 1968), the great American civil rights leader. Coretta was an active advocate for African-American equality, and a leader for the civil rights movement. She also was a singer who incorporated music into her civil rights work.

Coretta Scott was born in Marion, Alabama, the third of four children of Obadiah Scott and Bernice McMurray Scott. From age 10 she worked to increase the family's income. While in high school, she was lead soprano for the senior chorus. She also played trumpet and piano, and graduated valedictorian in 1945. She then enrolled at Antioch College in Yellow Springs, Ohio, where she studied music and was politically active in the Antioch chapter of the NAACP. Coretta transferred out of Antioch when she won a scholarship to the New England Conservatory of Music in Boston. Coretta met Martin Luther King while he was attending graduate school in Boston. On Valentine's Day 1953, the couple announced their plans to marry. They were wed on June 18, 1953. They moved to Montgomery, Alabama in September, 1954.

On September 1, 1954, Martin Luther King Jr. became full-time pastor of Dexter Avenue Baptist Church in Montgomery. Coretta gave up her plans to become a classical singer in favor of supporting her husband in his ministry and struggle for African-American civil rights. They welcomed their first child, Yolanda on November 17, 1955. The couple would be blessed with four children in years following. Martin became involved in the Montgomery Bus Boycott, resulting in threats against his life. In the process, the couple began to believe in nonviolent protests as most effective way to express opposition, which they understood to be the Biblical way.

Coretta and her husband joined Ralph Abernathy in a courtroom on September 3, 1958. Martin was arrested for "loitering" and "failing to obey an officer." A few weeks later, Martin was stabbed by an assailant, and had to be hospitalized for a short time. Having recovered, Martin and Coretta accompanied Lawrence Reddick on a five-week tour of India, where Martin spoke frequently and Coretta sang enthusiastically.

On January 30, 1956, the King family suffered a house bombing. In 1960 Martin was jailed for picketing in a department store, and then sent back to jail three days later for driving with an Alabama license while being a resident of Georgia-this time for four months of hard labor. Robert Kennedy obtained his release from prison, and John Fitzgerald Kennedy, on the presidential campaign trail, called to encourage him.

The Kennedy support brought a brief reprieve for Coretta and Martin, until early in November 1963, when they went together to march in a Women Strike for Peace rally in New York. Sadly, that day was ruined by news of the assassination of President Kennedy in Dallas, Texas. Meanwhile, J. Edgar Hoover of the FBI had threatened to mail tapes, alleging improper extramarital incidents against her husband.

During the Lyndon Johnson presidency Caretta continued to work hard to pass the Civil Rights Act of 1964. Caretta complained that the Civil Rights Movement had been dominated by men, with little room for women, whom even Martin felt had their primary place at home. Caretta participated in a Women Strike for Peace protest in Washington in January 1968, with over *5,000* women marching.

Martin Luther King Jr was shot and killed in Memphis, Tennessee on April 4, 1968. Caretta learned of the shooting after being called by Jesse Jackson. A large number of telegrams attempting to comfort her arrived, most notably one from the mother of Lee Harvey Oswald, the alleged assassin.

Caretta now broadened her focus to include women's rights. She also founded the Martin Luther King, Jr. Center for Nonviolent Social Change in Atlanta. She published her memoirs, *My Life with Martin Luther King, Jr.* in 1969. Based in large measure on her efforts, in 1986, Martin Luther King, Jr. Day was made a federal holiday. During the 1980s, Caretta participated in a number of sit-in protests in Washington, DC that prompted nationwide demonstrations against South African racial policies, i.e., apartheid. She also endeavored to end the war in Vietnam, and to end capital punishment. She vehemently opposed the 2003 invasion of Iraq.

Her efforts to further social justice resulted in Antioch College creating the Caretta Scott King Center as a place to address issues of race, class, gender, diversity and social justice. On January *30, 2006,* she died at a rehabilitation center in Mexico, after suffering a stroke and ovarian cancer.

BIBLIOGRAPHY

Gelfand, Dale Evva. *Caretta Scott King: Civil Rights Activist.* New York: Chelsea Clubhouse, 2005.

King, Caretta Scott. *My Life with Martin Luther King, Jr.* London: Puffin, 1969.

McPherson, Stephanie Sammartino. *Caretta Scott King.* Minneapolis, MN: Twenty-First Century Books, 2007.

Stanley M. Burgess

Glossary

Apostle: One of the group made up of the twelve male disciples chosen by Jesus to preach the gospel; a missionary of the early Christian Church, especially of the first Christian mission to a country or region; one who pioneers an important reform movement, cause, or belief; one who is the "first to the tomb, and the first to spread the word to the other apostles" (Mary Magdalene).

Apostolic Fathers: A church father of the first- or second-century CE who was believed to have received personal instruction from the twelve apostles or from their disciples.

Apostolic Succession: The theory of a continuing line of descent from the apostles to the present day church transmitted through episcopal consecration. By tradition the patriarchates of Rome and Antioch were founded by the apostle Peter and Alexandria by the evangelist Mark. Rome has always made the strongest claims to continued apostolic succession.

Arminian theology: Jacobus Arminius (1560-1609) taught that Divine sovereignty was compatible with human free will, and the Jesus Christ died for all and not only for the elect. A more liberal view of theology than strict Calvinism. John Wesley held an Arminian position, as contrasted with George Whitefield's Calvinist teachings.

Azusa Street Revival: The term given to events that ran from 1908-1913 in and around the Apostolic Faith Mission in Los Angeles, California. Classical Pentecostals have tended to seed this revival as generating the modern Pentecostal movement worldwide, although we now know that

Pentecostalism as a movement has always existed from the first century CE onwards, trans spatially and trans-temporally. At Azusa Street participants, led by William Seymour, experienced ecstatic spiritual experiences, such as glossolalia, dramatic worship services, and interracial mingling. Azusa Street spawned missionary activity in virtually all parts of the world.

Bogomils: Radical dualists in the Balkans (ninth through fifteenth century CE) who taught that the world and the human body were the work of Satan, with only the soul being the work of God. They rejected Church sacraments, all of the Bible except the New Testament and Psalms, and marriage. For them, sin is a "sexually transmitted disease."

Camisards: A fanatical group of French Protestants (early eighteenth-century CEL) who were persecuted by King Louis XIV for their perceived excesses, included ecstatic inspiration and prophecies. In England, they were known as the "French Prophets."

Cappadocian Fathers: Three brilliant philosopher-theologians who lived as contemporaries in Asia Minor (now Turkey): Basil the Great, Gregory of Nazianzus, and Gregory of Nyssa. Their influence led to the final defeat of Arianism at the Council of Constantinople (381) and the full acceptance of the Holy Spirit as an equal member of the Divine Trinity.

Cathars: A group of dissenters in twelfth and thirteenth century France who claimed to be restoring the purity of the Church. They were radical dualists, who rejected Church sacraments, priestly leadership, marriage, and the doctrines of bodily resurrection, hell, and purgatory. In place of the sacraments, they instituted the *consolamentum,* a baptism of the Holy Spirit by the laying on of hands. The Cathars were persecuted to extinction by the Inquisition.

CE/BCE: CE refers to "Common Era" and is the equivalent of AD ("in the year of our Lord"). BCE refers to "Before the Common Era" and is equivalent to BC.

Charism: Greek word meaning a free, graciously conferred gift. *Charismata* is the plural of *charism*. In the New Testament these terms usually refer specifically to gifts derived from the Holy Spirit.

Charismatic/s: Charismatics are those who attest to an experience of spiritual renewal through the power of the Holy Spirit. They are so-named because they put special emphasis on spiritual gifts, including speaking in tongues (glossolalia, xenoglossia, heteroglossia, and glossographia), prophecy, healing, and exorcism. Charismatics are from older denominations, whether Protestant, Roman Catholic, or Orthodox, and as such can be distinguished from newer Classical Pentecostals (twentieth and twenty-first centuries). Independent Charismatics (previously known as "Nee-Charismatics" are those individuals who claim to be neither Pentecostal or denominational Charismatic, but evidence the same emphasis on spiritual gifts and exuberant worship services.Independent Charismatics have become the most numerous of the three groupings.

Catholic Reformation: Earlier called the "Counter Reformation." One of three categories of sixteenth century reform: the Protestant Reformation, the Catholic Reformation, and the Radical Reformation. Catholic reform found expression in the deepening of lay piety, the reform of old religious orders and the rise of new orders, that were dedicated to the revival of spiritual life and service to others. It was spawned by Renaissance humanism, and later sponsored by a reformed papacy that worked with a church council held at Trent.

Church fathers: Any of the early writers in the Christian church who formulated doctrines and codified religious observances.

Church mothers: A term little used, although numerous women began Christian denominations (e.g., Ann Lee and Aimee Semple McPherson), and otherwise influenced Christianity. Such groups as the Church of God in Christ highly honor their Church mothers, who serve as ministers and assist others. In a very real sense, this is the subject of the present tome.

Classical Pentecostals: Modern renewalists who emphasized glossolalia as the primary spiritual gift was well as evidence of spirit baptism. They see themselves as restorers of the first-century church. Rather than remaining in the mainstream churches, Classical Pentecostals formed new fellowships.

Confessor: One who has suffered for the faith but was not martyred outright.

Ecstasy: A mystic or prophetic state or trance, a rapturous delight

Edict of Nantes: An declaration (1598) of French King Henry IV, granting religious and civil rights to the Huguenots (French Protestants).

End-times: An expression used by individuals inclined to apocalyptic thought. Refers to the end of the world or of an age.

Feminism: The theory of political, economic, social, personal, and religious equality of the sexes. It is in direct opposition to patriarchy.

Fleece, put out a: To invoke *God's* help in making a decision by calling on God to show a designated sign. See Judges 6:11-40.

Fundamentalism/ist: The fundamentalist movement is militantly Evangelical, originating in the United States in 1920 in opposition to liberalism and secularism. Usually it has opposed Pentecostalism, although the more moderate Evangelicals have embraced Classical Pentecostals.

Gifting: The term used to describe Spirit-endowment with gifts as enumerated in 1Corinthians 112 and 14 and Isaiah 11:1-2.

Glossolalia: Better known as "speaking in other/unknown languages."

Glossographia: Writing in unknown languages. Perhaps for the deaf and those unable to speak. See Hildegard of Bingen for an example.

Hagiography: The writing of the lives of the saints (the "holy ones").

Heteroglossia: Speaking in a variety of known languages.

Imagio Christi: Achieving perfection by following Christ.

Levitation: From the Latin levitas or "lightness," the process by which an object is held aloft, without mechanical support, in a stable position.

Martyr: One who has died for the faith.

Matriarchy: Matriarchy is a social system in which women hold primary power and predominate in roles of leadership in the Church, the family, political leadership, moral authority, social privilege, and control of property. Most of Matriarchies today are in African Initiated Tribes, but examples are also to be found in India, especially in Kerala (earlier Travancore-Cochin).

Montanists: An apocalyptic movement founded in Phrygia (in what is now Turkey) in the latter half of the second century CE by a prophet named Montanus.

Patriarchy: Patriarchy is a social system in which men hold primary power and predominate in roles of leadership in the Church, the family, political leadership, moral authority, social privilege, and control of property.

Paulicians: A group of radical dualists in the Byzantine Empire, beginning in the seventh century CE.

Pelagians: Those Christians who taught that humans can take the initial and fundamental steps toward salvation by their own efforts. It is named after the British theologian Pelagius who taught in Rome in the late fourth and early fifth centuries CE.

Protestant Reformation: Includes the movements named after the magisterial or teaching Reformers-Luther, Zwingli, and Calvin-in the sixteenth century CE, as well as a large number of smaller groups who also protested the teachings of the Roman Catholic Church. It is disputed whether the Church of England was Protestant.

Protomartyr: The first martyr in a given region.

Radical Reformation: The sixteenth century Reformation involved not only the Protestant magisterial Reformers and the Catholic Reformers, but also "radicals" including nonconformists, visionaries, and others who rebelled against both Catholics and mainstream Protestants.

Renewal Movement: The classical Pentecostals, Charismatics, and Independent Charismatics (previously known of as "Nee-Charismatics") who in the twentieth and twenty-first centuries CE emphasized the presence and power of the Holy Spirit in their personal religious experience, in enthusiastic worship, and in their wide range of spiritual gifts.

Revocation of the Edict of Nantes: Provisions of the Edict of Nantes were increasingly infringed in the seventeenth century until the edict was revoked by King Louis XIV in the Edict of Fountainebleau on October 18, 1685.

Venerable: A monastic saint.

Venerable-martyr: A martyred monastic.

Virgin-martyr: An unmarried, non-monastic, chaste female martyr.

Wonderworker: A saint renowned for performing miracles, also called "miracle-worker."

Xenoglossia: Speaking in a language that the speaker has never studied.

Lightning Source UK Ltd.
Milton Keynes UK
UKHW010114100223
416722UK00012B/834/J